Mosaic 2
Listening/Speaking

Mosaic 2

Listening/Speaking

4th Edition

Jami Hanreddy
University of Wisconsin, Milwaukee

Elizabeth Whalley
San Francisco State University

McGraw-Hill/Contemporary

A Division of The McGraw-Hill Companies

Mosaic 2 Listening/Speaking, 4th Edition

Published by McGraw-Hill/Contemporary, a business unit of The McGraw-Hill Companies, Inc., 1221 Avenue of the Americas, New York, NY 10020. Copyright © 2002, 1996, 1990, 1985 by The McGraw-Hill Companies, Inc. All rights reserved. No part of this publication may be reproduced or distributed in any form or by any means, or stored in a database or retrieval system, without the prior written consent of The McGraw-Hill Companies, Inc., including, but not limited to, in any network or other electronic storage or transmission, or broadcast for distance learning.

Some ancillaries, including electronic and print components, may not be available to customers outside the United States.

This book is printed on recycled, acid-free paper containing 10% postconsumer waste.

2 3 4 5 6 7 8 9 0 CUS CUS 0 9 8 7 6 5 4 3 2 1

ISBN 007-232986-6
ISBN 0-07-118018-4 (ISE)

Editorial director: *Tina B. Carver*
Series editor: *Annie Sullivan*
Developmental editor: *Annie Sullivan*
Director of marketing and sales: *Thomas P. Dare*
Project manager: *Genevieve Kelley*
Coordinator of freelance design: *David W. Hash*
Interior designer: *Michael Warrell, Design Solutions*
Photo research coordinator: *John C. Leland*
Photo researcher: *Amelia Ames Hill Associates/Amy Bethea*
Typeface: *10.5/12 Times Roman*
Printer:

Dedication

To the memory of Fred Goldstein, Rufus Rufty Rusty Russell III, Cindy Strauss, and Gertrude and Stanley Whalley.

For Freddy, who shared my love of puns as well as the grand metaphor.
And for Joe and Gracie whose love consummately provides the context for these efforts.

The acknowledgements and photo credits for this book begin on page 199 and are considered an extension of the copyright page.

www.mhcontemporary.com/interactionsmosaic

Mosaic 2
Listening/Speaking

Mosaic 2 Listening/Speaking

Boost your students' academic success!

Interactions Mosaic, 4th edition is the newly revised five-level, four-skill comprehensive ESL/EFL series designed to prepare students for academic content. The themes are integrated across proficiency levels and the levels are articulated across skill strands. The series combines communicative activities with skill-building exercises to boost students' academic success.

Interactions Mosaic, 4th edition features

- updated content
- five videos of authentic news broadcasts
- expansion opportunities through the Website
- new audio programs for the listening/speaking and reading books
- an appealing fresh design
- user-friendly instructor's manuals with placement tests and chapter quizzes

In This Chapter gives students a preview of the upcoming material.

Chapter 2

Danger and Daring

IN THIS CHAPTER

Lecture:	Hooked on Thrills
Learning Strategy:	Noting Specific Details
Language Function:	Saying *Yes* and *No*

Did You Know?

- The first heart transplant took place in Cape Town, South Africa, in 1967 and was performed by Christiaan Barnard. The patient, Louis Washkansky, lived for only 18 days after the surgery.
- 74,000 Americans are waiting for a transplant. A new name is added to the waiting list every 18 minutes.
- 261 medical institutions in the United States operate organ transplant programs.
- 25 different organs and tissues can be transplanted including heart, lungs, kidney, liver, corneas, bone, and cartilage.
- 90% of American say they support the concept of organ donation, but urgently needed organs are actually donated only 1/3 of the time.
- One donor can provide organs, bone, and tissue for 50 people.
- More than 60% of all organ recipients are between the ages of 18 and 49.

PART 1   Getting Started

Sharing Your Experience

1   Discuss the following questions as a class or in small groups.

1. The choices of several famous men and women are described here. What are the advantages and disadvantages of these decisions? In similar circumstances, would you have made the same choices?

Buddha   Socrates

a. Buddha left his family and gave up all his worldly possessions; he vowed to sit in meditation until he achieved enlightenment for the sake of all human beings.

b. Socrates chose to accept his unjust punishment of drinking poison rather than escape from prison and live in hiding.

Did You Know? offers a variety of interesting facts to spark students' interest in the topic.

Part 1 Getting Started activates students' prior knowledge through prelistening questions and a vocabulary preview.

PART 2   Predicting Exam Questions

Most students want to get good grades. One strategy for getting good grades is to predict which questions an instructor will ask on an exam.

Information Likely to Be on Exams

1. Any point the instructor tells you will be on the exam or anything the instructor says would make a good exam question.
2. Information that the instructor repeats directly from the textbook or class readings.
3. Things stated more slowly or more loudly than other things. (Instructors often slow down or speak louder when they want to point out something important.)
4. Key facts.

Examples:
For a course about the history of civil rights conflicts:
   Who was Martin Luther King?
For a business management course:
   What should you say if you don't want to recommend someone for a job and do want to avoid a lawsuit?

5. Information about recent research, especially the instructor's own research. (Instructors want to make sure their students are up-to-date. Also, asking questions about data that cannot yet be found in the library is a good way to find out if students have been attending class.)
6. Information on handouts

Before You Listen

1   **Considering the Context.** The lecture in this chapter is for a training course for resident advisors (RAs). Resident advisors are students living in dormitories (dorms) who receive special training and then are paid to assist new students. They answer questions students may have about campus life and help resolve conflicts in the dorms. In small groups discuss the following questions:

1. Would you like to live in a dorm? Why or why not?
2. What questions do you think a resident advisor needs to be able to answer?
3. What kinds of conflicts do you think people might have in dorms? How would you handle

Learning strategies include using lecture organization to identify main ideas, using different outline forms, understanding and using figurative language, listening for comparisons and contrasts, listening for causes and effects, distinguishing between fact and opinion, predicting exam questions, and thinking critically.

Before You Listen prepares students for the lecture by having them consider and discuss the topic and predict main ideas of the lecture.

Listen

3 Taking Notes on Causes and Effects. Read through the partial outline of causes and effects. Listen to the Webcast. Take notes by completing the outline.

Causes	Effects
1a. Japanese products are easy to get.	1. Americans buy many Japanese products.
1b. Japanese products are _____	
1c. Japanese products are _____	
2. _____	2. American companies are losing business.
3. _____	3a. Some leaders in business, labor, and government want protective taxes and _____
	3b. Other leaders say the United States should _____
4. U.S. manager encourages individual initiative.	4a. Separate people moving up from _____
	4b. Keep clear division between _____

Note-taking strategies include using different outline forms, abbreviating, using illustrations, using target expressions to help understand lectures, and using cohesive devices as markers.

---

6 Evaluating Speakers in Context. With some speakers, it's easier to determine the main points than with others. And in everyday interactions with friends, family, or co-workers, there are times when we all have difficulty getting to the point. To research this issue:

1. Choose three people from the following list and find an opportunity to listen to each one speak without interruption for several minutes. Many of them can be heard on the radio or TV.

artist	religious speaker	politician	teacher
businessperson	news reporter	scientist	three-year-old child
close friend	parent	shopkeeper	

2. As you listen, note the main points and then consider these questions:
   - Which of the three speakers was the most long-winded?
   - Which one got to the point in the shortest time?
   - Did any of the speakers talk on and on so much that you felt they never got to the point? If so, which one(s)?
   - With which speaker was it easiest to get the gist of what was being said?
   - With which speaker was it hardest to get the gist of what was being said?

3. Share your responses to these items with your classmates and give brief descriptions of your three subjects, including approximate age and educational background. Did you notice any patterns? For example, did you and your classmates discover a relationship between profession and long-windedness? Or perhaps between age and not getting to the point? Were there any particular topics about which most subjects tended to "beat around the bush" (talk around the subject but not exactly on the subject)?

PART 3   Requesting the Main Point

A scene from the classic American film *Mr. Smith Goes to Washington*

Getting to the point quickly is generally a goal of most English speakers, but not all of them. Some speakers are intentionally long-winded. For example:

- A United States senator who does not want a bill to be passed may talk on and on, day and night, to delay the vote on the bill.
- Someone who is shy and timid about a particular issue might beat around the bush, talking all around the subject, to delay having to face it.

Talk It Over offers a variety of speaking activities, including role-plays, interviews, presentations, small-group discussions, and pairwork.

Language function practice takes students from identifying and understanding functional language to using it in everyday and academic settings. Some useful functions include requesting the main point, persuading and giving in, acquiescing and expressing reservations, and taking and keeping the floor.

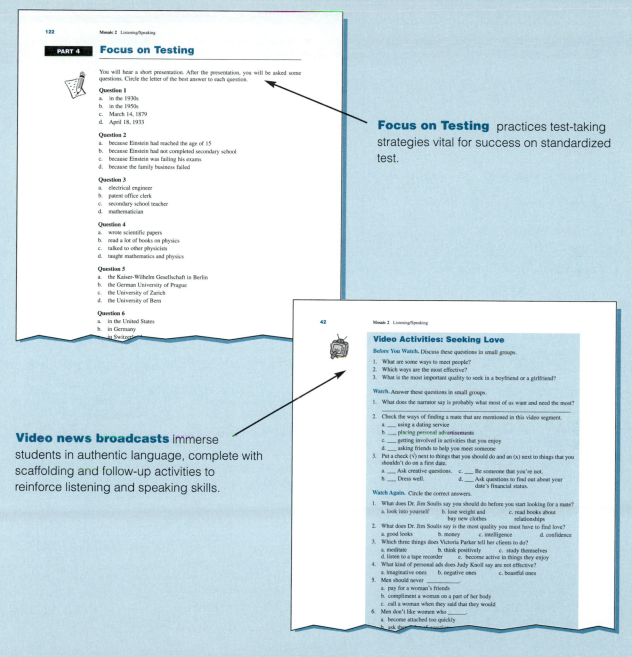

Focus on Testing practices test-taking strategies vital for success on standardized test.

Video news broadcasts Immerse students in authentic language, complete with scaffolding and follow-up activities to reinforce listening and speaking skills.

Don't forget to check out the new *Interactions Mosaic* Website at www.mhcontemporary.com/interactionsmosaic.

- Traditional practice and interactive activities
- Links to student and teacher resources
- Cultural activities
- Focus on Testing
- Activities from the Website are also provided on CD-ROM

Mosaic 2 Listening/Speaking

Speaking Tasks	Focus on Testing	Lecture Topics	Video Topics
■ Discussing educational experiences ■ Evaluating a lecturer's style ■ Sharing your language learning autobiography ■ Evaluating speakers in context ■ Requesting the main point ■ Role-playing conversations	■ Questions about a presentation	■ To School or Not to School	■ The School of Success
■ Discussing thrillseekers ■ Speaking from a prepared outline ■ Saying *yes* and *no* ■ Completing a survey about taking risks	■ Questions about a news feature	■ Hooked on Thrills	■ Extreme Sports
■ Discussing adolescence ■ Discussing abbreviations ■ Decoding abbreviations ■ Creating messages using abbreviations ■ Expressing congratulations and condolences ■ Sharing cultural expressions ■ Role-playing dialogues	■ Questions about a conversation	■ Becoming a Man, Becoming a Woman	■ Seeking Love
■ Discussing the solar system ■ Sharing scientific theories ■ Using illustrations to enhance descriptions ■ Giving a scientific report ■ Using formal expressions to admit a lack of knowledge ■ Using informal expressions to admit a lack of knowledge	■ Questions about an American Indian folktale	■ The Origins of our Solar System	■ Abduction by Aliens
■ Discussing transitions ■ Discussing free will ■ Making analogies ■ Determining the subjects of analogies ■ Role-playing dialogues ■ Guessing situations and emotions	■ Questions about a presentation	■ The Stages of Life – A View from Shakespeare	■ College Graduation
■ Discussing dreams ■ Comparing and contrasting dreams ■ Analyzing dreams ■ Interviewing about dreams ■ Expressing the positive view ■ Debating as optimists and pessimists ■ Responding to complaints positively	■ Questions about a conversation	■ Dreams and Reality	■ Social Phobia

(continued on next page)

Mosaic 2 Listening/Speaking

Speaking Tasks	Focus on Testing	Lecture Topics	Video Topics
■ Discussing jobs and work ■ Discussing advances in technology ■ Discussing technology and society ■ Describing innovations ■ Persuading in informal situations ■ Debating work-related issues ■ Role-playing situations requiring persuasion	■ Questions about a radio interview	■ Japanese and American Business Management	■ Telecommuting
■ Discussing laws of nature ■ Discussing breakthroughs ■ Sharing past experiences ■ Describing scientific processes ■ Giving and receiving compliments ■ Discussing compliments in context ■ Discussing inappropriate compliments	■ Questions about a presentation	■ Discovering the Laws of Nature	■ Advances in Medicine
■ Discussing music ■ Sharing your knowledge ■ Role-playing a critic ■ Presenting facts and expressing doubts ■ Completing conversations	■ Questions about a music review	■ The Rise of Rock 'n' Roll	■ Women in Jazz
■ Discussing conflicts ■ Discussing dorm life ■ Evaluating exam questions ■ Asking and answering exam questions ■ Acquiescing and expressing reservations ■ Discussing conflicts and resolutions	■ Questions about a discussion	■ Dealing with Conflicts	■ A Strike
■ Discussing principles ■ Discussing medical resources ■ Discussing the lecture ■ Understanding and using reference words ■ Presenting your point of view	■ Questions about a human interest story	■ Organ Transplants	■ Stealth Surgery
■ Visualizing the future ■ Thinking critically by analyzing responses ■ Evaluating critically ■ Gathering and reporting research ■ Predicting the future ■ Role-playing reunions	■ Questions about a presentation	■ The Future	■ Concept Cars

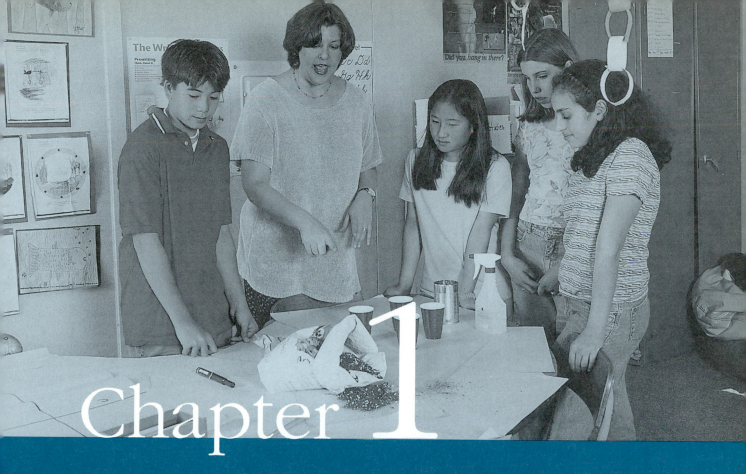

Chapter 1

Language and Learning

Did You Know?

- High school students in the United States spend an average of 38 hours per week in the classroom. In Russia the figure is 52 hours, and in Japan it's 59 hours.
- In the United States, reading, writing, and arithmetic are considered the most important school subjects for young children. These three skills are often referred to as the three Rs: reading, 'riting, and 'rithmetic.
- The number of children currently being taught at home in the United States is over 1.2 million and is growing steadily.

PART 1

Getting Started

Sharing Your Experience

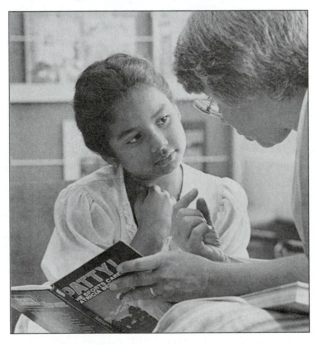

 1 Discuss the following questions in small groups. Think back to the time when you were in elementary school and share your recollections with your classmates.

1. Who was your favorite teacher? How old were you? Why was he or she your favorite? Share a specific incident that explains why you liked that teacher so well.
2. Who was your least favorite teacher? Why? How old were you? Share an anecdote that explains why you disliked this teacher.
3. In what ways has school been exciting? Disappointing?

4. Do you feel you would know less, the same amount, or more if you had not gone to school? Why? If you hadn't gone to school, how do you think you would have learned things? From your parents, your parents' friends, your friends, your siblings, television, radio, movies, books, computers?

5. Do you think everyone should be required to go to school? Why or why not?

Vocabulary Preview

2   **Vocabulary in Context.** The speaker uses the following words in the lecture. After the list are six statements that teachers might make to describe students. Fill in the blank in each statement with the appropriate word from the list.

5. enthusiastic	*extremely pleased or excited*
4. genius	*a person with great intelligence and/or ability*
6. to get away from it all	*to retreat from the stress of daily activities*
1. gifted	*very capable and inventive; talented*
2. moody	*frequently appearing disagreeable, unpleasant, or sad to others*
7. nonconformist	*a person who refuses to follow established customs*
3. obedient	*follows orders*

1. In nursery school, Rudy Thomas could sing his ABCs on key without missing a note. He played the piano without being taught. He made up beautiful songs by himself. By the time he was six, he must have spent six hundred hours at the piano. He probably will be a great composer or performer one day, because he's musically _____.

2. Sometimes Barbara Michaels is happy, but more often she seems sad or grumpy. She is so _____ that it is difficult for her to make any friends.

3. I think George Redfern is the kind of student that many teachers like. He does whatever he is told without asking any questions and never gets into trouble. I, however, find this kind of student difficult. I don't like students who are so _____. They are so dull. I much prefer students who challenge me.

4. Nancy Burke's IQ is over 165. She completed high school by the time she was 12 years old. She graduated with highest honors from the university when she was 16 and completed her PhD in astrophysics at age 21. Her parents say that by the time she was three months old, they could already tell that she was a _____.

5. It's so nice to have Michael Jones in class. He is always cheerful and seems to like everyone. It's clear that he really enjoys school because he is so _____ about all the classes and activities.

6. I think that Penny Mattson is working too hard. I know she has her TOEFL exam next week, but she needs _____ and relax a little or she might get sick.

7. Instead of doing term papers for her political science class, Patsy usually creates some sort of dance performance that illustrates her main arguments and includes all the supporting details. She is really a _____. I'm surprised the professor allows her to change the course requirements in that way.

PART 2

Understanding Main Ideas

In most lectures, several main ideas are presented. These are the concepts the speaker wants the audience to remember. Most often the lecturer also provides a general, or thesis, statement that includes all the main concepts. When a lecture is well organized, with a clear beginning, middle, and end, the main ideas are usually easy to pick out. When a lecture is not well organized, understanding the gist of what is being said can be difficult. Some lecturers are long-winded, taking a long time to come to the point. Others talk on and on and never seem to come to the point at all.

The Model Lecture Has Three Parts

1. Introduction
   Usually the general, or thesis, statement is included here. Sometimes the main ideas are mentioned, but not fully explained.

2. Body
   The main ideas and examples are always presented here.

3. Conclusion
   Traditionally this section contains a summary of all the main ideas. The general, or thesis, statement will be repeated, or it may be introduced here for the first time.

Before You Listen

1 Considering the Topic. Discuss the following questions in small groups.

1. Think about your classmates during your first eight years of school. Which ones had artistic talent? Did those students like or dislike school? Why?
2. Think about your classmates who were talented in science or math. Did those students like or dislike school? Why?
3. Based on your group discussion, can you draw any conclusions? Share your findings with the rest of the class.

Listen

2 Listening for Main Ideas. Listen to the lecture once all the way through. Then listen again. This time, listen for the main ideas in the introduction, the body, and the conclusion of the lecture. Stop the tape or CD after you hear each of the following sentences and write the main idea of the part of the lecture that you have just heard.

Stop 1 These questions are very important ones for you as future teachers to consider.

_____

_____

Stop 2 Mark Twain, Charlie Chaplin, and Vincent van Gogh are examples of what we expect to find.

_____

_____

_____

Huck Finn and Tom Sawyer, two of Mark Twain's characters, frequently stayed away from school.

Mark Twain was not a very obedient student and had very negative experiences in school.

Stop 3 He [Wordsworth] did well in math, history, and literature courses and felt he had a free and happy life at school.

_____

_____

_____

Stop 4 Even though these scientific giants experienced conflicts between the demands of school and the development of their own minds, we should not jump to conclusions.

_____

_____

_____

Stop 5 He [Fleming] passed his medical school entrance examinations with higher marks than any other student.

_____

_____

_____

After You Listen

3 **Evaluating a Lecturer's Style.** Discuss the following questions about the lecture with your classmates:

1. Do you think the lecture was well organized? Poorly organized? Why?
2. Was the lecturer long-winded and taking too much time to get to the point? Did the lecturer *ever* get to the point?

4 **Comparing Notes.** Share the main ideas that you wrote down with your classmates. Did you find it easy or difficult to pick out the main ideas? Why?

Talk It Over

5 **Sharing Your Language Learning Autobiography.** Think about the variety of experiences you've had as you've been learning English. Begin with the point at which you didn't know a single word and continue through the present.

In Small Groups

Use the following questions as a guide to present your "English autobiography." Speak for two to three minutes. As you listen to your classmates' autobiographies, note the main points.

1. When were you first exposed to English? How old were you?
2. Where were you when you first began to learn English?
3. Have you been learning the language continuously since then, or were you interrupted for some reason?
4. Did you study this language in school? If so, where and when? What approaches or methods did your teachers use? Were any of your teachers native speakers of the language? Do you think this made a difference? Why or why not?
5. Have you had opportunities to speak this language outside the classroom with friends or family? Have you had a close boyfriend or girlfriend or perhaps a husband or wife who spoke the language?
6. Were you exposed to more than one dialect of the language? Do you think this helped or hindered your language acquisition? Why?

As a Class

Share some of the main points of these autobiographies. Were the main points dealing with personal feelings similar, or were they different? In what ways?

6 **Evaluating Speakers in Context.** With some speakers, it's easier to determine the main points than with others. And in everyday interactions with friends, family, or co-workers, there are times when we all have difficulty getting to the point. To research this issue:

1. Choose three people from the following list and find an opportunity to listen to each one speak without interruption for several minutes. Many of them can be heard on the radio or TV.

artist	**religious speaker**	**politician**	**teacher**
businessperson	**news reporter**	**scientist**	**three-year-old child**
close friend	**parent**	**shopkeeper**	

2. As you listen, note the main points and then consider these questions:

   - Which of the three speakers was the most long-winded?
   - Which one got to the point in the shortest time?
   - Did any of the speakers talk on and on so much that you felt they never got to the point? If so, which one(s)?
   - With which speaker was it easiest to get the gist of what was being said?
   - With which speaker was it hardest to get the gist of what was being said?

3. Share your responses to these items with your classmates and give brief descriptions of your three subjects, including approximate age and educational background. Did you notice any patterns? For example, did you and your classmates discover a relationship between profession and long-windedness? Or perhaps between age and not getting to the point? Were there any particular topics about which most subjects tended to "beat around the bush" (talk around the subject but not exactly on the subject)?

PART 3

Requesting the Main Point

A scene from the classic American film *Mr. Smith Goes to Washington*

Getting to the point quickly is generally a goal of most English speakers, but not all of them. Some speakers are intentionally long-winded. For example:

- A United States senator who does not want a bill to be passed may talk on and on, day and night, to delay the vote on the bill.

- Someone who is shy and timid about a particular issue might beat around the bush, talking all around the subject, to delay having to face it.

Other people are unintentionally long-winded; they will talk for a long time and then ask a question such as "Am I talking too much?" or "Does this make any sense?" Still others talk on and on, never coming to the point at all.

If a speaker is long-winded or is not getting to the point, you may want to ask for the main point. If the speaker is a friend or family member, you might use one of the following informal expressions.

Requesting the Main Point (Informal)

The following expressions are very informal and can seem rude or too aggressive in many situations, even with family or friends.

■ Get to the point, will (would) you please?
■ I don't get it. What are you talking about?
■ Oh, come on! Stop beating around the bush and get to the point.
■ So, what are you trying to say?
■ So, what's the (your) point?
■ What are you driving at?
■ What are you getting at?

If the speaker is not a close friend, but is an acquaintance—a supervisor or a teacher, for example—you must be careful how you ask for the main point so that you don't offend the person. In these or other sensitive situations, when you wish to be more polite, use one of the following more formal expressions.

Requesting the Main Point (Formal)

One of these expressions:

■ Excuse me.
■ I'm sorry.
■ Pardon me for interrupting, but . . .

Followed by one of these:

■ I didn't quite catch the point. Could you go over it again, please?
■ I didn't follow that last part. Could you give the main point again, please?
■ I didn't understand the point you were making. Could you say it again, please?
■ I don't quite understand what you're getting at.

1 **Listening for Appropriate Expressions and Tone of Voice.** In the following conversations you will hear expressions for requesting the main point used politely and impolitely. Sometimes the tone of voice is what makes the difference. Listen to the speakers and answer the questions. Then compare your answers in small groups.

Conversation 1

Randy tries to tell Sandy some interesting news.

1.   Was this conversation friendly or unfriendly? __friendly__

2.   Was it formal or informal? __informal__

3.   Was Sandy polite or impolite? __impolite__

Conversation 2

Professor Draper is talking about the midterm exam.

1.   Was the student's request for the main point polite or impolite? __impolite__

2.   What would you have said in the same situation? _____

Conversation 3

Professor Werner and Richard discuss an upcoming field trip.

1.   Did Richard handle the situation well? __Yes__

2.   Was he polite or impolite? __polite__

2 **Requesting the Main Point.** Listen to another version of the lecture "To School or Not to School." In this version, some of the main points have been omitted. During the lecture, stop the tape or CD at each pause and take turns asking for the main point. Practice requesting the main point by using an appropriate expression.

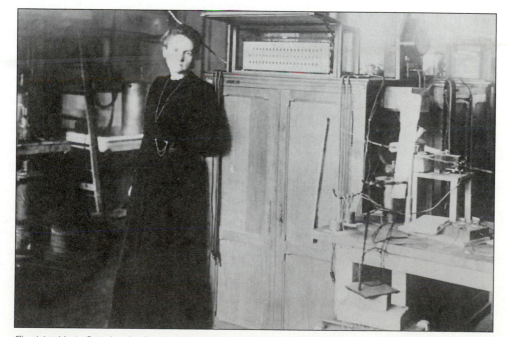

Physicist Marie Curie loved school and was a star pupil.

Talk It Over

3   **Role-Playing Conversations.** Look at the following incomplete conversations. Only Speaker A's first turn in the conversation is provided. With a partner, decide which of you is Speaker A and which is Speaker B, and complete each of the conversations. The first one has been partially completed as an example.

1.   Speaker B will ask for the main point on his or her first turn. Speaker A can choose to answer right away or to continue the conversation for a while before giving the main point.
2.   Take turns being Speaker A and Speaker B to create a variety of conversations.
3.   Try making up a few conversations of your own, using these as models.
4.   Select the conversation that you and your partner enjoyed most and present it to the class.

Conversation 1

A: Good morning, professor. Did you hear about that terrible accident on the highway last night? The traffic was backed up for hours. I hope everyone was okay. I'll bet a lot of people were late getting home, too. Probably a lot of people couldn't do some of the things they'd planned to do 'cause they got home so late. You know, almost everything closes by nine o'clock—like the public library and everything and…

B.   Stop beating around the bush, Jorge. What's your point?

A: Well, so I was one of the people, and I was late and…

B: Get to the point, please. I'm late for class.

A: I don't have my homework.

B:

A:

Conversation 2

A.   Yes—about your art project—well, oil paint is an interesting medium; the variety of textures one can achieve with oil paints is remarkable. And paper cups—yes, paper cups *do* have some interesting possibilities. And these coat hangers—it never occurred to me to use them like this. So your sister told me you're not sure whether you're going to major in art or not. Fred Carlson went through the same thing. Have you ever met Fred? He works over in the career counseling center now.

B.

A.

B.

Conversation 3

A: Dad, I'd like to talk to you about something. I went over to the registrar's office yesterday. And, you know, Joan works over there. The line was really long—all the way out the door and around the building. I hadn't decided which classes to sign up for yet, but I figured that I had plenty of time to do that while I waited in line. And then I bumped into Joan and we started talking. You know, she's had the most interesting life, and she never even went to college!

B:

A:

B:

Conversation 4

A: Do you remember that book you loaned me last week? The biography of Albert Einstein? Well, I was reading the chapter about how he developed the theory of relativity, and the phone rang. It surprised me because it was so early. No one usually calls before eight o'clock. I didn't want to get up to answer it because the chapter was so interesting. Did you know that he was only a patent clerk – he wasn't even a professor yet – when he developed that theory?

B:

A:

B:

PART 4

Focus on Testing

Understanding spoken English on standardized listening comprehension tests, such as the TOEFL, is more difficult than listening in most other contexts. During a standardized test, you cannot interact with the speaker to get clarification or rewind the tape to listen again. You get only one chance to listen for the important information. The Focus on Testing exercises in this book will help you practice for this type of test.

You will hear a short presentation. After the speaker finishes talking, you will hear a series of questions. Circle the letter of the best answer to each question.

Question 1

a.   language and learning
b.   artificial intelligence
c.   the human brain
d.   intelligent behavior

Question 2

a.   intelligent behavior
b.   a machine
c.   the human brain
d.   the environment

Question 3

a.   when you must remember and process a lot of information
b.   when you must answer a lot of questions
c.   when you must use primitive reasoning
d.   when you must act intelligently

Question 4

a.   the mysteries of the human brain
b.   logical rules
c.   intuition
d.   language and learning

Video Activities: The School for Success

Before You Watch. Discuss these questions in small groups.

1. Which of these things do you think are most important for students' academic success? Why?
    a. their school   b. their home life   c. their parents

2. What can parents do to help their children be more successful in school?

Watch. Answer these questions in small groups.

1. What is the name of the school featured in the video?_____

2. Who takes classes at this school?_____

3. Which of these things does George Frasier think causes failure in schools?
    a. Children watch too much television.
    b. Schools don't have enough money.
    c. Parents are not paying enough attention to their children.

4. Circle the things that George Frasier says that parents must give their children.
    a. love   b. attention   c. discipline   d. support   e. values

Watch Again. Listen for these words and say what they mean.

1. *Link* means the same as _____.
    a. connect   b. establish   c. separate

2. *Maintain* means the same as _____.
    a. begin   b. finish   c. continue

3. *Nurturing* means _____.
    a. talking to   b. taking care of   c. leaning on

4. *Structured* means _____.
    a. having rules   b. being free   c. safe

After You Watch. Discuss these questions with your class.

1. How much responsibility do you think parents should take for their children's education?
2. Do the schools have any right to tell parents what to do in their homes?

Chapter 2

Danger and Daring

Did You Know?

- Annie Taylor, the first person to go over Niagara Falls in a barrel, went over the falls on October 24, 1901. She expected to become rich and famous, but she didn't and died poor. You can see pictures of her and other daredevils if you visit the Daredevil Museum in Niagara Falls, New York.

- Many people around the world are interested in extreme sports such as rock climbing, extreme skiing, bungee jumping, and skysurfing. One unusual extreme sport, underwater hockey, is played in Australia, Belgium, Canada, Columbia, France, Holland, Japan, South Africa, the United Kingdom, the United States, and Zimbabwe.

- Rock climbing is an extreme sport that is sometimes used to help children with attention deficit disorder (ADD). These children have difficulty paying attention and concentrating. When rock climbing, the climber must pay close attention to every move in order not to fall. The children enjoy the excitement of this sport and learn how to focus their attention.

- Freediving is an extreme sport in which divers compete to see who can go the deepest on just one breath. An Italian, Umberto Pelizzari, dove 236 feet on one breath of air. The really dangerous part is coming back to the surface. About 55 freedivers in European countries die each year.

- The fastest human team sport is freeflying. A team jumps out of an airplane and falls through the air at an average rate of 160 to180 miles per hour. A few teams have reached the highest speed on record of 250 miles per hour.

PART 1   # Getting Started

Sharing Your Experience

In small groups, discuss the following items.

1   Read and discuss this news article. Then share the highlights of your discussions with the rest of the class.

Stunt Jump Thwarted

A police helicopter and emergency services officers yesterday prevented Tony Vera, who described himself later as a stunt man and magician, from leaping off the Manhattan tower of the Brooklyn Bridge.

Clad in a loincloth and a straitjacket, Mr. Vera, who had climbed to the top of the tower, stood on top for several minutes, having trouble fastening the straitjacket. A police helicopter hovered close to the bridge, preventing him from making a wide leap, while emergency services officers made their way to the top.

The officers grabbed Mr. Vera and led him down to safety, and he was hustled off by the police. But before they did, Mr. Vera said: "I want some excitement in my life. I'm going to do it again. I just want to jump."

New York Times, September 13, 1980.

2 Do you know of any people who seek thrills by facing unnecessary danger? If so, what type of thrill-seeking activity is most common? Share your answers with your classmates.

Vocabulary Preview

3 **Vocabulary in Context.** The following words are used in the lecture in this chapter, but the speaker does not define them. Read the definitions and fill in the blanks in the sentences with the correct forms of the words.

daredevil	*one who fears nothing and will attempt anything*
hullabaloo	*excitement; chaotic activity*
irresistible	*too strong to oppose or withstand*
to motivate	*to give encouragement or a reason for action*
to pull off	*to accomplish something very difficult*
seeker	*person who looks for something*
stunts	*difficult or dangerous actions*
to take up	*to begin a new hobby or activity*

Thrillseeker David Blaine frozen in a block of ice.

1. Are you willing to take great risks? Do you seek out extremely dangerous situations? If so, you are a(n) _____.

2. Do you know of anyone who loves climbing mountains? To such a person, an offer to be a member of an expedition to Nepal to climb Mount Everest would probably be _____.

3. Have you ever seen a rock star whose fans scream and jump up and down whenever they see the star? This star causes a lot of _____ wherever he or she goes.

4. Have you ever tried to figure out why people do the things they do? If so, you are looking for what _____ people.

5. Do you know someone who looks for thrilling experiences all the time? This person could be called a thrill _____.

6. Have you ever accomplished something very difficult? What was the most important fact that helped you _____ this task?

7. What is the most exciting thing you do on a regular basis? When did you first _____ this activity?

8. Because people love to watch other people do dangerous things, many people are able to earn a lot of money doing _____ for an audience.

PART 2

Noting Specific Details

Once you have learned to pick out the main ideas in a lecture, your next step is to note the specific details. You will need these details later to answer questions on all types of exams: multiple choice, short answer, and essay. To listen for and note specific details, it is helpful to notice how the lecture is organized.

Lecture Organization and Note Taking

If the lecture is organized in the standard way, that is, if it contains three sections—introduction, body, and conclusion—listen for and note the main ideas in each of these sections. The following information will help you decide which specific details you should write in your notes.

1. If the introduction to the lecture is a summary of what you learned in the previous class session, take notes on this material again. These notes will be an added reminder of what the lecturer thinks is important.

2. If the introduction to the lecture is just a general introduction or an attention getter (a fact, a saying, a story, or a joke), you don't need to write this material down unless you might like to use it later.

3. Next, listen for information in the body of the lecture. You will probably hear the most details in this section. Write down as much information as you can in your notes, but don't worry if you can't get everything. Just put a question mark in the margin and ask questions later.

4. As you listen to the conclusion, continue to make your notes as complete as possible. Most conclusions won't contain any new information, but be ready in case the instructor has forgotten to include an important detail earlier and decides to mention it in the conclusion.

Which Outline Form Should You Use?

One good way to organize the main points and specific details is to use a formal outline. Look at the following examples. The one on the left is more commonly used, but many note takers find the one on the right easier to use because they don't need to remember when to use the capital and lowercase letters or roman and arabic numerals.

Outline Using Roman Numerals, Arabic Numerals, and Letters

I.   Introduction
    A. Main point
    B. Main point
    C. Main point

II.   Discussion/body
    A. Restatement of main point A
      1. Specific detail
      2. Specific detail
      3. Specific detail
        a. Further detail of A3
        b. Further detail of A3
    B. Restatement of main point B
      1. Specific detail
        a. Further detail of B1
        b. Further detail of B1
      2. Specific detail
    C. Restatement of main point C
      1. Specific detail
      2. Specific detail
        a. Further detail of C2
        b. Further detail of C2
      3. Specific detail

III.   Conclusion
    A. Summary of IIA
    B. Summary of IIB
    C. Summary of IIC

Outline Using Only Arabic Numerals

Introduction
(in paragraph form, a paraphrase of the lecturer's introductory remarks)

1.   Main point
    1.1   Specific detail
    1.2   Specific detail
    1.3   Specific detail
        1.3.1 Further detail of 1.3
        1.3.2 Further detail of 1.3

2.   Main point
    2.1   Specific detail
        2.1.1 Further detail of 2.1
        2.1.2 Further detail of 2.1
    2.2   Specific detail

3.   Main point
    3.1   Specific detail
    3.2   Specific detail
        3.2.1 Further detail of 3.2
        3.2.2 Further detail of 3.2
    3.3   Specific detail

Conclusion
(in paragraph form, a paraphrase of the lecturer's concluding remarks)

Alternative Note-Taking Strategies

Of course, formal outlines such as the examples shown here work best for note taking when the lecturer carefully organizes the material into introduction, body, and conclusion; uses one of these types of outlines as speech notes; and then sticks to the outline during the talk. But many lecturers do not follow these rules. Some add bits of information here and there as they think of them during the lecture. Other lecturers do not use an outline format when preparing their talks. In these cases, you may need alternatives to the formal outline in order to note main points and specific details well.

Here are five different ways to organize your notes. Use the one that feels the most comfortable and useful to you.

1. This method of note taking is most useful when the main points and details are long phrases and sentences.

    Main point
            Detail
            Detail
            Detail
    Main point
            Detail
            Detail
            Etc.

2. This method of note taking is most useful when details are symbols, statistics, single words, or very short phrases.

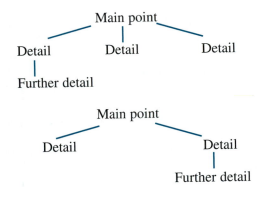

    Etc.

3. The following method is especially useful when the lecturer tends to back up and give specific details on points mentioned earlier in the lecture. If you leave enough space to add more details later, note taking during this type of lecture should not be difficult.

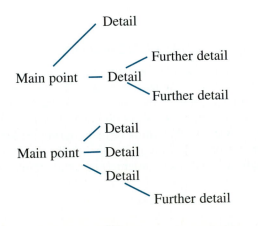

    Etc.

4. This method is useful when the details precede the main point.

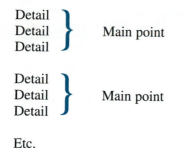

Etc.

5. This method is especially useful if the lecture is not well organized or if the lecturer does not state the main points clearly or digresses frequently. By putting all the main points on the left and details on the right, you can match them up with arrows later and double check to see if something you thought was a main point was really a detail, and vice versa.

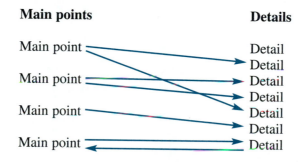

Adding Visual Cues to Your Notes

In addition to using these basic systems of note taking, many note takers find it helpful to set things off visually by using different-colored inks or by framing certain items in boxes or circles.

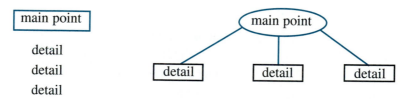

Before You Listen

1 **Considering the Topic**. Discuss the following questions in small groups.

1. Many thrill seekers claim that they engage in dangerous activities only for personal satisfaction—that they are concerned only with increasing their self-esteem. Some critics say, however, that money is the real motive behind the most daring of these activities and that if there were no publicity or fame and fortune, there would be no daredevils to perform dangerous stunts. Why do you think people do dangerous daredevil stunts?

Phillipe Petit balanced on a cable between two buildings 1,350 feet above the street for 45 minutes.

Skateboarding competitions have become extremely popular with thrillseeking men and women.

2. Which groups do you think are more likely to engage in thrill-seeking activities and why?

> Men or women?
> Young children or teenagers?
> Young adults or middle-aged people?
> Rich people or poor people?
> A visitor to a foreign country or a person at home?

Listen

2 **Listening for Specific Details**. The lecturer discusses the types of people who choose to face danger and what it means to be "hooked on thrills."

1. Listen to the beginning of the lecture and decide whether you should take notes on the introduction.

Your decision: I should _____ should not _____ take notes on the

introduction because _____

2. Listen to the lecture all the way through from the beginning. Take notes using one of the two lecture outline forms on page 17 or one of the five alternative note-taking methods shown on pages 18–19. Note as many specific details as you can.

_____

_____

_____

_____

_____

_____

_____

_____

_____

_____

_____

3. Did the note-taking method you chose work well for this particular lecture? If not, choose another method and listen again to note the main points and specific details.

After You Listen

3 **Comparing Notes.** Compare notes with your classmates and share your feelings about the note-taking methods you used.

Talk It Over

4 **Speaking from a Prepared Outline.** Prepare a brief talk on a daredevil stunt that you have heard about or read about and present your talk to the class. You may need to use the Internet or make a trip to the library.

As you speak:
■ Use notes that you have made in outline form.
■ Have your classmates take notes in outline form.

After you have finished speaking:
■ Compare the notes you spoke from with the notes other students made.
■ Do you and your classmates have the same main points and details? If not, discuss the differences and why you think they occurred.

PART 3

Saying Yes and No

When we are asked if we would like to do or have something, we have three basic ways to respond: *yes, no,* and *maybe.*

■ *Maybe* is a neutral word meaning that at a later time your answer may be *yes* or *no. Maybe* is exactly in the middle of the scale between *yes* and *no,* and there are no ways of saying *maybe* that are either stronger or weaker. Some alternative expressions for *maybe* are *perhaps* and *possibly.*

■ *Yes* and *no* can be expressed in a variety of ways. Depending on how close to or far away from *maybe* your feelings are, you may choose either a weaker or stronger expression to say *yes* or *no.*

Stronger Yes	*Weaker Yes*
Absolutely!	I think so.
Definitely!	I'm considering it.
For sure!	I'll think about it.
Great!	Most likely I will.
I'll say!	OK. (with unenthusiastic intonation)
OK! (with excited intonation)	OK, if you really want me to.
Sure thing!	Probably.
You bet!	That might be a good idea.

Stronger No	*Weaker No*
Are you kidding?	I don't think so.
Forget it!	I doubt it.
Never!	I'd rather not.
No way!	Not likely.
Not on your life!	Probably not.
Nothing doing!	That's probably not such a good idea.
Not for all the tea in China!	

1 **Listening for** *Yes* **and** *No* **Expressions.** Listen to the following conversations and note the various ways in which the speakers say *yes* and *no.* Fill in the blanks in each conversation. When you are finished, compare your answers in small groups.

Conversation 1
Ted and Paul are discussing their plans for the weekend.

Ted: . . . You want to go with us?

Paul: _____

Ted: . . . Take it and you'll be ready to go with us.

Paul: _____

_____

_____

Ted: . . . I know lots of people who've done it.

Paul: _____

_____

_____

Ted: . . . The course is only 20 bucks.

Paul: That's not too bad.

_____

_____

Ted: . . . You've got the money don't you?

Paul: _____

_____

Conversation 2

Terry and Lynn are discussing vacation possibilities.

Terry: . . . Wouldn't that be great? Let's go!

Lynn: _____

_____

Terry: . . . Think how strong and brave you'll feel at the end.

Lynn: _____

_____

_____

Terry: . . . You'll be a better person for it.

Lynn: I won't climb a mountain! _____

_____

_____

Lynn: . . . Wanna go out to dinner?

Terry: _____

_____

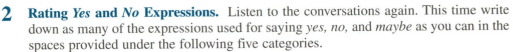

2 **Rating *Yes* and *No* Expressions.** Listen to the conversations again. This time write down as many of the expressions used for saying *yes*, *no*, and *maybe* as you can in the spaces provided under the following five categories.

stronger *yes*   weaker *yes*

_____

_____

_____

_____

stronger *no*   weaker *no*

_____

_____

_____

_____

maybe

_____

_____

_____

_____

3 **Saying *Yes* and *No*.** In the lecture there are four statements from Marvin Zuckerman's Sensation-Seeking Survey. Listen to the lecture again. As you hear each of these statements, write down the expression that best indicates how strongly you agree or disagree with it. Discuss your answers with your classmates.

1. _____

_____

_____

2. _____

_____

_____

_____

3. _____

_____

_____

_____

4. _____

_____

_____

_____

Talk It Over

4   **Answering Survey Questions.**   Are you adventurous? Do you like to take risks and try new things? Or are you more cautious and not particularly interested in new adventures? Take a survey test and find out.

1. Work with a partner. Take turns giving and taking the test provided here.
   1. The test giver reads each item to the test taker.
   2. The test taker responds to each item, using expressions from the boxes on page 22.
   3. The test giver puts a check in the appropriate column for each answer.
   4. When you both have completed the test, look in the appendix on page 194 for scoring instructions.
   5. Add up your scores and see how you each "measure up" on the risk-taker ruler on page 27.
   6. Share your ratings with the class – if you dare!

2. Make up a few of your own risk-taker test questions to ask each other. Begin your questions with these or similar phrases:
   1. Would you ever ....?
   2. How would you like to ....?
   3. How about ....?

3. Answer the questions using the expressions that best represent your immediate reactions to the questions. Share your questions and answers with your classmates.

Risk-Taker Test

Question	Response				
Would you ever . . .	**Strong yes**	**Weak no** yes	**Maybe**	**Weak no**	**Strong no**
1. try a new popular but unusual haircut?		✓			
2. try a very unusual food with a familiar name (for example, chocolate-covered ants?)	✓				
3. try a very unusual food with an unfamiliar name?		✓			
4. explore a recently discovered island?	✓				
5. go alone to see a band at a club?	✓				
6. play in a band that goes on tour to another country?	✓				
7. volunteer to be the first passenger in a newly designed 2-seater airplane?			✓		
8. try sky surfing?		✓			
9. try to climb a 15,000-foot mountain?			✓		
10. try Motocross mountain biking?	✓				
11. parachute from a plane onto a beautiful, sweet-smelling meadow?	✓				
12. parachute from a plane onto the top of a skyscraper?		✓			
13. try skydiving stunts?		✓			
14. sail across the Pacific Ocean from San Francisco to Japan in a boat without a motor?					✓
15. dive off a 40-foot cliff in Hawaii into the cool blue water below?			✓		
16. go out on a blind date?	✓				
17. go to a small party where you know only 2 of the 7 people there?	✓				
18. go to a party of 60 people where you know only the host?			✓		
19. drive a race car at 150 miles per hour?		✓			
20. volunteer to take part in an experiment to test the effects of a new drug on humans?					✓
21. go to a country where you could not read, write, or speak the language at all and where you did not know anyone?		✓			
22. cross the street against a red light?					✓
23. eat a dessert for breakfast?	✓				
24. take part in a traditional cultural dance while visiting another country?	✓				
25. volunteer to make a speech in front of a large group of people?			✓		

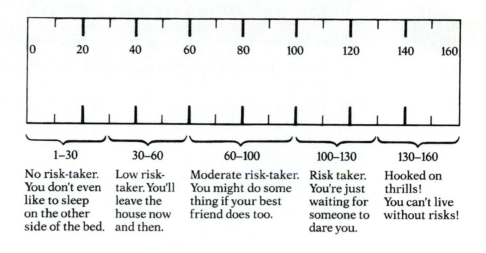

1–30	30–60	60–100	100–130	130–160
No risk-taker. You don't even like to sleep on the other side of the bed.	Low risk-taker. You'll leave the house now and then.	Moderate risk-taker. You might do something if your best friend does too.	Risk taker. You're just waiting for someone to dare you.	Hooked on thrills! You can't live without risks!

PART 4　# Focus on Testing

Listen to the short news program. After the news feature, you will be asked some questions. Circle the letter of the best answer to each question.

Question 1

a.　a popular sport among all young people in California
b.　a very dangerous sport in France
c.　a sport for young daredevils and thrill seekers
d.　a sport that requires a lot of special training

Question 2

a.　jump feet first from high places
b.　jump from bridges, cranes, and balloons
c.　jump into the water below
d.　jump up into the sky

Question 3

a.　hot-air balloons
b.　parachutes
c.　special suits
d.　cords that are like giant rubber bands

Question 4

a.　to show courage and ensure a good crop of yams
b.　to test the strength of the vines
c.　to test the strength of their ankles
d.　to be daredevils and thrill seekers

Video Activities: Extreme Sports

Before You Watch. Discuss these questions in small groups.

1. What is the most dangerous sport you have tried? Why did you try a dangerous sport?

2. What do you know about hang gliding and paragliding? Describe these sports.
3. Have you ever meditated? What was it like?

Watch. Complete the sentences.

1. People enjoy hang gliding and paragliding because they are _____.
   a. peaceful
   b. good exercise
   c. safe

2. Hang gliding and paragliding are similar to _____.
   a. riding in a plane
   b. going up in a rocket ship
   c. flying like a bird

3. Tandem rides are for _____.
   a. one person
   b. two people
   c. three people

Watch Again. Answer these questions in small groups.

1. What is the name of the place that many people go to hang glide? _____

2. The narrator says, "To you and me it might be intimidating; to the veteran, it's blissful."
   a. What is *it*?
   b. Who are the veterans?
   c. What are other words for *intimidating*?
   d. What are other words for *blissful*?

3. Check the words that are used to describe hang gliding.
   a. spiritual   b. holy   c. dreamlike   d. natural   e. ethereal

After You Watch. Discuss these questions with your class.

1. Have you ever or would you ever go hang gliding or paragliding? Why or why not?

2. Have you ever had an experience similar to the ones described in the video segment?

Chapter 3

Sex and Gender

PART 1

Getting Started

Sharing Your Experience

1 Do you remember entering adolescence? What was that time like for you? In small groups, discuss the following questions.

A quinceañera party is a traditional celebration in some Latin families when a girl reaches the age of 15.

1. Did you participate in any ceremony marking the change from childhood to adulthood (for instance, a graduation ceremony, a religious ceremony, or a social event)? If so, describe it.
2. Did you change school levels at about this time?
3. What new interests did you develop?
4. Were you called by any new name or nickname?
5. What changes in responsibilities and relationships do you remember occurring after you reached puberty? For example, did you have greater responsibilities in your home? What were they? What about the community? Did your relationships with your friends or neighbors change? If so, how?

Vocabulary Preview

2   **Vocabulary in Context.**   The following words are some key terms used in the lecture. The definitions match the way the words are used by the lecturer. Use the correct forms of the words to complete the sentences in the letter from Pam to Nancy.

confirmation	*a religious ceremony recognizing the transition to adulthood*
equilibrium	*the state of being in balance*
fasting	*abstaining from food*
humiliation	*the lowering of the pride or dignity of a person*
infected	*the condition of being diseased with a germ or virus*
isolation	*the state of being alone*
navel	*the location on the body where the umbilical cord was attached to the fetus; the belly button*
ordeal	*an extremely difficult experience, usually involving physical and/or emotional stress or pain*
suitor	*a male who courts a female*
tribal	*characteristic of a tribe or group having a common ancestor or leader*

Thursday, October 16

Dear Nancy,
Well, here I am at home, sick in bed. All I've got is a sore throat, but the way Mom is acting, you'd think I was _____ with the plague or something. I don't think keeping me in _____ away from everybody else is really necessary. Nobody will catch what I have if I don't kiss them — ha! Ha!

I hate just lying around. I'm getting so fat it's _____ just to look in the mirror. Man! Guess I'd better give up junk food and maybe even stop eating for a week or so. But _____ is such an _____ it's really tough to stop eating for a whole week. I wonder if I can make it. I don't think you can die from hunger in only a week, though!

We have a foreign exchange student living with us for a month. Her name is Desta. She is very nice and has been telling me about customs in her country. In one _____ rite of passage, girls our age are separated from everyone for a period of time, and then there is a ceremony to celebrate their becoming an adult. Desta says this helps the girls adjust to the physical and emotional changes in their lives. The puberty rites help them to maintain their _____ instead of becoming unbalanced as they go through all these changes.

Desta has made some interesting dishes from her country, and she taught me some words in her language—like the words for boyfriend and girlfriend. And guess what! I've got a _____, a real boyfriend! Herman asked me out! And he calls me every day. He's even invited me to his sister's _____ ceremony and the party afterwards. But I'm not sure my Dad will let me go to the party, because it goes too late. Sometimes he treats me like I'm still attached to him and Mom by a cord at my _____ or something. Oh, well. Maybe next year!

Well, got to go now. Still have homework to do. (Ugh!) Write soon!

Love,
Pam

PART 2

Abbreviating—When and How

Creating Your Own Abbreviations

The best way to accurately note a lecturer's ideas is to use the same words the lecturer uses as often as possible. Writing down every word the lecturer says is almost impossible. To *abbreviate* means "to shorten." Knowing when and how to abbreviate will help you quickly and accurately take down the information. Later, when you are writing exams or papers, you can put the information into your own words.

Four Main Ways to Abbreviate

1. Leave out whole words, word endings, vowels, or other letters.

2. Use only the first letter, or first two or three letters, of a word.

3. Use symbols to replace words or letters.

4. Change word order.

For example, if the instructor says, "You will be expected to learn all about many ceremonies, perhaps over fifty, by the end of the term," you might write:

know 50 ceremonies by end of term

or

learn > 50 ceremonies

Or, if the instructor says, "A greater number of males than females are born to the Yuma tribe each year," you might shorten the sentence to:

Yuma tribe: males born > females each year

or

Yuma tr.: m. born > f. ea. yr.

If you prefer using symbols as much as possible, the previous example might look like this:

> # ♂ than ♀ / yr. for Yuma

Can you guess what the instructor must have said from the following examples?

Rts. of pas. Impt. all cults.

Rts. f. @ 10 yrs.; m. @ 12 yrs.

When you abbreviate, you must be careful not to use the same abbreviation for two different things. For example, if the instructor is talking about *transitions* in life and *transmissions* of knowledge, you shouldn't use *trans.* as the abbreviation for both words. Write two abbreviations you could use instead:

_____ and _____

Similarly, you should not use *ord.* as the abbreviation for both the words *ordeal* and *order*. Write two abbreviations you could use instead:

_____ and _____

Here's another example. Instead of writing *boy, male,* or *man*, you can usually use the symbol ♂ and instead of writing *girl, female,* or *woman*, you can usually use the symbol ♀ . But if an anthropology lecturer is discussing particular differences between what boys and men in the tribe are allowed to do, for example, it wouldn't be helpful to use ♂ for both. Write two abbreviations you could use instead:

_____ and _____

Naturally, you will develop your own system of abbreviations as you go along. But some systems seem to work well for most everyone. For example, some students use a small raised *g* to shorten all *-ing* words such as:

fastᵍ (fasting) _____

humiliatᵍ (humiliating) _____

isolatᵍ (isolating) _____

Some students also like to keep a key to their abbreviations at the top of the page. For example:

m. = married   M = males _____

_____

unm. M go off w. tribal elders to spend time fastᵍ. _____

_____

_____

Some Useful Abbreviations

Here are three lists of abbreviations. The first contains some of the most common word-level abbreviations; the second features items that are particularly useful for taking down homework assignments; and the third includes symbols. Even if you don't use any of these abbreviations in your own note taking, examining the list can help you develop your own system.

Commonly Used Abbreviations

a. answer	**alt.** altitude, alternate	**Amer.** American
Amers. Americans	**atm.** atmosphere, atmospheric	**av.** average
ave. avenue	**b.** born	**b.p.** boiling point
¢ cents	**c.** about (from Latin *circa*)	**cf.** compare (from Latin *confer*)
co. company	**ct.** count	**cu.** cubic
d. deceased, died	**dept.** department	**doz.** dozen
Dr. doctor	**ea.** each	**e.g.** for example (from Latin *exempli gratia*)
ff. following pages	**fr.** from	**ft.** feet
g. gram	**gal.** gallon	**id.** the same, identical (from Latin *idem*)
i.e. that is (from Latin *id est*)	**jr.** junior	**m.** married
mod. modern	**n.b.*** note well (from Latin *nota bene*)	**no(s).** number(s)
pd. paid	**pop.** population	**re.** regarding, concerning
rel. religion	**ret.** retired, returned	**riv.** river
s. son	**sc.** science	**sr.** senior
stat. statistics	**terr.** territory	**yr.** year

*N.b. is a good abbreviation to use as a note to yourself, indicating something important.

Abbreviations for Homework Assignments

ch. chapter	**p.** page
ev. #'s even numbers	**pp.** pages
1 learn	**q.** question(s)
od. #'s odd numbers	**st.** study

Mathematical and Other Symbols

one **1**	because **∴ , bec., b/c**	means, causes **→**
two **2, etc.**	before **b/4**	is caused by **←**
first **1st**	equal to **=**	plus, over **+**
second **2nd**	not equal to **≠**	minus **−**
third **3rd**	identical to **∫**	money **$**
fourth **4th, etc.**	hence, therefore **∴**	percent **%**
about, approximately **~**	intersection **∪**	question **?**
and **& or +**	more than **>**	there is **∃**
at **@**	less than **<**	

Before You Listen

1   **Discussing Abbreviations.**

1.   In small groups, share any note-taking abbreviations and symbols that you use. Write down any that are not in the boxes. Share them with the rest of the class.

_____

_____

_____

_____

2.   Ask your instructor what symbols and abbreviations he or she uses most often. Add these to your list.

Listen

2   **Taking Notes Using Abbreviations.** Listen to the lecture and take notes. Abbreviate whatever you can. At the pause, stop the tape and discuss the answers to the lecturer's questions.

_____

_____

_____

_____

_____

_____

After You Listen

3 **Comparing Notes.** Compare your notes with your classmates. If you see any abbreviations your classmates used that you think would be useful, put them on the board. Use these new abbreviations as you listen to the lecture and take notes a second time.

Talk It Over

4 **Decoding Abbreviations.** We encounter abbreviations and symbols in a variety of situations every day. As a class, decide what these abbreviations stand for.

1. ASAP (on a business memo)_____

2. FYI (on a business memo) _____

3. ANML DOC (on license plate)_____

4. SOS _____

5. Tom. clld. @ 7, cl. bk. _____

6. H2O_____

7.

_____

8.

_____

9.

_____

10.

_____

5 **Guessing about "Found" Symbols.** Look for examples of symbols and abbreviations in your daily life. (You'll probably need to spend a couple of days looking.) Bring them to class, put them on the board, and have your classmates guess where you found them and what they mean.

6 Creating Messages Using Abbreviations.

1. People sometimes have abbreviated messages on the license plates on their cars. In small groups, write messages for license plates. Use only the number of letters allowed in your state or area. Have your classmates guess their meanings.

2. Then create two messages that you could use on a T-shirt. Put these on the board and have your classmates guess what these T-shirt messages are.

PART 3

Extending Congratulations and Condolences

Many rites of passage are happy occasions such as birthdays, graduations, and weddings. At these times we offer *congratulations*. In contrast, when someone loses a job or suffers the death of a parent, spouse, child, or close friend, we offer *condolences* for the loss.

Expressions for Extending Congratulations

When you wish to congratulate someone, you can say "Congratulations" and add a phrase expressing good wishes appropriate to the particular occasion.

Congratulations! (plus one of the following)

For something new, such as a baby, job, car, an award, a raise, an engagement:

I'm so happy for you!	I'm so pleased for you!
I'm thrilled for you!	I'm tickled for you!
That's wonderful (terrific, great)!	That's great news!
It couldn't have happened to a nicer person!	

For birthdays:

May you have many more.	May you have a hundred more.
Many happy returns (of the day).	I wish you all that you wish for yourself.

For weddings:

(I wish you) All the best in the years to come.
All the best to you both.
May you have a long and prosperous life together.

For graduation:

I'm sure you'll have much success in the years to come.
I know you've got a great future ahead of you.

Expressions for Extending Condolences

On occasions of loss and grief, you should choose the most appropriate and sensitive words to express your feelings and offer comfort.

One of these expressions:

I'm so (terribly, extremely) sorry.

I can't tell you how sorry I am.

My thoughts are with you
(and your family)

My condolences to you .
(and your family)

All my sympathy to you in this
trying time.

*Followed by one of these
(optional):*

Is there anything I can do?

Let me know if there's anything you
need.

Can I help out in any way?

If there's anything I can do to help,
please don't hesitate to ask.

If you don't feel comfortable with any of the expressions of condolence, just be honest and put it this way:

I'm sorry. I just don't know what to say.

    or

I can't express how sorry I am.

1 **Listening for Sincere and Insincere Congratulations.** When you extend congratulations or condolences, you must use the appropriate tone of voice as well as the right words. For example, if your tone of voice is not genuinely happy or expresses indifference, your enthusiastic words of congratulations will never convince listeners that you are truly happy for them.

Listen to the following short conversations. In each conversation, the second speaker offers congratulations to the first. In some conversations, the second speaker is sincere (his or her tone of voice is enthusiastic) and in others he or she is indifferent (not enthusiastic). Listen to each conversation and circle the word that best describes the *second* speaker. When you are finished, compare your answers in small groups.

Conversation 1		**Conversation 4**	
sincere	indifferent	sincere	indifferent

Conversation 2		**Conversation 5**	
sincere	indifferent	sincere	indifferent

Conversation 3		**Conversation 6**	
sincere	indifferent	sincere	indifferent

2 **Listening for Expressions of Congratulations.** Listen to the following conversation in which congratulations are given. In the spaces provided, write down all the expressions of congratulations you hear. Compare answers with your classmates.

_____

_____

_____

_____

3 **Listening for Expressions of Condolences.** Listen to the following conversation in which condolences are given. In the spaces provided, write down all the expressions of condolences you hear. Compare answers with your classmates.

_____

_____

_____

_____

4 **Expressing Congratulations and Condolences.** During the first portion of the lecture, the instructor and students mention a variety of occasions for which congratulations or condolences might be appropriate. During the rest of the lecture, the instructor mentions a few more. Listen to the lecture and note other occasions that might require either congratulations or condolences. Compare notes with your classmates. Then as a class, choose expressions that would be appropriate for each of the situations in your notes.

Occasions requiring congratulations or condolences	**Appropriate expressions**
_____	_____
_____	_____
_____	_____
_____	_____
_____	_____
_____	_____

Talk It Over

5 **Sharing Cultural Expressions.** For the following occasions, think of expressions of congratulations or condolences in other languages. Then translate these expressions into English and share them with your classmates. How similar are these expressions to each other and to the ones in English?

1. An engagement: _____

2. A wedding (to the newly married couple): _____

    _____

3. A pregnancy: _____

4. The birth of a baby: _____

5. A graduation: _____

6. A job promotion: _____

7. A new purchase (a car or a house): _____

    _____

8. A retirement party: _____

9. A job loss: _____

10. The death of a friend: _____

11. The death of a relative: _____

12. A serious accident: _____

6 **Writing and Role-Playing Dialogues.**

1. Work with a partner to write dialogues for a few of the following situations requiring congratulations and condolences. In each situation, you must decide what might be said before and what might be said after the congratulations and condolences. Change partners and write a few more.

1. Congratulations! I'm so happy for you. When do you expect the new arrival?
2. I'm so sorry. How did it happen?
3. I'm so sorry. How sad you must feel. Is there anything I can do?
4. Congratulations! Who's the lucky person?
5. Congratulations! And what are your future plans?
6. Congratulations! What's his/her name?
7. I can't tell you how sorry I am. How's your mother doing?
8. Congratulations! I'm so pleased for you! When do you start?
9. Congratulations! That's great news! What time?
10. I'm sorry. I just don't know what to say. Please call me if you need anything.
11. Oh, that's terrible. I'm so sorry. Do you have any other possibilities?

2. Rehearse and present dialogues to the class.

| PART 4 | # Focus on Testing |

You will hear a short conversation. After the conversation you will be asked some questions. Circle the letter of the best answer to each question.

Question 1

a. a professor
b. a doctor
c. a student
d. a friend

Question 2

a. that they are too much
b. that they sound like a good idea
c. that they are a strange idea
d. that that climbing mountains is fun

Question 3

a. What seems normal is all a matter of what you're used to.
b. What seems OK is based on your cultural perspective.
c. Cultural norms never change.
d. Western rites of passage may seem strange to a tribal culture.

Question 4

a. their first date
b. their next date
c. his driver's license
d. cars

Video Activities: Seeking Love

Before You Watch. Discuss these questions in small groups.

1. What are some ways to meet people?
2. Which ways are the most effective?
3. What is the most important quality to seek in a boyfriend or a girlfriend?

Watch. Answer these questions in small groups.

1. What does the narrator say is probably what most of us want and need the most?

   _____

2. Check the ways of finding a mate that are mentioned in this video segment.
   a. ____ using a dating service
   b. ____ placing personal advertisements
   c. ____ getting involved in activities that you enjoy
   d. ____ asking friends to help you meet someone

3. Put a check (√) next to things that you should do and an (x) next to things that you shouldn't do on a first date.
   a. ____ Ask creative questions.   c. ____ Be someone that you're not.
   b. ____ Dress well.   d. ____ Ask questions to find out about your date's financial status.

Watch Again. Circle the correct answers.

1. What does Dr. Jim Soulis say you should do before you start looking for a mate?
   a. look into yourself   b. lose weight and   c. read books about
                                 buy new clothes   relationships

2. What does Dr. Jim Soulis say is the most quality you must have to find love?
   a. good looks   b. money   c. intelligence   d. confidence

3. Which three things does Victoria Parker tell her clients to do?
   a. meditate   b. think positively   c. study themselves
   d. listen to a tape recorder   e. become active in things they enjoy

4. What kind of personal ads does Judy Knoll say are not effective?
   a. imaginative ones   b. negative ones   c. boastful ones

5. Men should never _____.
   a. pay for a woman's friends
   b. compliment a woman on a part of her body
   c. call a woman when they said that they would

6. Men don't like women who _____.
   a. become attached too quickly
   b. ask them a lot of questions
   c. make a lot of money

After You Watch. Discuss these questions with your class.

1 How do you meet people?
2. What do you think is the best way to find a boyfriend or girlfriend?

Chapter 4

Mysteries Past and Present

Did You Know?

■ In the early 1980s, a U.S. scientist, Alan Guth, proposed the "big bang" theory of the origin of the universe. According to Guth, the universe was formed when some extremely condensed matter exploded and expanded to millions of times its previous size.

■ The length of a month ranges from 28 to 31 days because of early theories about the universe. Ancient peoples created the calendar of months using a system based on the apparent movements of the moon and the stars.

■ There are many different calendars currently in use around the world, including the Chinese, Vietnamese, Hebrew, Hindu, and Islamic.

■ After the sun, the star closest to Earth is Alpha Centauri. It is 260,000 times further away from us than the sun.

PART 1

Getting Started

Sharing Your Experience

In small groups, discuss the following items.

1 Look at the diagram of the solar system. How many planets can you identify? Which planet is closest to the sun? Which one is farthest away? Which one is closest to the earth? Label the diagram as well as you can. The number of moons or natural satellites is written as a numeral next to each planet.

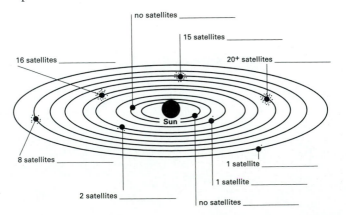

no satellites _____

15 satellites _____

16 satellites _____

20+ satellites _____

Sun

8 satellites _____

1 satellite _____

1 satellite _____

2 satellites _____

no satellites _____

2   Share stories, myths, or folktales that you have heard about the origin of the solar system. What similarities and differences are there among these creation stories?

Vocabulary Preview

3   **Vocabulary in Context.** Each of the following sentences provides a context for key words and phrases from the lecture. Read the sentence for each word or phrase and write your own definition. Then compare your definitions with your classmates.

(to) bear in mind	elements	mass
bottom line	(to) get right down to it	sphere
dense	hypothesis; to hypothesize	electromagnetic field
lump		

1. A magnet is a piece of metal that can attract iron. When a piece of metal is made into a magnet by using an electric current, the magnet is called an electromagnet. In outer space we find places where there are entire <u>electromagnetic fields</u>.

   An <u>electromagnetic field</u> is _____ .

2. To demonstrate to the class the relative sizes of the planets, the instructor took balls of different sizes and placed them at various distances from a very large ball, which represented the sun. These <u>spheres</u> were of many different colors, and the students were very interested in what the colors indicated about the planets.

   <u>Sphere</u> mean_____

3. When we study objects in space, we are often concerned with the size or volume of the object and what it is made of. We want to know, for example, if the <u>mass</u> is a solid or a liquid.

   <u>Mass</u> means _____

Modern astronomer Edwin P. Hubble.

4. Astronomers develop theories of the origin of the planets. They take certain ideas or theories and <u>hypothesize</u> about what the results would be if these ideas were correct. These results or conclusions then need to be tested to see if the ideas are actually correct. Unfortunately, it is often difficult for an astronomer to get enough money to test the <u>hypothesis</u>. He or she may struggle for years before raising the necessary money.

   <u>Hypothesis</u> means _____

   _____

   To <u>hypothesize</u> means _____

   _____

5. "Take these small pieces of clay," the instructor told the students, "and put the <u>lumps</u> together to build your own model of the solar system. Of course, you don't have to use clay. You could use <u>lumps</u> of dough or papier mâché if you prefer."

    <u>Lump</u> means _____

6. Another question astronomers ask about objects in space is this: How <u>dense</u> is the object? They need to know how close the molecules in the object are to each other. Often they use special photography to find the answer.

    <u>Dense</u> means _____

7. Scientists make guesses about what objects in space are made of. Their guesses are based on what they already know about the frequency of certain <u>elements</u> in the universe. They have a good idea ahead of time how much iron, hydrogen, or mercury will be found in objects in space.

    Besides iron, hydrogen, and mercury, examples of <u>elements</u> are _____

8. "<u>Bear in mind</u>," said the professor as a reminder to the students, "that we'll have an astronomy quiz each Thursday from now to the end of the term; put it on your calendars so you remember."

    To <u>bear in mind</u> means _____

9. "You must have a passing average to pass this course," he went on. "The <u>bottom line</u> is that no one with less than a 70 average passes." (See No. 10 for an additional example of the use of <u>bottom line</u>.)

    <u>Bottom line</u> means _____

10. "You know," said the astronomy professor, "you'll learn a lot about astronomy in this course. Astronomers have learned an enormous amount in the last hundred years. But when you <u>get right down to it</u>, what we've learned is that what we don't know is far greater than what we do know. The <u>bottom line</u> is that our ignorance is greater than our knowledge."

    To <u>get right down to it</u> means _____

| PART 2 |

Using Illustrations in Note Taking

Many students have difficulty remembering important information from a lecture. The best solution to this problem is to take notes. Research has shown that students who take notes using the lecturer's own words as much as possible do better than students who take notes using their own words.

To take good notes, however, you don't need to write down every single word the lecturer says. For example, you can abbreviate (See Chapter 3 Part 2). You can also use diagrams and pictures to illustrate what the lecturer says. There is a saying, "A picture is worth a thousand words," and a simple drawing can often replace several sentences in your notes.

A good time to use illustrations is when the lecturer is speaking about something easy to draw. Another good time is when the lecturer is talking about the relationships between two or more objects or ideas. For example, a lecturer says, "Consider two stars. The second one is about twice as big as the first. Now think about the smaller one rapidly approaching the larger one." In this case, you might draw something like this:

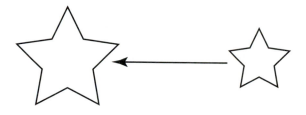

Or you might draw it this way:

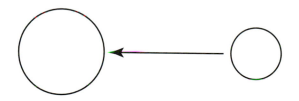

Later, the lecturer may add, "Now, let's call the larger star LS and the smaller star SS." You then label the stars. Note: You should label your drawing even if the lecturer does not tell you what label to give. Your drawing would now look like one of these drawings.

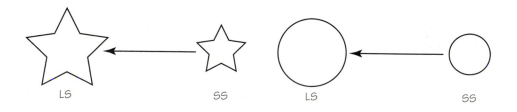

Label drawings carefully in order to avoid confusion later. The circles in the second drawing, for example, could be stars, planets, satellites, novas, or snowballs. When you reread your notes, you want to be able to distinguish the planets from the stars.

For example, if the lecturer says, "According to Tycho Brahe, planets travel in concentric circles around the sun, but then travel as a unit around the earth," you might draw and clearly label a diagram like this one.

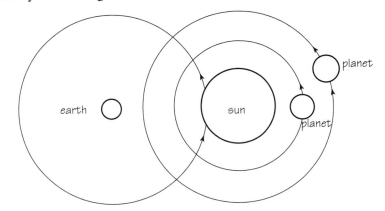

Note: In addition to making your own drawings and diagrams, you should always copy drawings and diagrams your instructor uses into your notes.

Before You Listen

1 **Discussing Scientific Theories.**   In groups of three or four, discuss the following questions.

1. What scientific theories about the origin of the solar system did you learn in school? How many theories does your group have? Summarize each group's scientific theories about the origin of the solar system and list them on the board.

2. Can your group think of any other ways that the solar system might have been formed? Share these ideas with the class.

Listen

2 **Using Illustrations in Note Taking.**   Listen to the lecture once through to become familiar with the scientific concepts introduced. Then look at the hypotheses on the next page. Some of them have been illustrated for you as examples. Listen to the lecture again and fill in the missing illustrations and labels.

1. Descartes's vortices theory
   a. Hot cloud of dust and gases

b. Cooling cloud becomes central body with smaller bodies revolving around it

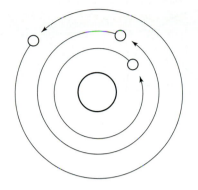

2. Kant and Laplace's nebular hypothesis

3. Jeans and Jeffries's gravitational attraction hypothesis

4. Alfvén's plasma-nebular hypothesis
    a. Rotating protostar set off thermonuclear reaction

b.   At first, the disk turned much more slowly than the center sphere

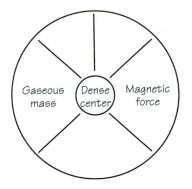

c.   Later, the disk gained speed until it was faster than center sphere, and cooling caused lumps to form, which eventually became planets and moons

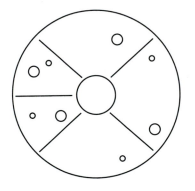

d.   Planet and moons formed according to chemical composition of the lumps

After You Listen

3   **Comparing Notes.**   Compare your illustrations with a partner. Each pair of students in the class should put at least one illustration on the board. As a class, discuss the good points of each of the illustrations.

Talk It Over

4   **Using Illustrations To Enhance Descriptions**.   Make up a description of an uncharted, new solar system.

1.   In pairs, imagine that you and your partner are traveling in a space capsule toward a new solar system. When you arrive, describe to each other what you see out the window of the space capsule as you pass through this new solar system. Be sure to include the following:

■   the size of the sun in relation to the planets

■   the number and size of planets in relation to each other

■   the distance of each planet from the sun

■   the number of moons each planet has (if any)

■   any unusual characteristics of any of the planets (for example, any planet that always faces the sun so that half the planet is in darkness)

■   any other objects, such as spaceships and meteors

2.   Make a drawing of what you both described.

5   **Giving a Scientific Report.**   Put a barrier between you and your partner or sit back-to-back.

1.   Imagine that you are a space explorer and your partner is your contact at Mission Control. Choose one of the planets from the uncharted solar system that you explored in the previous exercise. Describe to Mission Control what you see on both sides of the planet as you circle it in your spaceship. Give enough information so that your partner at Mission Control can take clear

notes, for example, "On one side of the planet I see three large bodies of water, and the funny thing is that they are all shaped like letters of the alphabet. The first, at the upper left, is shaped like an E. The second, right below it, is shaped like an R, and the third, in the upper right, is shaped like a G. The land masses all have mountains in the middle that seem to be made entirely of some sort of shiny metal. All around the mountains are meadows of crystal. There are seven cities, all on the plains . . ."

2. When your partner, taking notes at Mission Control, has a good "picture" of the planet, change roles and do the activity again.

3. When everyone in the class has finished, a few pairs of students can read their descriptions to the entire class. As the descriptions are given, class members can take turns drawing the various features of the planets on the board or on paper.

PART 3   # Admitting a Lack of Knowledge

In the United States and Canada, a person's ability to admit a lack of knowledge is valued. Students often criticize an instructor who is unwilling to admit ignorance and praise an instructor who is willing to admit ignorance. The same is true for how students view each other.

Formal Ways to Admit a Lack of Knowledge

One of these:	*Followed by one of these:*
I'm afraid…	I can't remember.
I'm sorry but…	I can't/couldn't tell you.
	I don't know.
	I don't remember.
	I forget.
	I have no idea.
	I just don't know.
	It's slipped my mind.
	I'm not sure.

If you add a reason for your lack of knowledge, your words will sound more polite. For example:

a: Can you tell me where the post office is?
b: No, I'm afraid I couldn't tell you. I'm new here myself.

Informal Ways to Admit a Lack of Knowledge

The following expressions are used frequently among friends, but may sound rude in other contexts.

Beats me.

(I) Can't/couldn't even begin . . .

Don't ask me.

(I) haven't (got) a clue.

(I) haven't the foggiest (idea).

I have no idea.

How do I know?

I give up!

It's beyond me.

I'm sure I don't know.

1 Listening for Formal and Informal Expressions.   Listen to the following conversations in which one person admits a lack of knowledge. In some conversations, the second speaker is more formal, and in others he or she is more informal. Listen to each conversation and circle the word that best describes the *second* speaker. When you are finished, compare your answers in small groups and discuss the conversations. Do you think in any of the conversations the second speaker is actually rude?

Conversation 1

formal   informal

Conversation 2

formal   informal

Conversation 3

formal   informal

Conversation 4

formal   informal

Conversation 5

formal   informal

Machu Pichu

2 **Listening for Expressions Admitting a Lack of Knowledge.** Listen to the lecture and write the expressions the lecturer and students use to express their lack of knowledge.

Talk It Over

3 **Using Formal Expressions to Admit a Lack of Knowledge.**

1. Think of an unexplained phenomenon or mystery (e.g., the Loch Ness monster, the Bermuda Triangle, Easter Island, UFOs, crop circles, ghosts, Machu Picchu, Bigfoot) that you know about and write ten questions about it. Try to have five questions that people will probably be able to answer and five that they won't.

     Examples:
     Where is Stonehenge? (England)
     How did the Druids move the rocks at Stonehenge? (No one knows.)

2. Choose a partner and take turns asking and answering the questions. Answer the questions if you can, but when you can't, admit your lack of knowledge by using a variety of formal expressions from the explanation box.

3. When you finish, change partners and do the activity again. Then change partners several more times if time permits. You may want to eliminate some of your questions and add a few others for variety as you go along.

4 **Using Informal Expressions to Admit a Lack of Knowledge.** Think about some less mysterious questions such as:

■ Where's the cap for the toothpaste?
■ Where are the car keys?
■ Why are some fire engines painted red and others green?
■ When will they fill that big hole in the street in front of the school?

Jot down ten questions of this type, then ask and answer the questions with a partner as you did in the previous activity. Respond using informal expressions from the explanation box. Practice using various tones of voice from polite to irritated to rude. Use your acting skills and have fun.

PART 4 # Focus on Testing

You will hear a short American Indian folktale. After the folktale, you will be asked some questions. Circle the letter of the best answer to each question.

Question 1

a. Coyote
b. Silver Fox
c. Coyote and Silver Fox
d. Coyote, Silver Fox, and the rest of the animals

Question 2

a. They decided to make things.
b. They decided to dance.
c. They decided to make the world.
d. They decided to whirl around.

Question 3

a. They sang and hopped.
b. They danced and ran.
c. They ran and jumped and hopped and skipped.
d. They sang and danced and jumped and skipped.

Question 4

a. The Story of a Traveler
b. The Story of How the World Was Made
c. The Story of How Not to Become Lonely
d. The Story of a Silver Fox

Video Activities: Abduction by Aliens

Before You Watch. Discuss these questions in small groups.

1. Do you think that people from other planets have visited Earth? Have you ever seen a UFO? (Unidentified Flying Object)
2. Abduct means the same as _____.
   a. borrow   b. kidnap   c. visit

Watch. Answer these questions in small groups.

1. Ruth Foley says that she _____.
   a. has been abducted by people from outer space
   b. was born in outer space
   c. she has visited other planets

2. What do the abductors look like? Write a description.

   _____

   _____

   _____

3. According to Ruth, what is the abductors' purpose?
   a. to perform medical tests
   b. to ask people about life on Earth
   c. to tell people about their planet

4. People in Indiana say that _____ burned the ground near a house in Indiana.
   a. an abductor   b. a light   c. a spaceship

5. The author of Secret Life _____ abductions really happen.
   a. isn't sure if   b. is positive that   c. doesn't believe that

Watch Again. Write answers to these questions.

1. How old was Ruth Foley when she was first abducted? _____
2. Who once saw Ruth being abducted? _____
3. What was the year of the abduction in Indiana? _____
4. How long did it take for the grass to grow on the burned spot? _____
5. Who is John Mack and what did he write? _____
6. What does John Mack believe? _____

After You Watch. Discuss these questions with your class.

1. Do you believe Ruth Foley's story? Why or why not?
2. Have you ever heard or read of any other stories of UFOs? Describe them.

Chapter 5

Transitions

Did You Know?

■ Some people like change and some don't. Everett Rogers of Michigan State University divides people into five basic categories. Which type are you?

■ "Innovators" are adventurous and eager to try new things. They are usually young and don't care too much what others think. (2.5% of the population)

■ "Early Adopters" are often respected leaders within the established social system. People ask for their opinions before adopting new ideas. (13.5%)

■ "Early Majority" people are followers rather than leaders. They make changes only after a lot of their friends do. (34%)

■ "Late Majority" people are doubtful of change and cautious about adopting new ideas. They have little influence on the actions of others. (34%)

■ "Resisters" are very suspicious of new ideas and generally think things were better in the past. They are not curious and do not take risks. (16%)

PART 1

Getting Started

Sharing Your Experience

1   Everyone experiences transitions in life. These might include changing schools, getting married, or just getting older and facing new responsibilities and privileges. In small groups, discuss two transitions that you've faced and what they meant to you. When you were going through these transitions, did you feel in control or did you feel caught by the circumstances and events surrounding these times?

Vocabulary Preview

2   **Vocabulary in Context.**   Match the definitions on the right to the underlined words in the sentences on the left.

____ 1.	We shouldn't be surprised that it is difficult to figure out other people's <u>motives</u> for the things they do when we can't even figure out our own.	a. compelled to do something
____ 2.	People who believe that we are like puppets and have little control over our lives may feel that our efforts in life will produce only "sound and <u>fury</u>" and in the end will not mean anything.	b. reasons for doing something
____ 3.	Some children will <u>whine</u> on and on until their parents finally can't stand it anymore and will give them whatever they want.	c. to say something indirectly
____ 4.	Some people believe that <u>passion</u> is the cause of much suffering in life, while others believe that <u>passion</u> is the only thing that makes life worth living.	d. to frighten by showing power or making threats
____ 5.	Extremely confident and strong-willed people can easily <u>intimidate</u> others who are shy and less confident.	e. a soft but irritating noise made through the nose and used to complain
____ 6.	The man was so <u>driven</u> by ambition that he rarely went home from work until 10 or 11 at night.	f. intense emotion
____ 7.	He <u>beat around the bush</u> for 15 minutes before he finally directly said, "Due to changes in the company, you're fired."	g. anger; rage

3   **Using Vocabulary.**   As a class or in small groups, discuss the following questions.

1. Did you ever feel as if you were *in a rut* and want to make a major change in your life? If so, when? Why?

2. Do you think it's important *to make a name for yourself* in life? Why or why not?

3. What are some of the things you would do *at the drop of a hat*? (For example: Help a friend in trouble? Eat a piece of chocolate cake? Go for a swim in the ocean?)

4. There's a fine line between honesty and rudeness. But sometimes you have to speak out and say something in a straightforward manner, in other words, *put it bluntly*. When was the last time you had to do this? What were the circumstances? What did you say?

5. Sometimes it seems that certain laws of irony operate in the universe. For example, Jeremy called Susan to invite her to a party and left a message about the party with her roommate. When Susan called back two hours later, Jeremy rushed to answer the phone and fell and broke his arm. It was bad enough that he had broken his arm, but *to add insult to injury,* it turned out that Susan was planning to go to the party with someone else instead. What have been some of the ironies in your life, or cases in which insult was added to injury?

Understanding and Using Figurative Language

Life is like a river, always changing, yet ever the same. This expression is an example of figurative language; that is, language used to create an image and not meant to be taken literally. An analogy is one type of figurative language. It is a comparison, showing the logical relationship between two things. A metaphor is another type of figurative language. It is similar to an analogy because it shows the relationship between two things, but it is different because it says that one thing "is" another thing and not just similar to it. Some examples of analogies and metaphors are:

1. An idea is like a seed.

2. History is merely gossip. — *Oscar Wilde*

3. Love is food for the soul, but jealousy is poison.

4. Life is a disease. The only difference between one man and another is the stage of the disease. — *George Bernard Shaw*

Analogies and metaphors can be paraphrased as equations. For example, the four previous examples can be represented by the following equations:

1. idea = seed   3.   love = food for the soul

2. history = gossip   4.   life = disease

Analogies and metaphors make language more interesting and vivid and are powerful ways to make your ideas understandable. They do not have to be complex; in fact, they can be quite simple. It is common for people to use analogies and metaphors to help others understand what they are trying to say. Therefore, it is important for you to be able to recognize them and to know the difference between literal and figurative language as you develop your listening skills.

Expressions Often Used in Making Analogies

about the size of a	as (big) as	mean(s)
are almost like	is the same as	seem(s) like
are similar to		

Before You Listen

1 **Considering the Topic.** In small groups discuss the following:

1. Do you think people have much influence over their own growth and development (physical, mental, and emotional)? Or do you think that "free will" does not exist and that human beings are like puppets whose strings are pulled by forces beyond their control? Why?

2. Assume for the moment that you *do* direct your own life, or "pull your own strings" as the expression goes. What do you personally want to achieve to feel successful? (Give at least one example.) What are the steps you plan to take to make this happen?

3. Consider the following quotations about time. What do you think they mean? Does any one of them hold particular significance for you? Why? If you can, tell about an event or time in your life when one of these quotations might have been significant. Let your classmates guess which quotation best applies to the situation you describe.

Time wasted is existence, used [it] is life —*Henry Wadsworth Longfellow*

I recommend you take care of the minutes, for the hours will take care of themselves —*Lord Chesterfield*

Unhappy is he who trusts only to time for his happiness —*Voltaire*

Listen

Public Radio Newsletter

Transitions in Literature Series
Program 6

Jacques's Speech from *As You Like It*

Jacques from Shakespeare's
As You Like It.

All the world's a stage,
And all the men and women merely players.
They have their exits and their entrances,
And one man in his time plays many parts.
His acts being seven ages. At first the infant,
Mewling and puking in the nurse's arms,
Then whining schoolboy, with his satchel
And shining morning face, creeping like a snail
Unwillingly to school. And then the lover,
Sighing like a furnace, with a woeful ballad
Made to his mistress' eyebrow. Then a soldier,
Full of strange oaths, and bearded like a pard,
Jealous in honor, sudden and quick in quarrel,
Seeking the bubble reputation
Even in the cannon's mouth. And then the justice,
In fair round belly with good capon lined,
With eyes severe, and beard of formal cut,
Full of wise saws and modern instances,
And so he plays his part. The sixth age shifts
Into the lean and slippered Pantaloon,
With spectacles on nose and pouch on side,
His youthful hose, well saved, a world too wide
For his shrunk shank, and his big manly voice,
Turning again toward childish treble, pipes
And whistles in his sound. Last scene of all,
That ends this strange eventful history,
Is second childishness and mere oblivion,
Sans teeth, sans eyes, sans taste, sans everything.

2 **Listening for Figurative Language.**

1. Listen to the lecture once all the way through and note the main ideas.
2. Then play it again and make a mark in the box each time you hear an analogy or a metaphor.

Analogies and Metaphors	Total Number

3. Listen to the lecture a third time. As you listen, complete the following analogies or metaphors. Use the lecturer's words if you can. Otherwise, complete them in your own words.

Examples: Life is like a giant _puzzle_.

A Buddhist would probably see transformation or change as _an opportunity for spiritual growth_.

1. We seem to be afraid that all our planning, and struggling for success are simply _____
_____.

2. One of the most disturbing visions is the idea that we are just _____
_____.

3. Or even worse, what if we are just _____
_____.

4. The seven stages of life are _____
_____.

5. The schoolboy creeps to school like _____
_____.

6. When the lecturer says the hero burns with desire, he means that desire is like _____
_____.

7. The young hero thinks that becoming a man means _____
_____.

8. The young soldier grows a beard so he will look as fierce _____
_____.

9. As the man grows older, he loses the clear voice of youth. Now his voice _____
_____.

10. Reaching old age, the man has almost come full circle. He is now like _____ again.

After You Listen

3 **Comparing Answers.** After each of the three parts of Activity 2, compare your answers with your classmates. Discuss the meaning of each analogy and metaphor.

Talk It Over

4 **Making Analogies.** In small groups, think of as many analogies as you can for each of the following items. One way to do this is to create free associations: that is, to see what pops into your head when you hear each item. Then make an analogy comparing the item with the idea that just came to you. Or you may prefer to be more deliberate and analytical in devising your analogies.

> **Example:**   time
>
>   time = change
>
>   Time is like a river, constantly changing yet always the same.

1. love	6. sorrow	11. youth
2. infatuation	7. life	12. old age
3. passion	8. death	13. a friend
4. a realist	9. a woman	14. imperfection
5. a man	10. perfection	15. ambition

5 **Determining the Subjects of Analogies.**   Share some of your group's analogies with the rest of the class by playing the following guessing game. Consider all the analogies your group created and select a few favorites. Now substitute the pronoun *it* for the subject of each of these analogies and see if the rest of the class can guess which item you are talking about.

> **Example:**   *It* is like a river, constantly changing yet always the same.
>
>   Question: What is *it*?
>
>   Answer: Time.

PART 3

Making Negative Statements or Comments Politely

Many times there is only a fine line between honesty and rudeness. This is especially true when what is being said is negative or critical. The negative comment may be based on accepted fact, or it may be just a personal opinion, in which case the thin line between honesty and rudeness becomes even thinner. Therefore, when you feel you must make a negative statement and you don't want to offend the listener, you can use one of the following expressions with a sympathetic tone of voice.

If the expression and the negative statement following it are not delivered in a sympathetic, sincere tone, they will not have the desired effect. For example, if your voice sounds sarcastic, angry, or impatient, your words will convey only these feelings and you will sound rude.

Polite Expressions for Making Negative Comments

Actually, I hate to say this, but . . .

For some reason . . .

Frankly, I don't like saying this but . . .

I'm afraid . . .

I'm sorry to tell you . . .

It could be said that . . .

Let's face it . . .

Not to beat around the bush . . .

This is difficult/hard to say, but honestly . . .

To be frank . . .

To be honest with you . . .

To put it bluntly . . .

To tell the truth . . .

---

1 **Listening for Appropriate Tone of Voice.** You will hear three pairs of conversations. Each of the pairs uses exactly the same words, but each version has a different meaning because of the tone of voice used by one of the speakers. Listen to each conversation and answer the questions.

Conversation 1A

1. Is Gloria really concerned about Ted? _____
   Is Mickey? _____

2. How do you know?_____
   _____
   _____

3. How would Ted feel if he overheard this conversation?_____
   _____

Conversation 1B

1. Is Gloria really concerned about Ted now? _____
   Is Mickey? _____

2. How do you know? _____
   _____
   _____

3. How would Ted feel if he overheard this conversation? _____
   _____

Conversation 2A

1. How does the father feel about not going to his daughter's wedding? _____
   _____

2. How do you know? _____
   _____
   _____

3. What reason might he have for not going? _____
   _____

Conversation 2B

1. How does the father feel about not going to his daughter's wedding?
   _____

2. How do you know? _____
   _____

3. What reason might he have for not going? _____
   _____

Conversation 3A

1. Does Jane like Paul's artwork? _____

2. How can you tell? _____
   _____

3. Does Jane like Paul? _____

4. How can you tell? _____
   _____

Conversation 3B

1. Does Jane like Paul's artwork? _____

2. How can you tell? _____
   _____
   _____
   _____

3. Does Jane like Paul? _____

4. How can you tell? _____
   _____
   _____
   _____

2   Listening for Expressions That Introduce Negative Statements.   In the lecture, the instructor uses various expressions to introduce negative statements or comments. As you listen to the lecture, write down as many of the expressions as you can. What can you tell about the lecturer's attitudes from the tone of voice used with each one? Share your responses with the class.

1. Let's face it. (for Activity 2) _____

   Time and change always bring our decline and eventual death. (for Activity 3) _____

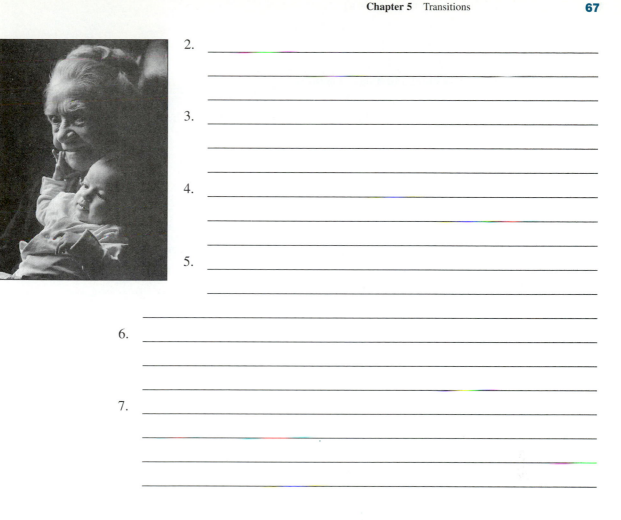

2. _____

_____

_____

3. _____

_____

_____

4. _____

_____

_____

5. _____

_____

_____

6. _____

_____

_____

7. _____

_____

_____

_____

3   Listening for Negative Statements.   Listen to the lecture again. This time write the negative statement that follows each of the introductory expressions you wrote for Activity 2. You may paraphrase these negative statements if you wish. Share your responses with the class.

Talk It Over

4   Role-Playing Dialogues.

1. Choose a partner and together select one of these situations as the basis for a role-play.
2. Invent two characters who might find themselves in this situation and decide which of you will play each one.
3. Select an attitude and tone of voice for each character from the second list. The characters can use the same tones of voice or different ones.
4. Role-play a dialogue in which the characters talk about the situation they find themselves in. Practice introducing negative comments using the expressions on page 65. (See the following sample dialogue.)
5. If time permits, choose another situation, another set of characters, and new tones of voice and do a new role-play.

Situations

1. the birth of a baby
2. a child's first day at school
3. a child skipping class
4. a child pretending to be sick so he or she won't have to go to school
5. graduating from school
6. cheating on an exam
7. being interviewed for a job
8. getting offered a job you don't want
9. getting fired
10. retiring
11. falling in love with someone who doesn't love you
12. getting divorced
13. getting married
14. changing careers
15. becoming a widow or widower
16. a situation of your choice

Tones of voice

1. sad	8. hurt	15. nervous
2. angry	9. vengeful	16. passionate
3. depressed	10. shy	17. confused
4. delighted	11. sarcastic	18. envious
5. excited	12. guilty	19. mean
6. frightened	13. powerless	20. amused
7. loving	14. powerful	

Sample dialogue

Situation: birth of a baby. Terry speaks in a *depressed* tone and Francis is *amused*.

Terry: Did you hear what happened after Jennifer's baby was born?

Francis: No! What happened?

Terry: Well, after seeing the baby, Jennifer's husband went home and cried.

Francis: You're kidding! Why?

Terry: Well, to put it bluntly, their baby is really ugly. Isn't that depressing?

Francis: No, not particularly. Let's face it: All newborn babies are ugly.

Terry: To tell the truth, I agree with you. It's a wonder more fathers don't go home and cry after they see their babies for the first time.

Francis: Well, why waste tears so soon? By the time they're teenagers, the parents will really have reasons to cry!

5 **Guessing Situations and Emotions.** With your partner, present a dialogue to the rest of the class, but do not tell your classmates which situation or emotions you have selected. After you've finished, let them guess.

PART 4 # Focus on Testing

You will hear a short presentation. After the presentation you will be asked some questions. Circle the letter of the best answer to each question.

Question 1

a. 5%
b. 40%
c. 8%
d. 85%

Question 2

a. the first stage
b. the second stage
c. the third stage
d. the fourth stage

Question 3

a. Hindu women are considered to be both divine and inferior.
b. Hindu women are expected to go through the same Dharma stages as men.
c. Hindu women are traditionally expected only to serve their husbands.
d. Hindu women are traditionally expected to have no interests outside the home.

Question 4

a. Samnyasa
b. Brahmacarya
c. Dharma
d. Vanaprasthya

Video Activities: College Graduation

Before You Watch. Discuss these questions in small groups.

1. Have you ever attended a graduation ceremony? What happened at the ceremony?
2. How many years do people usually have to study to become doctors?

Watch. Circle the correct answers to the following questions.

1. Why is Mrs. Christianson so happy?
   a. She's graduating from college.
   b. Her son is becoming a doctor.
   c. She has just immigrated to the United States.

2. Louis Christianson says that his mother gave him a love of _____.
   a. education
   b. medicine
   c. Mexico

3. Louis decided to become a doctor _____.
   a. when he was young
   b. in high school
   c. after high school

Watch Again. Match the speakers to the quotations.

Quotations	Speakers
____ 1. I'd love to share with you some stories about the medical students soon to be physicians before you.	a. narrator
____ 2. I did a major in philosophy, so I had no plans to go to medical school.	b. graduation speaker
____ 3. Nine years ago Christianson was graduating from Madison High School.	c. Mr. Christianson
____ 4. I still see him as my baby.	d. Louis Christianson
____ 5. We are delighted.	e. Mrs. Christianson

After You Watch. Discuss these questions with your class.

1. Why do we have graduation ceremonies? What is their importance?
2. If you were planning a graduation ceremony, would you change anything or keep it completely traditional?

Chapter 6

The Mind

Did You Know?

■ Adult humans begin dreaming about 90 minutes after they fall asleep. Dreams continue to occur about 90 minutes apart and total nearly two hours per night. With approximately five dreams a night, humans will have about 136,000 dreams in a lifetime, spending a total of six years in a dream state.

■ The dream state is called REM (rapid eye movement) sleep because when they dream, most people's eyes move rapidly as if they were watching an exciting movie.

■ REM sleep is a combination of very light sleep and very deep sleep. The person in a REM state is sleeping lightly enough to be aware of light and noises in the room. However, the REM sleeper is not able to move any part of the body at all.

PART 1   Getting Started

Sharing Your Experience

1   As a class or in small groups, discuss these questions.

1. How often do you remember your dreams?

2. When are you most likely to remember your dreams? After you've eaten a large meal? After seeing an exciting movie? At the end of a stressful day?

3. Do you believe dreams help people deal better with daily life? If so, how?

Le Libérateur by René Magritte

Hand with Reflecting Sphere by M.C. Escher

Time Transfixed by René Margritte

Vocabulary Preview

2   Definitions.   You may already know the meanings of some of the following words. However, the words you know may be different from the ones your classmates know. In small groups, match the definitions on the right with the words on the left.

_____ 1. chaotic
_____ 2. to conceptualize
_____ 3. the downside
_____ 4. fleeting
_____ 5. flexibility
_____ 6. in tune with
_____ 7. to manipulate
_____ 8. perception
_____ 9. trivial
_____ 10. the upside
_____ 11. to visualize

a. unimportant; ordinary
b. to form mental images
c. the ability to bend; ability to adjust
    to new situations
d. the positive side; good part
e. disorganized; in a state of confusion
f. vanishing quickly
g. insight gained through the senses;
    observation
h. to manage (people, numbers, stocks, and so
    forth) skillfully for one's own profit
i. in harmony with; in agreement with
j. to form theories, ideas, or concepts
k. the negative side; bad part

3   Vocabulary in Context.   Work with a partner. First choose roles and read the following telephone conversation together. Then read it a second time, pausing to replace the underlined words with some of the expressions introduced in Activity 2.

Telephone Conversation

Stacy: Hi, Hank. What's up? How's the psych course going? Is it interesting?

Hank: Yeah. The chapter this week is pretty interesting.

Stacy: Oh yeah? What's the topic?

Hank: It's about dreams.

Stacy: What's so interesting about dreams?

Hank: Well, for one thing, it's hard to come up with new theories about dreams. To form new theories is difficult because there are so many current theories.

Stacy: Like what?

Hank: Well, for one thing, there's the theory that dreams reflect reality.

Stacy: What do you mean by that?

Hank: Some philosophers say that there is no way to prove that those quickly disappearing images we have in our sleep may be just another form of this crazy, unorganized world we live in. They say that our view of the world, which we get through sight, sound, touch, taste, and smell, may actually be changed through dreams.

Stacy: That sounds like it might not be unimportant. What else did you learn?

Hank: Well, that in some cultures forming an image that comes in a dream is considered to be no different from reality. And people in those cultures hold on so strongly to this belief that they react in waking life as though the dream were true. They seem to have no <u>willingness to adjust or change their minds</u> on this matter. For example, a Zulu man reportedly broke off a friendship after he dreamt that his friend intended to harm him.

Stacy: I wonder how that would work in our culture. People would try to <u>control and guide</u> their dreams so they could make their waking hours happier, don't you think?

Hank: I guess so. You'd really have to understand the workings of the mind to be so <u>in harmony with</u> your dreams like that, wouldn't you?

Stacy: Yeah, I guess you would.

Hank: Hey, listen. Enough about school. You want to catch a movie Thursday night?

Stacy: Sure. What did you have in mind?

Hank: Renoir's *The Grand Illusion* is playing at the Fine Arts. Want to see it?

Stacy: Sure, come by for me at 6:00.

Hank: Okay, see you then. Bye.

Stacy: Bye.

PART 2

Listening for Comparisons and Contrasts

In Chapter 5, you learned about using analogies for comparison - that is, looking at the similarities between two things. English speakers commonly use analogies both in formal and informal situations. For example, in a lecture on the nature of dreams you might hear:

Dreams are like smoke. You can't quite hang on to them, and they go away so quickly that you can barely remember them.

In a casual conversation a friend might say:

> In my dream last night the clouds were like human heads, each one smiling and wearing a funny hat. I woke up laughing.

Another way of looking at the relationship between two things is to point out the differences between them, that is, to contrast them. In this chapter we will look at how analogies can be used for both comparison and contrast.

Comparisons and contrasts are indicated in four main ways: (1) through words that signal comparison, (2) through words that signal contrast, (3) through pairs of antonyms within a single statement, and (4) through tone of voice. Below are some examples of each type of indicator.

Expressions That Signal Comparison

again	in a similar way
also	likewise
and so does . . .	similarly
equally important	the same way (as)
in a like manner to . . .	

Expressions That Signal Contrast

although / though / even though	meanwhile
but	nevertheless
by (in) contrast	on the contrary
conversely	on the other hand
however	whereas
instead	yet

Pairs of Antonyms

Antonyms can be used to show contrast when the speaker is talking about one topic or idea.

Fortunately . . .	Unfortunately . . .
The advantages are . . .	The disadvantages are . . .
The best part is . . .	The worst part is . . .
The positive features are . . .	The negative features are . . .

Tone of Voice

Word stress and intonation can also indicate comparison and contrast. For example, in the following sentences, comparison is indicated by stressing the words *mind* and *body* and by using rising intonation at the end of the first sentence and falling intonation at the end of the second. Try it.

The *mind* repairs itself during sleep.
The *body* repairs itself during sleep.

1 **Listening for Comparison and Contrast in Informal Conversations.** The following conversations contain examples of each type of indicator. Listen to the conversations once and discuss them with a partner. Then listen a second time and list which indicators of comparison and contrast were used by the speakers. When you are finished, compare your answers in small groups.

1. Otto and Henry _____

    _____

2. Judy and Paula _____

    _____

3. a teaching assistant and students _____

    _____

Before You Listen

2 **Considering the Topic.**   Have you ever dreamed about something that later actually happened? For example, you might have dreamed about receiving a gift or seeing a car accident and then had the exact same thing happen in real life. Share your stories in small groups.

Listen

3 **Listening for Comparison and Contrast in a Lecture.**   Listen to the lecture to get the main ideas. Also write down any words or phrases that might signal a comparison or a contrast.

Illustration from Ursula LeGuin's novel *The Lathe of Heaven*

_____

_____

_____

_____

_____

The following chart lists some of the comparisons and contrasts in the lecture. Listen to the lecture again and fill in the chart as you listen.

Dreams vs. Reality

	Comparison	**Contrast**
1. Dreams and waking life	Both waking images and dreams are inspirations for scientists, artists _____ _____	Dream images are more subtle than waking experiences _____ _____
2. Two types of dreams	✕	_____ _____ _____ _____ _____
3. Dr. Haber's reaction to George and other people's reaction to George	✕	_____ _____ _____ _____ _____
4. George and Dr. Haber	_____ _____ _____ _____ _____	_____ _____ _____ _____ _____
5. The lathe of heaven and a child playing with a tape recorder	_____ _____ _____ _____ _____	✕
6. Our concept of time and LeGuin's concept of time	✕	_____ _____ _____ _____

After You Listen

4 **Comparing Responses.**   Share your answers to Activities 2 and 3 with your class-mates. At what points in the lecture are comparisons and contrasts *not* introduced by the usual signal words? Which comparisons are marked by intonation changes?

Talk It Over

5 **Comparing and Contrasting Dreams.**   Ursula LeGuin suggested that reality can-not be controlled. Similarly, dreams cannot be controlled, which may be one reason we can learn about our hopes, beliefs, and feelings from our dreams. Some dreams are symbolic; others are more straightforward representations of actual events.

In this activity you will be comparing and contrasting two dreams stimulated by the same event. First read Situation 1 and the two dreams. Then discuss the following questions as a class. Then do the same for Situations 2 to 5, stopping to discuss each in turn.

1. How are the dreams similar?
2. How are the dreams different?
3. Which one is more symbolic and which is more related to actual events? Why do you feel this way?

Situation 1

You and a friend read the following story in a newspaper: The Hotel Ritz has been robbed. Three gunmen, posing as doctors, entered the hotel in Dallas. Because there was a medical convention in the hotel at the time, the gunmen were undetected and made a clean getaway.

Dream 1: A doctor is examining you, but instead of being in an office, you are in your car. All of a sudden, the doctor pulls out a gun.

Dream 2: You have invited a few friends for dinner. You are making the final prepara-tions in the kitchen. As you reach for the butter, it turns into a pistol.

Situation 2

The atmosphere at school has been chaotic because final examinations will be given next week. Of course, students are studying intensely. You're especially worried about your economics final because your instructor is hard to understand and reminds you of a rhinoceros.

Dream 1: While you are in the library with your economics book, you notice a rhi-noceros chewing a textbook on the table next to yours. Nobody but you seems to notice.

Dream 2: You are reading a paperback in bed with your stereo playing very loudly. Everything is fine. All at once, your normally well-behaved dog jumps on the bed and begins howling and will not stop.

Situation 3

Two men in the office are arguing about administrative policies. Jim, who has worked there longer, wants the promotion, but the offer was made to Michael, a newer employee who has been working for Jim. No seniority system exists.

Jim's dream: A rock band is playing in the cafeteria, and everyone is eating pink and green food with stars on it. Jim asks the band to play some folk music, but the band members ignore him. He tries to buy some of the pink and green food with stars on it, but the young man at the cash register says he's too old to eat this food and asks him to leave.

Michael's dream: Michael has a conversation with Jim and apologizes for the argument. Jim forgives him and announces that he has a new job at twice the salary at a Japanese company just opening down the street.

Situation 4

You have read in the newspaper about a group of skiers who have been missing for two weeks. Rescue teams fear the worst because avalanches have been occurring daily this winter.

Dream 1: You are jogging in shorts and a T-shirt. The weather changes drastically, and it begins to rain. To make matters worse, you are eight miles from home.

Dream 2: You are walking in the snow thinking about how fresh and clear the air is. Your warm clothing feels too heavy and tight all of a sudden. Soon you are having trouble breathing. Your hat keeps falling down over your eyes, and your collar creeps up over your mouth. You wake up gasping for air.

Situation 5

Tom reads in the paper that since it is the last Sunday in October, he must set his clock back one hour.

Dream 1: He dreams that he wakes up in the morning and everything is backward. He walks backward to the bathroom to brush his teeth and sees the back of his head in the mirror. He feels like he is putting on his clothing correctly, but when he looks down it is all backward. The car goes in reverse to work, and at the end of the day when he climbs into bed he finds his head where his feet usually rest.

Dream 2: Tom dreams that he is an hour early for a major appointment with a man named Mr. Timekeeper. Mr. Timekeeper is very impressed that Tom is so early and gives Tom four million dollars' worth of business.

6 **Analyzing Dreams.**   In this activity you will be doing some more dream analysis, this time as part of a team of "psychoanalysts" analyzing patients' dreams. Work in groups of three or four to analyze each patient. Then discuss your findings with the other groups.

1. How are each group of dreams alike, and how are they different?

2. Which dreams represent a single major issue and which deal with several different issues in the person's life?

3. What does each dream mean?

Patient 1

Peter is a 38-year-old used-car salesman who has recently filed for bankruptcy. His wife has threatened to leave him unless he gets out of debt.

Dream 1: He jumps off the Eiffel Tower but is picked up by a stork and carried to the Caribbean.

Dream 2: He is at his bank making a night deposit when two female outlaws hold up the bank and leave him tied up and bound with a scarf so that he cannot talk.

Dream 3: He flies to Italy to order lasagna, but can find only pizza. As he enjoys the pizza, a helicopter lands across the street and two men get out and offer him $77,000.

Patient 2

Martin, from Denver, Colorado, marries Sulin from France and they live and work in Paris for three years. Then they move back to Denver.

Dream 1: Martin dreams he is back in Paris at their apartment talking to the neighbors.

Dream 2: Martin dreams he is alone in an airplane, and all the signs and control indicators are labeled in French. He picks up an equipment manual, which is written in French, and realizes he can't read it.

Dream 3: Martin goes to the office in Denver and finds that all the people there are his coworkers from France. None of them speaks English, and all of them need his help. He speaks French perfectly and easily arranges housing for his coworkers. When he finishes, everyone cheers and they pick him up on their shoulders and carry him around the office.

Patient 3

An elderly man, Mr. Hill, describes these dreams.

Dream 1: Mr. Hill dreams he is in college taking courses and living in the dorms. Although he does very well, no one notices or sees him.

Dream 2: Mr. Hill is a young man working on his father's ranch. Everyone is looking at the blue sky and hoping for rain.

Dream 3: Mr. Hill meets his first grandchildren. They are twins, a boy and a girl. The boy looks like him and the girl looks like his deceased wife.

Patient 4

Tina is a freshman at Santa Barbara City College, majoring in computer science.

Dream 1: Tina is in a computer store selecting a word processor. As she walks up to look at one, it changes into an ice cream sundae. The second one changes into a bicycle, the third into a small swimming pool, the fourth into a refrigerator, and the fifth into a sculpture of a dancer. She leaves the store feeling worried that she'll never find a computer that will stick around.

Dream 2: Tina walks into class feeling very good, confident about the exam she is about to take. She sits down, and the instructor passes out the exam. She takes one look at it and can't remember anything.

Dream 3: Tina is at a party and three men come up to her and ask her to dance. She can't decide what to do.

7   Interviewing People about Dreams.   If possible, ask a native speaker of English about a dream he or she remembers. Or ask someone to tell you in English about a dream he or she has had.

1. Find out as much as you can about the dream.
2. Share your findings with your classmates.
3. Discuss whether anyone could have had this dream or only a native speaker of English? Why?

Expressing the Positive View

People often need others to listen to their complaints. It is quite common, for example, to find ourselves listening to the complaints of family, friends, or colleagues about something that has gone wrong at home, at school, at work, or at a shop.

To console or cheer up the unhappy person, we can suggest ways to look at the problem as though it were "all for the best." This ability to look at the bright or positive side of an issue is useful in both informal conversations and formal discussions.

Statements that demonstrate a positive view are often introduced in one of three ways:
(1) by expressions that signal contrast (See page 75.)
(2) by expressions that present a positive view
(3) by comparing this situation with one that is even worse.

Below are some examples of each type of indicator.

Expressions That Present a Positive View

Yes, that's true, but just think . . .
Well, try to look at it this way.
It's just as well, because . . .
It's all for the best, because . . .
Well, look at the bright side.
But, on the bright side . . .
But at least . . .
The upside of this is . . .

Comparing a Situation with One that is Worse

Just imagine if . . .
Yes, but things could be worse! What if . . .
You think that's bad? I heard about a person who . . .
Yes, but look at it this way.
On the other hand, . . .

1 Listening for the Positive View.   Listen to the following conversations and answer the questions. Share your answers to the questions with your classmates. Can you imagine yourself responding similarly to any of the speakers? Why or why not?

Conversation 1
Gary and Julius

1. What expression does Gary use to help Julius "look at the bright side"?

_____

_____

2. Is Gary's suggestion amusing?

_____

_____

Why or why not? _____

_____

_____

Conversation 2
Christine and Eric

1. What does Eric suggest doing instead of going to the picnic?

_____

2. What expression does he use to introduce this suggestion?

_____

3. Do you think Eric was glad the picnic was rained out? _____

Why or why not? _____

_____

Conversation 3
Clara and Joyce

1. What is Joyce's complaint? _____

2. What does Clara suggest? _____

_____

3. What expression does Clara use to introduce her suggestion? _____

4. Was Clara able to convince Joyce to see the bright side? _____

How do you know this? _____

_____

2   **Summarizing the Positive View.**   Listen to the lecture as you complete this exercise. Listen specifically for situations that might be considered negative or unpleasant. Read through the following six statements. They are paraphrases of parts of the lecture. After each statement, write a summary of the positive response to the situation given in the lecture. Be sure to include the optimistic expression that the speaker uses in your response.

1.   Often our dreams seem trivial and useless.

   On the other hand, many breakthroughs in science and inspirations in the arts come during dreams.

The Alvin Ailey Dance Company

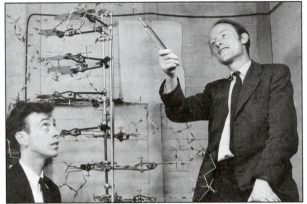

Crick and Watson with a model of the DNA double helix structure.

2.   After Coleridge's writing was interrupted by a visitor, he could not remember the rest of the poem he had created in a dream.

   _____

   _____

   _____

3.   And one night last week I dreamed about hot dogs piled up on a bridge—no useful images for scientific discoveries or artistic creations there that I can figure out.

   _____

   _____

   _____

4.   Every time George dreams a new reality, each person has a new set of memories to fit this new reality. They remember nothing of the old reality.

   _____

   _____

   _____

5. Dr. Haber has been trying to use George's dreams to change the world.

_____

_____

_____

6. Dr. Haber dreams that everything is gray - the people, the buildings, the animals, and the plants.

_____

_____

_____

3   **Comparing Answers.**   Share your answers to Activity 2 with your classmates. Then discuss the following: Is it easier to understand a lecture that presents contrasting points of view or a lecture that presents only one point of view? Why or why not?

Talk It Over

4   **Debating as Optimists and Pessimists.**   In this activity, you will have a chance to become an extreme optimist, looking only on the bright side, or an extreme pessimist, who can see only the dark side. Form teams and debate the positive and negative sides of the topic you choose. Your instructor or a neutral classmate can serve as moderator. Each team gets a point for each good argument it presents for or against a particular point of view.

1. Form teams of three or four persons. Then find another team to be your opponents in a debate.
2. Work with the other team to choose one of the topics from the list to debate. Decide which team will take the positive point of view and which will take the negative.
3. Spend ten minutes preparing for the debate. Imagine what the other team's position will be and come up with arguments against their point of view.
4. During the debate, take turns with the other team in presenting and then defending your point of view. (Those presenting the positive side can use expressions from this section. Those presenting the negative side can use the expressions from Part 3 of Chapter 5.)
5. If time permits, stay on the same teams, choose a new topic, but take the opposite point of view. This time around, pessimists become optimists and optimists become pessimists.

Topics

1. hypnosis
2. mind-altering drugs such as LSD
3. telepathy
4. memorization as a method of study
5. many years of intense study on a particular subject, excluding all other areas of study
6. controlling anger at all times
7. being totally honest at all times
8. daydreaming
9. treatment of mental illness with drugs
10. experimenting with mind-altering situations such as sleep deprivation or total sensory deprivation

5 Responding to Complaints Positively.   A conversation that is just one complaint after another is called a gripe session. A gripe session can be a good thing because it helps everyone get feelings out into the open. Participants may also feel better because of the support and sympathy they receive. Sometimes, however, a gripe session may go on for a long time without producing positive results. At times like this, we welcome the optimist who helps everyone see the bright side and get back on a positive track.

1. In small groups, choose a topic from the following list.
2. Complain all you want and say all the negative things you can about the topic.
3. After a few minutes, try offering a more optimistic view of the situation using some of the expressions from this section.
4. Choose another topic and begin again. Cover as many different topics as time permits.

Suggested Topics

1. dormitory or cafeteria food
2. bureaucracies / red tape
3. politicians / politics
4. traffic / parking
5. roommates
6. single life / married life
7. final exams / writing papers
8. going to the dentist
9. music / art
10. people who...
11. the high cost of...
12. the quality of...
13. the university system in my country
14. selfish people
15. staying up late at night to party

CITY OF MILWAUKEE PARKING TICKET				
LICENSE PLATE NUMBER	MAKE	MODEL	YEAR	COLOR
BUR 4956	Honda	Accord	2001	Blue

Location: _N. Stowell Ave._   Time: _10:00 a.m._

Fine: _$15.00_   Reason: _Parked in a "No Parking" zone_

Issued by: _Officer J.B. Maloney_

PART 4   # Focus on Testing

You will hear a short conversation. After the conversation you will be asked some questions. Circle the letter of the best answer to each question.

Question 1
a. dreaming
b. studying
c. eating
d. reading

Question 2
a. He's been reading a boring book.
b. He's been losing touch with reality.
c. He's been up late partying.
d. He's been up late studying.

Question 3
a. She sat with Brian in the garden.
b. She gave Brian a pink rose.
c. She brought Brian some refreshments.
d. She said that Brian looked rested.

Question 4
a. because he didn't like cookies
b. because he wasn't sure who brought the cookies
c. because he was losing touch with reality
d. because the girl in the dream brought the cookies

Question 5
a. to share refreshments with the girl in the dream
b. to share refreshments with his girlfriend, Kelly
c. to share refreshments with the famous Dr. Freud
d. to share refreshments with a lovely young lady

Video Activities: Social Phobia

Before You Watch.   Answer these questions in small groups.

1. A phobia is _____.
    a. a need   b. a fear   c. an idea

2. What kinds of phobias do you know of?

Watch.   Answer these questions in small groups.

1. What kind of phobia does Katherine Whizmore suffer from? _____

2. Circle the things that people with this disorder believe.
    a. People are judging them all of the time.
    b. People want to physically hurt them.
    c. People are unfair to them.

3. Which kinds of treatments help these people?
    a. education about their illness
    b. antidepressant drugs and behavioral therapy
    c. surgery

Watch Again.   Choose the correct answers.

1. By the age of twenty, Katherine Whizmore was afraid to _____.
    a. go to work   b. cross the street   c. go shopping alone

2. How many Americans suffer from this disease?
    a. 100 million   b. 1 million   c. 10 million

3. This disease usually begins in _____.
    a. college   b. high school   c. junior high school

4. Panicked means _____.
    a. confident   b. very frightened   c. sick

5. Impaired means _____.
    a. afraid   b. extraordinary   c. injured

6. Scrutiny means _____.
    a. correction   b. inspection   c. destruction

7. Harshly means _____.
    a. fairly   b. kindly   c. cruelly

8. Struggle means to _____.
    a. fight   b. give up   c. win

After You Watch.   Discuss these questions with your class.

1. Do you know anyone who is very shy or afraid in public? What happens to them? What do they do about it?

2. What kinds of situations make you feel nervous or shy?

Chapter 7

Working

Did You Know?

An American business consultant, W. Edwards Deming, played an extremely important role in the economic growth of Japan after World War II. His principles, which American businesses were slow to adopt, are as follows:

- Quality is defined by the customer.
- Quality comes from improving the production process, not by sorting out and eliminating defective products.
- Long-lasting quality improvement comes from working "smarter" rather than from working longer or harder or faster.
- Change and improvement must involve *everyone* in the organization.
- Ongoing training of all employees is the key to continuous improvement of processes and products.
- Replacing warnings and slogans with education and self-improvement programs for employees leads to greater productivity.

PART 1

Getting Started

Sharing Your Experience

In small groups, discuss the following items.

1 What images does the term *work* bring to mind? Do you imagine bored people watching the clock? Or do you imagine an excited group of people working cooperatively on a project that will benefit all of them? In small groups, share your attitudes about work by answering the following questions:

1. Have you or anyone you know ever had a job that you thought was wonderful? What was the job and what made it so good?

2. Have you or anyone you know ever had a terrible job? What was the job and what made it so bad?

3. What do you think the perfect job would be? Create a fantasy job in your mind and share it with your group. What is it? Where is it? What are the hours? How much do you earn? Who are your coworkers?

2 Each person has a slightly different definition of job satisfaction. Read the items in the following list and rank them from 1 (for most important) to 10 (for least important) according to your criteria for job satisfaction. Add some new criteria if you wish. Compare your answers with those of your classmates. What new criteria did students add? What category did most people rank first? Last?

_2_	mental challenge	_6_	flexible working hours
_5_	good pay	_3_	cooperative decision-making involving both workers and management
_8_	health and hospital care		
_7_	long paid vacations	_1_	opportunities for advancement
_4_	friendly coworkers	_7_	individual recognition
___	other _____		

3   Discuss with your classmates how you think most Americans would rank the categories in Activity 2. If possible, interview three to five Americans who work in a variety of situations to check your assumptions. Then discuss the results of your interviews with your classmates.

Vocabulary Preview

4   **Sharing Definitions.**   You may already know the meanings of several of the following words. However, the words you know may be different from the ones your classmates know. Pool your knowledge and match the definitions on the right with the words on the left.

_b_ 1. to assemble	a. the belief that the interests of the individual are more important than those of the group
_e_ 2. consensus	b. to put together
_f_ 3. consultant	c. the highest price
_j_ 4. dispute	d. new idea, method, or device
_a_ 5. individualism	e. group opinion
_i_ 6. initiative	f. person who gives expert advice
_d_ 7. innovation	g. maximum number allowed
_h_ 8. interdependence	h. mutual reliance or support
_g_ 9. quota	i. ability and willingness to start things
_c_ 10. top dollar	j. disagreement

5   **Vocabulary in Context.**   Fill in the blanks with the appropriate forms of the words from the vocabulary list. Note: You will not use every word on the list.

When an American company finds itself in economic trouble, its stockholders become uneasy, and quick action is essential. It is common practice for specialists to be called in to help find a solution for the company's problem. In fact, this situation has just occurred at a major corporation. A _3._____ has been hired by XYZ to find out why sales have declined in recent months. In order to learn more about the company's problems, the consultant has arranged a meeting with company managers. This consultant wants to be sure that he understands the existing philosophy before he introduces any _7._____ or makes any changes.

According to the company philosophy, each worker is expected to take the _6._____ on a new idea; workers are not led by the hand. However, once the individual devises the idea, a _2._____, or collective agreement, is needed before the idea can be carried out. Once there is agreement about an idea, costs are carefully analyzed to judge whether the idea fits with the general plan. Then, if the project is determined to be worthy of company effort, a team is _1._____. This cooperation, or _8._____, among workers makes the company's managers proud. The company's cooperative policies have been working well up until the past few months; workers have been content, and few _4._____ have occurred among the workers. Because the working conditions are so favorable, the sales slump must be caused by other factors. At least that is the assumption the consultant will start with.

Listening for Causes and Effects

When businesspeople and researchers look at a successful company, they often ask themselves: What factors make the company successful? To answer this question, they examine various factors to decide which ones seem to be related. Then they determine if the relationship is one of cause and effect rather than just chance.

For example, one automobile dealership sells more cars than any other dealer. The other dealers wonder why. They look at many factors: location of the showroom, business hours, prices of the cars, and the amount of money paid to salespeople.

When the dealers discover that the showroom location of each dealership is similar, the business hours are similar, and the prices of the cars are similar, but that the amount of money paid to the salespeople is greater at the most successful dealerships, they suspect a cause-and-effect relationship.

Seeing cause-and-effect relationships can help us find solutions to problems in all aspects of life, from business to academic life, from group to individual situations. Therefore it's no surprise that instructors present causes and effects as they lecture. In explaining cause-and-effect relationships, lecturers generally use two approaches.

Method 1: The Straightforward Approach

The lecturer clearly lists the causes and the effects that are involved in a situation. If a lecturer uses Method 1, the best note-taking system is to put all of the causes on one side of the page and the effects on the other. For example, consider the following notes on the garbage collectors' strike in New York City from a lecture on labor unions and management.

Labor Unions and Management: NYC Garbage Collectors' Strike

Causes		Effects	
1a.	low wages	1.	workers strike
1b.	long hours		
1c.	dirty working conditions		
2.	strike	2a.	city looks ugly
		2b.	areas smell bad
		2c.	tourist business is lost
		2d.	disease breaks out
3.	picketers throw rocks at scab workers	3a.	25 persons are arrested
		3b.	bad feelings increase between management and employees

Method 2: Implied Connections

Method 2 is less obvious than Method 1. Causes and effects are presented as a series of facts with implied connections rather than clearly stated ones. It is the student's job to recognize the implications and make the connections. If a lecturer uses Method 2, being familiar with cause-and-effect expressions can help you find the connections. You can also go back to your notes later and determine which bits of information are causes and which are effects. You can then show connections between causes and effects with numbers, arrows, or any other system you'd like to use.

Causes, effects, and their relationships are frequently signaled by the following expressions.

Expressions Signaling Causes

because
for
since

Expressions Signaling Effects

as a consequence
as a result
consequently
hence
so
therefore
thus

Expressions Signaling a Cause-and-Effect Relationship

as a consequence of . . .
as a result of . . .
due to the fact that . . .
due to this
due to this fact
for this reason
if . . . then
when . . .then

Before You Listen

1 **Considering the Issue.** Discuss the following questions in small groups.

Under what conditions do you think it is important for workers to cooperate and rely on each other? Under what conditions is an interdependent work situation better than one in which each person does a separate task?

2

Filling Out a Survey.   Before listening to the Webcast on Japanese and American Business Management, fill out the following Audience Survey.

Audience Survey

How Would You Run a Doorbell Company?

For each item circle either a or b.

1. Supervision of production; wages
    a   Use a supervisor. Have a supervisor record the number of doorbells each worker assembles; pay each person according to how many he or she produces.
    b. Don't use a supervisor. Have a team of workers assemble the doorbells. Record the number of doorbells assembled by a production team of several workers without a supervisor and provide equal bonuses for each member of the team when more than a specific number are produced.

2. Raises and promotions
    a   Give frequent raises and promotions to workers who work fastest. Give frequent raises and promotions to workers who work hardest. Give fewer rewards to the others.
    b. Give few but regular promotions and raises to everyone on the basis of age and number of years with the company.

3. Slow work periods
    a   Hire many workers during periods when the demand for doorbells is heavy; fire unnecessary workers when business slows down. Don't reduce pay of those who remain employed.
    b. Give all employees lifelong employment guarantees. Reduce pay and hours for both labor and management, but fire no one when business slows down.

4. Quality control
    a. Have an outside inspector responsible for quality control. The outside inspector is someone who is not involved in the production process.
    b. Make the work team responsible for quality control. Give extra money or time off for excellent records. Encourage team cooperation by giving awards and public praise.

5. Changes and improvements in the system
    a   Use outside consultants to get new ideas for improving electronic doorbells. Reward individual workers who make usable suggestions. To avoid disagreements among workers, let management decide on all changes.
    b   Use work teams to get new ideas. Have regular discussion meetings of the work team. Make changes slowly, only after workers and management agree.

Listen

3   **Taking Notes on Causes and Effects.** Read through the partial outline of causes and effects. Listen to the Webcast. Take notes by completing the outline.

Causes	Effects
1a. Japanese products are easy to get.	1. Americans buy many Japanese products.
1b. Japanese products are _____ .	
1c. Japanese products are _____ .	
2. _____ _____	2. American companies are losing business.
3. _____ _____ _____	3a. Some leaders in business, labor, and government want protective taxes and _____ _____ .
	3b. Other leaders say the United States should _____ _____ .
4. U.S. manager encourages individual initiative.	4a. Separate people moving up from _____ _____ .
	4b. Keep clear division between _____ _____ .

Causes	Effects
5. Japanese manager encourages group efforts.	5a. _____ _____ _____ .
	5b. _____ _____ .
6a. Japan is a small country.	6. _____ _____
6b. Japan is isolated.	
6c. Japan is _____ _____ .	
7a. The United States is _____ _____	7. Business practices that are competitive and free from roles may not be as good for modern industrial production as Japanese practices are.
7b. The United State has _____ _____	
7c. The United States has _____ _____	
7d. The people in the United States like _____ _____	
8a. William Ouchi says the United States should strengthen the bond between workers and their companies by providing _____ _____	8a. Then United States productivity will _____ _____ .
8b. _____ _____	8b. And in the long run, these reforms will lead to _____ _____ .
8c. _____ _____	8c. _____ _____
8d. and _____ _____	8d. _____ _____
	8e. and _____

Causes	Effects
9a. IBM, Intel, Procter and Gamble, and Hewlett-Packard have _____ _____ .	9a. Decrease in _____ _____ .
9b. _____ _____ .	9b. and _____
9c. and _____ _____ _____ .	9c. Increase in _____ _____
	9c. and _____ _____
10. U. S. companies adopt the Japanese philosophy of business organizations.	10. Ouchi claims _____ . _____ .

After You Listen

4   **Comparing Notes.**   Compare your outline notes with a partner or with the class.

5   **Discussing Advances in Technology.** The items in the following three pictures are available through mail-order catalogs in the United States. Each one represents a technological advance that has had a noticeable effect on the work we do. Can you think of any other technological "toys" that have had an important effect on how work is accomplished? Share your ideas with the class.

SONY

Mavica MVC-CD1000

- 1600 x 1200, 1024 x 768 and 640 x 480 pixel Recording Modes
- 10 x Optical Zoom Viewfinder & 2.5" LCD Monitor
- 3" Mavica CD-R Disc (156 MB)
- 6-60mm f/2.8 (35 Equiv 39-390mm) Zoom Lens • SteadyShot optical Picture Stabilization • 2x digital zoom
- Program Aperture, Shutter or Manual Comp • Pop up & External Flash Jack
- Auto, Manual Focus • MPEG Movie mode • NTSC Video Out
- USB Port • 52mm Filt. Diam.
- 5.5 x 5.25 x 8.3 " • 34.9 oz.

New Low Price

Panasonic.

DVD-RV31K/31S DVD/CD Player

- Component Video Out
- 10 Bit Video D/A Converter
- Advanced Virtual Surround Sound
- Hi-Speed Smooth Motion Scan: 5 Speed up to x100
- Outputs f/DTS and Dolby Digital Decoders
- 16.9 x 3.9 x 10.6" • Weighs 6.4 Lbs. Model DVD-RV31S Silver Chasis

free VisorPhone offer

Buy any Visor handheld and get VisorPhone FREE when you activate service

Now, for a limited time, when you buy a Visor handheld you can get VisorPhone FREE when you activate service!* So you can make calls and surf the web from almost anywhere—plus stay unbelievably organized. Because VisorPhone with your Visor handheld is an integrated mobile phone, wireless web device and Palm OS organizer all in one. But hurry! This offer is good only at **Handspring.com!**

Ready to save?

Talk It Over

6 **Discussing Technology and Society.**   Look in some current magazines, mail-order catalogs, and business or scientific journals. Cut out or copy a few pictures and descriptions of high-tech items that are used in the workplace. Bring these pictures to class and use them to do this activity.

1. In small groups read the descriptions aloud and talk about the benefits of using this device.
2. Decide whether or not this device could have a major effect on our lives. If so, would it be a positive or a negative effect?
3. Decide which of these devices might cause the most dramatic effect on society as a whole. Why do you think so?

7 **Describing Innovations.**   In small groups, share your answers to the following questions.

1. If you could design something to make your work (at school, at home, or on the job) easier, what would it be? Describe it.
2. How would it affect society as a whole?

Share a few of your group's most beneficial or most imaginative designs with the whole class.

PART 3 # Persuading and Giving In

Persuading

The most effective way to persuade someone to agree with you is to present a strong argument. A persuasive argument may be purely logical and reasonable, or it may be based on feelings or emotions. In either case, you will need to give reasons why this particular argument or point of view is a good one.

To be persuasive, you can start off with a strong cause-and-effect statement. This can then be followed by additional support for your point of view. As you make additional points, use the expressions provided here to emphasize that you are introducing additional facts.

A Persuasive Statement of a Cause-and-Effect Relationship

More companies in this country should adopt Japanese-style management practices. A company in my town did this and doubled both productivity and sales.

Additional Points

Not only that, but the employees are much happier, so they are generally healthier and don't have to take off so many days because of illness. What's more, the food in the employee cafeteria is really terrific, so the employees don't have to eat in expensive restaurants or take time to make their own lunches.

Expressions Used to Strengthen Arguments

Along with that . . .	Moreover . . .
And another thing . . .	Not only that, but . . .
And I might add . . .	Not to mention the fact that . . .
Besides . . .	Plus the fact that . . .
Furthermore . . .	What's more . . .
In addition to that . . .	

Giving In

What do you do when someone has managed to persuade you to agree with his or her point of view? How can you let this person know that he or she has presented a convincing argument and you're ready to *give in?* In this case, the following expressions will be useful.

Expressions Used When Giving In

OK plus one of the following expressions:

Formal

I guess you're right (after all).
If you really insist.
I'll go along with that.
Maybe you are right.
Perhaps in this case (you're right).
You may have a point there.
(I guess) You've convinced me.

Informal

I give up.
I'll buy that.
I'm sold.
You win.
You're right.
You've sold me.

Accepting an Offer

Persuading and giving in can take place in situations other than formal discussions. For example, someone may try to persuade you to actually do something for them, not just to agree with their point of view. They may even offer something to give you a stronger reason to go along with their request. In the following example a person is making an offer to a coworker.

> Could you help me out? I'd really like to go to San Francisco for the weekend, but I've been scheduled to work on Saturday. Will you fill in for me on Saturday if I work for you on a day you want to take off to visit your mother?

When someone has been persuaded to accept an enticing offer, one of the following expressions is commonly used.

Expressions Used When Freely Accepting an Offer

Come to think of it . . .	On second thought . . .
If you insist . . .	That's an offer I can't refuse!
I'm sold!	You've sold me!
In that case . . .	You've talked me into it.
Now that you mention it . . .	When you put it that way . . .

Sometimes people will try to persuade you to do something for them by presenting the negative consequences that will result if you do not do what they are asking. In the following example a worker describes what will happen if a fellow employee doesn't go along with a request.

> Do you think you could work on Saturday? We all have to put in some extra time this week. If we don't, the project won't be finished on time and the company could lose the contract.

When someone reluctantly accepts an offer, one of the following expressions is commonly used.

Expressions Used When Reluctantly Accepting an Offer

Given that there seems to be no other choice . . .
If I absolutely have to . . .
If that's the only alternative . . .
If that's the only way . . .
If that's the way it's got to be . . .
If there's no other alternative . . .
If there's no other way . . .
If you insist . . .
Okay, just this once.
That's an offer I guess I'd better not refuse!
Well, under those circumstances . . .
When you put it that way . . .

1 **Listening to People Persuading and Giving In.** Listen to the conversation and answer the questions.

1. Where is the company executive from? _____

2. What does he want to do?_____

3. Who is he trying to persuade?_____

4. Who will work for the company?_____

5. Who will manage the company?_____

6. What does the company executive say about pollution problems?

_____

7. What is the mayor concerned about?_____

8. What enticing offer does the executive make?_____

9. Is the mayor persuaded?_____

2 **Listening for Expressions for Persuading and Giving In.** Listen to the conversation a second time, and write down all the expressions you hear for persuading and giving in. When you are finished, compare your answers in small groups.

Persuading   **Giving in**

_____   _____

_____   _____

_____   _____

_____   _____

3 **Listening for Expressions Introducing Persuasive Arguments.** Listen again to the Webcast comparing Japanese and American business customs.

1. As you listen, make a list of the expressions the speaker uses to introduce persuasive arguments. Then compare your list with your classmates' lists.

2. The two speakers in the discussion share a particular point of view. In one or two sentences, state their point of view. Did the speakers persuade you to agree with them? Why or why not? Share your answers with your classmates.

4 **Persuading in Informal Situations.** There is a cynical saying: "Everyone has a price." This means that if someone initially does not want to do something, his or her services can be "bought" for the "right price." As a class, have fun discovering your classmates' "prices" for various actions.

1. Ask another student in the class (or your instructor) to do something unusual or something to which they would usually say no. For example:

Will you pay for my trip to Paris next week?

Will you marry my brother tomorrow?

Will you do my homework for me?

2. When the student responds negatively (see page 22 for ways to say no), do not take no for an answer. Try to persuade your classmate by presenting various positive or negative consequences. For example:

Well, would you pay for my trip if I gave you a 1% interest in my company?

If you don't marry my brother, he will be heartbroken.

3. If your classmate still refuses to do what you've asked, you must continue to present consequences that are more and more positive or negative until your classmate finally gives in. For example:

If you don't pay for my trip, I will probably lose my entire business because I can't get to Paris to negotiate a big contract.

If you marry my brother, you will be married to the richest, kindest, and most handsome man in my country. He will be devoted to you all your life.

4. Then change roles so that your partner is now making a request of you.

5. If you work in small groups, let other students in on the laughter by sharing a few of your group's conversations with the rest of the class.

Talk It Over

5 **Debating Work-Related Issues.**   As a class or in smaller groups, form teams to represent opposite sides in debates on work-related issues. Choose from the following topics or create your own topics for debate. Use persuasive expressions to convince your opponents to accept your point of view. Give in each time your opponents present a convincing argument.

Debate Topics

1. Selecting children at a young age and training them for certain professions [is / is not] best for these individuals and for society as a whole.

2. Management [should / should not] involve itself in the personal life and well being of its employees.

3. Industrial spying [is / is not] justifiable.

4. White-collar jobs [should / should not] have more prestige than blue-collar jobs.

5. Women [should / should not] be allowed to do any job they choose if they meet the basic qualifications.

6. Robots in the workplace are a [help / hindrance] to the welfare of workers.

7. Trade unions [are / are not] the best means of solving problems in the workplace.

8. Companies [should / should not] be responsible for the costs of continuing education for employees.

6 **Role-Playing Persuasion.** In pairs, choose one of the following situations to role-play. Use the expressions for persuading and giving in as your characters express their views to each other. If time permits, change partners one or more times and do the activity again. Then present one of the role-plays to the class.

Situations

1. You love to ski and try to go to the mountains on the weekends as often as possible. Therefore, you support the idea of a four-day, ten-hour work week. A coworker, on the other hand, likes to play tennis every afternoon after work and wants to continue working five days a week for eight hours a day. The matter will be voted on by the employees tomorrow. Try to persuade your coworker to vote for the four-day workweek.

2. You are waiting for a plane at the airport. You start a conversation with a friendly Japanese woman sitting next to you. She works for an American camera company, perhaps Eastman Kodak, in Japan. You work for a Japanese camera company, perhaps Nikon, in Chicago. Each of you is happy with your work situation and tries to convince the other person that your company is the best.

3. You are interviewing for a management job with an American company. The interviewer is impressed with your background and seems to want to hire you. There have been problems in the relationship between workers and management at the company in recent years. When you start to suggest some changes based on Japanese management style, the interviewer says he doesn't think they need to change so much. Try to convince him that the company really does need to make some changes.

PART 4 **Focus on Testing**

You will hear a short segment from a radio interview. After the interview, you will be asked some questions. Circle the letter of the best answer to each question.

Question 1
a. small and large businesses that want to improve
b. small and large organizations that want to do a job well
c. small and large families that have a problem to solve
d. all of the above

Question 2
a. Gracie
b. June
c. the children
d. all of the above

Question 3

a. The garbage was disturbed every day.

b. The garbage was disturbed when everyone was home.

c. The garbage was disturbed when the family ate meat.

d. The garbage was disturbed almost every day.

Question 4

a. Understand the reasons for the problem.

b. Plan and implement a solution to the problem.

c. Collect data on the current situation.

d. Make plans for further improvement.

Question 5

a. They took Gracie out right away.

b. They stopped eating meat.

c. They gave Gracie a little of the garbage.

d. They gave Gracie some meat in her bowl.

Question 6

a. staying home at night with the dog

b. collecting weekly data about the dog

c. taking out the garbage and rewarding the dog

d. cleaning up the mess in the kitchen after dinner

Video Activities: Telecommuting

Before You Watch. Sometimes people work from home. What are some advantages and disadvantages of telecommuting? List them below. In small groups, discuss your answers.

Advantages to Workers		Advantages to Employers	
1. _____		1. _____	
2. _____		2. _____	
3. _____		3. _____	
Disadvantages to Workers		**Disadvantages to Employers**	
1. _____		1. _____	
2. _____		2. _____	
3. _____		3. _____	

Watch.   Take notes on the benefits of telecommuting from different perspectives.

1. As you listen, note the benefits of telecommuting from a worker's perspective.

_____

_____

_____

_____

2. As you listen, note the benefits of telecommuting from an employer's perspective.

_____

_____

_____

_____

Watch Again.   Answer these questions in small groups.

1. Listen for these numbers and write what each one represents.
    a.   20,000,000   _____
    b.   12,000 - 13,000 _____
    c.   10,000   _____
    d.   3,000 - 4,000   _____

2. The phrases *gridlock* and *bumper-to-bumper* refer to _____.
    a. traffic accidents
    b. slow traffic
    c. very heavy traffic

3. When someone is *goofing off,* they are _____.
    a. sleeping
    b. working
    c. playing

4. The expression *saving a bundle* means _____.
    a. saving a lot of money
    b. working harder
    c. getting work done faster

5. Another word for *telecommuter* is _____.
    a. telephoner
    b. telenetter
    c. teleworker

After You Watch.   Discuss these questions with your class.

1. Would you like to telecommute? Why or why not?

2. Do you think telecommuting will ever become commonplace?

File Name	Sample Name	Comments	Dye Set/Primer
H51R	tissue	V-v1.0.4 ds 24.1x2	DyePrimer{M13RP1}
H52R	tissue	V-v1.0.4 24.1x2	DyePrimer{M13RP1}
H53R	tissue	V-v1.0.4 24.1	DyePrimer{M13RP1}
H54R	tissue	V-v1.0.4 ds 24.1x2	DyePrimer{M13RP1}
H55R	tissue	V-v1.0.4 24.1x2	DyePrimer{M13RP1}

08/05/93 - Gel Info

tissue

Chapter 8

Breakthroughs

IN THIS CHAPTER

Lecture:	Discovering the Laws of Nature
Learning Strategy:	What to Do When You Don't Understand
Language Function:	Giving and Receiving Compliments

Did You Know?

- The word *physics* comes from the Greek word *physis*, which means "that which shows itself and becomes observable." So physics is the study of the observable world and what makes it work. It is the science of matter and energy.

- Chaos is "lawless behavior governed entirely by law." —*British mathematician Ian Stewart*

- Some scientists say that the major breakthroughs in 20th century science are relativity theory, quantum mechanics, and chaos.

- Edward Lorenz, a meteorologist, proposed Chaos Theory in 1960 to explain the difficulty in making accurate weather predictions.

- Chaos Theory tries to explain the fact that there are unpredictable results in systems. The most common example is the "butterfly effect." This is the idea that a butterfly in China could influence weather patterns in New York City. Chaos Theory says that a small occurrence can produce big results.

- Many scientists have been interested in the motion of fluids, especially complicated, irregular motion called turbulence. Eventually researchers made the connection between turbulence and chaos theory. The results of this research led to products that relate to everyday life.

- Gold Star Company claimed to create the first "chaos" washing machine in 1993. It was supposed to produce cleaner and less tangled clothes. Daewoo Company in South Korea says that it produced a washing machine based on Chaos Theory in 1990.

- You believe in a God who plays dice, and I in complete law and order. —*Albert Einstein*

PART 1

Getting Started

Sharing Your Experience

1   As a class, or in small groups, discuss the following questions.

1. In what ways did you learn in school about the laws of physics? For example, did you learn about these laws through textbooks? Lectures? Class discussions? Laboratory experiments? Which way worked best for you?

2. In your everyday life, what have you learned about the physical laws of nature? Share what you have learned and how you learned it.

Vocabulary Preview

2   **Multiple Meanings.**   Many English words have more than one meaning. Sometimes the meanings are quite similar, but often they are very different. The words in the following list are defined as they are used in the lecture. Look over these words and definitions. Then choose the sentences that use the words as they are defined in the vocabulary list.

to bleed	*to cut and then take blood from a patient as part of a cure*
cosmos	*the universe considered as an orderly system*
matter	*that which is material, physical; not mental or spiritual*
relative	*not absolute; dependent on something else*

1.   to bleed
   a.   He was very lucky. After the accident he was only bleeding from the nose.
   b.   Modern doctors have recently experimented with bleeding patients as a cure for certain ailments.
   c.   Don't put your new black T-shirt in the wash with your white clothes because it might bleed.

2.   matter
   a.   The brain has both gray and white matter.
   b.   It doesn't matter to me.
   c.   It's only a matter of time.

COSMOGRAPHIE.

3.   cosmos
   a.   He likes to read *Cosmos* magazine.
   b.   The cosmos flowers she planted in the garden came up late this year.
   c.   He often wondered about the nature of the cosmos.

4.   relative
   a.   My cousin Pete is my favorite relative.
   b.   Time and space are relative to each other.
   c.   He finished the exam with relative ease.

3   Vocabulary in Context.   The following words used in the presentation do not have multiple meanings. Look over these words and their definitions. Then pick out the sentences in the exercise that use the words correctly.

metaphysical	*having to do with the branch of philosophy that deals with the nature of truth and knowledge in the universe*
paradigm	*unifying idea or set of principles*
such and such	*a condition, person, place, thing, or time not specifically mentioned*
wild-goose chase	*unfruitful attempt*

1. metaphysical
    a. He had a metaphysical at the doctor's office.
    b. She metaphysicals on her way back to work.
    c. They were both interested in metaphysical ideas.

2. paradigm
    a. She met a paradigm at the party.
    b. Her paradigm was the model for all the research that followed.
    c. The paradigm, an early model of the parachute, had many faults.

3. such and such
    a. The instructor gave this example to illustrate the theory: If you were going at such and such a speed for such and such an amount of time through space, the amount of time that seemed to pass on earth might be quite different.
    b   He was such and such a difficult instructor that the student wondered if she should wait until someone else taught the physics course.
    c. They were not interested in metaphysical ideas such and such as these.

4. wild-goose chase
    a. During the mating season for geese, we often see one wild-goose chase another goose.
    b. The quest for a unified field theory encompassing all the laws of nature may turn out to be a wild-goose chase.
    c. It was their first wild-goose chase, and they were proud of their success.

PART 2

What to Do When You Don't Understand

Have you shopped for a computer, a DVD player, or some other high-tech machine lately? If so, you may have found it difficult to follow exactly what the salesperson was saying. Maybe you thought you should understand because you knew all the words the salesperson used, but you still just didn't get it.

If this has happened to you, don't worry. This happens to everyone, even native speakers. Anyone who is trying to understand a complex new subject or concept may have a problem with understanding even when every word is familiar. For example, when you listen to the lecture in this chapter, "Discovering the Laws of Nature," you may find that some of the concepts are difficult to comprehend, even though the words are not.

Strategies to Use When You Don't Understand

1. Don't panic. Remember that you're not alone. Your classmates are probably having difficulty, too.

2. Don't give up. Continue to concentrate on the topic. Try not to let your mind wander. Thinking about something you *do* understand about the topic usually helps.

3. When you feel lost, listen for key nouns and verbs in the next few sentences. These words carry most of the meaning.

4. Continue to take notes even though they may not be perfect. Any nouns and verbs you manage to write down will be useful later when you start asking questions to determine exactly what you missed.

5. Write down any negative terms such as *never* and *not*. Without these words, your notes may appear to say the opposite of what the speaker intended.

6. Try repeating to yourself the sentence or sentences you can't seem to understand. If this does not help, try punctuating the sentence differently or changing the rhythm, stress, or intonation patterns as you repeat it to yourself. Sometimes a small change is all it takes to jump from the muddle of incomprehension to the "Aha!" of understanding.

7. Familiarize yourself with the speaker's topic ahead of time. If you are in an academic class, complete the assigned readings before the lecture. If there are no assigned readings or if the readings are very difficult, try to find some general information on the topic from an encyclopedia, a magazine, or a textbook from a lower-level course.

Before You Listen

1   **Discussing Breakthroughs.**   Discuss the following as a class or in small groups.

1.   Can you describe any scientific breakthroughs?

2.   Breakthroughs or discoveries can happen in all areas of life, not just in science. Share with your classmates a nonscientific breakthrough that you (or someone you know) has made in his or her life.

2   **Discussing Scientific Concepts.**

1.   Briefly share your understanding of the following concepts:

energy	**motion**	**light**	**time**
gravity	**space**	**matter**	

2.   Select the concept that you understand best. Do you think that your understanding of this concept is more correct than the understanding of a student five years ago? 15 years ago? 50 years ago? 250 years ago? 2,500 years ago? Discuss why you feel this way.

Listen

3   **Practicing Notetaking Strategies.**

1.   Listen to the lecture and take notes. Try to use at least three of the strategies in the box on page 111 as you listen.

2.   Listen to the lecture again. Fill in any gaps in your notes as necessary. Use the strategies in the box as needed. Then look over your notes and paraphrase and/or summarize each of the major ideas to make sure that you really understand everything you wrote down.

Johann Kepler

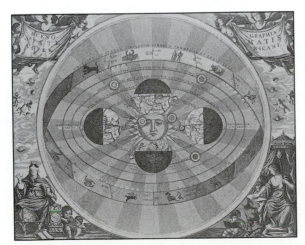

Copernican planetary system

Sir Isaac Newton

Galileo

After You Listen

4 **Comparing Strategies.** Compare with your classmates how well the strategies worked. Follow these steps:

1. Compare your summaries with your classmates.

2. Look at areas in your notes that may be incomplete and ask a classmate or your instructor for the missing information.

3. Discuss with your classmates which of the strategies worked best for you.

Talk It Over

5 **Sharing Past Experiences.** Earlier in this chapter, the example of the computer salesperson was given to represent ordinary situations in which you may understand the individual words someone uses, but you do not get the whole idea. In small groups, discuss the following:

1. What situations have you experienced where you understood each word but missed the main point of what someone was saying? What did you do? What was the result? Did you find a strategy you could use in the future (for example, asking for repetition, asking the speaker to give you an example or analogy, making eye contact with the speaker and raising your eyebrows or shrugging your shoulders)?

2. What techniques do instructors use to help you understand? Do they, for example, use study guides, charts, diagrams, or outlines?

3. What techniques do you use during conversations to present concepts that may be difficult to understand? For example, do you gesture with your hands? Do you draw diagrams?

6 **Describing Scientific Processes.**   As a class or in small groups, take turns describing what happens to energy and matter in the following everyday situations. Most of the vocabulary should be familiar, but the concepts may be a bit tricky. Use a basic physics book as a reference, if you wish, but don't make your explanations too technical.

1. blowing out a candle
2. riding a bicycle
3. grinding food in the garbage disposal
4. reflecting sunlight with a mirror onto a piece of paper
5. starting a car engine
6. planting a seed in a sunny garden

7. baking a cake
8. slipping on ice
9. rowing a boat
10. shooting an arrow
11. the turning of a windmill
12. the rising tides during a full moon

Giving and Receiving Compliments

Giving Compliments

Flattery

Flattery is the kind of compliment that sounds insincere. There is an old saying, "Flattery will get you everywhere." It means that some people like receiving compliments so much that if you flatter them a lot, they will do just about anything for you. Sometimes people say, "Flattery will get you nowhere with me." They mean that whatever it is you want, you won't talk them into it by giving them lots of compliments.

Sincere Compliments

People are often suspicious of flattery. Therefore, giving genuine compliments can be tricky. The keys to offering compliments appropriately are timing, number, and phrasing.

Timing

The person receiving the compliment will be more likely to feel it is sincere if it's deserved. Compliments are generally deserved when:

■ a person has accomplished something special.

■ a person is discouraged and you are reminding them of their good efforts and steady progress.

Number

How many compliments can you give at one time without overdoing it?

One's okay, and two are fine;
But stop at three, and draw the line.

Exception: If you give more than one compliment at a time to a superior at work or someone else in a position of authority, it may look like you are flattering them to gain favor or approval.

Phrasing

Take care to use adjectives and analogies that the person is pleased to identify with. For example:

Hank, you're really a *special* person. You have *a heart as big as the ocean*. Even though you're trying hard to complete your research, you still made time to raise money for the Homeless Children's Fund.

Expressions Used to Introduce Compliments

I don't mind saying . . .

I don't mind telling you . . .

I'd like to compliment you on . . .

If you ask me . . .

I've been meaning to tell you . . .

Just between you and me . . .

Receiving Compliments

Undeserved Compliments

Sometimes you may receive a compliment that you feel is undeserved. In this case, you may wish to be humble and say that the compliment is not true. However, do not deny or protest the compliment more than once or twice before you give in and accept the compliment graciously. Otherwise:

■ People might think you are "protesting too much," which could mean that you are really looking for even more compliments.

■ It might seem like you think the compliment is worthless, which could insult the speaker.

Inappropriate Compliments

Occasionally you may receive a compliment that you feel is inappropriate.

■ If the compliment is not offensive, you may either say a polite "thank you" or simply ignore it.

■ If the compliment is offensive, you should consider telling the person so and/or reporting the incident to a friend or superior.

Expressions Used to Receive Compliments

A simple "thank you" is always an appropriate and gracious response to a compliment. If you feel this is not enough, add one of the following expressions:

Coming from you, that's a real compliment.

Coming from you, that means a lot.

Do you really think so? How nice (sweet, kind) of you to say that.

I appreciate you saying that.

I'm really glad (pleased) you think so.

I'm really glad (pleased) you feel that way.

I'm very flattered.

That (Your opinion) means a lot to me.

That's nice to hear.

That's very kind (nice, sweet) of you.

Thanks, I needed that!

You've made my day!

What a nice (lovely, sweet) thing to say!

To show modesty you can say:

Oh, I can't take all the credit for that.

    Or

_____ deserves as much credit as I do.

1 **Listening for Appropriate and Inappropriate Compliments.** You will hear four conversations; the first two involve an instructor and some students, and the last two include several senior citizens. These conversations contain examples of both appropriate and inappropriate ways of giving compliments. Listen to each conversation, and answer the questions following it. Then compare answers with your classmates.

Conversation 1

Ron and Mr. McGovern are in the hall after class.

1. Ron's compliments to Mr. McGovern are inappropriate. What's wrong with Ron's timing?_____

2. What's wrong with the number of compliments?_____

3. What's wrong with the phrasing? _____

Conversation 2

Sandra and Mr. McGovern are in the professor's office during office hours.

1. Are Sandra's compliments to Mr. McGovern appropriate?_____

2. Why or why not? Consider location of the interaction, number of compliments, and phrasing in your answer. _____
_____
_____

Conversation 3

Helen, Larry, and Martin are chatting at a retirement home.

1. How does Larry first compliment Helen? _____
_____

2. What is Helen's response? _____
_____

3. Why do you think she says this? _____
_____

4. How does Martin compliment Helen? _____

5. How does Helen respond this time? _____

6. What do Helen and Larry tell Martin about his dancing? _____
_____

7. Who looked beautiful on the dance floor? _____

8. How does Martin feel about the compliments from Helen? _____
_____

Conversation 4

Later in the day at the retirement home Helen, Martin, and Larry continue chatting.

1. What's wrong with Martin? _____

    _____

2. Is the compliment Martin gives Helen appropriate? _____

3. How does Helen accept this compliment? _____

4. How does Larry try to cheer Martin up? _____

    _____

5. What does Helen say to encourage Martin? _____

    _____

6. Does it work? _____

7. How does Martin respond? _____

8. What does he mean by this? _____

    _____

2   **Giving and Receiving Compliments.**   Choose a partner for this activity. Listen to the lecture again. This time stop the tape each time you hear the speaker mention a breakthrough or other accomplishment, and do the following.

1. Pretend that your partner is the person the speaker is talking about. Imagine that you now have the opportunity to compliment this person on his or her achievements. Take this opportunity to really flatter him or her.

2. Let your partner respond to your compliments. Then continue listening to the tape.

3. When you stop the tape next time, change roles with your partner. This time *you* will pretend to be the person who made the breakthrough and your partner will compliment *you*.

4. Continue taking turns in this way as you listen to the rest of the tape.

5. When the lecture is finished, discuss which terms you used to give compliments, and how you felt as you were giving and receiving compliments in English.

3 **Discussing Compliments in Context.**

1. Listen to a TV soap opera or comedy.

2. Each time you hear a compliment, jot it down. Also note the context, the situation, and the response.

3. Listen until you hear at least three compliments.

4. Bring your notes to class. Describe to your classmates the situations, compliments, and responses you noted. Did you or your classmates hear any inappropriate compliments? If so, list them.

    _____

    _____

    _____

5. What made them inappropriate?

    _____

    _____

    _____

4 **Discussing Inappropriate Compliments.** Have you ever received an inappropriate compliment? If so, share this information with your classmates.

■ What was the situation?
■ What was the compliment?
■ How did you respond?
■ If you could do it all over again, would you respond differently?

5 **Researching the Language around You.** For the next day or two, pay particular attention to any compliments that you give, receive, or overhear.

Answer the following questions. Then share the results of your research with your classmates.

1. What was the relationship of the people involved? _____

    _____

    _____

2. What were their attitudes toward each other? _____

    _____

    _____

    _____

3. What expressions did they use to give or receive compliments? _____

    _____

    _____

    _____

4. Were any expressions used that were new to you? _____

   If so, what were they?_____

   _____

   _____

   _____

5. How many compliments did you give in one day? _____

   _____

6. How many compliments did you receive? _____

   _____

7. Describe any situations in which you thought the compliments were inappropriate.

   _____

   _____

   _____

8. Describe any situations in which you thought someone refused a compliment and "protested too much." _____

   _____

   _____

   _____

9. Do you think that consciously observing the behavior of giving and receiving compliments caused you to give more compliments than usual, fewer compliments than usual, or had no effect on the number of compliments you usually give? _____

   Why? _____

   _____

   _____

   _____

Talk It Over

6 **Complimenting Colleagues.** Be part of a "cutting edge" team on the verge of a real breakthrough. Then present your breakthrough invention to the world!

1. In small groups, imagine that you are a team of scientists living in the year 2200. You have recently made some important discoveries about the relationship of energy and matter. It is now your team's task to put these theories to practical use. You must design a device that converts energy into matter. As you brainstorm your ideas, make whatever drawing or diagrams you need to illustrate your ideas to your teammates.

2. As you work together, there should be opportunities to compliment your teammates on their ideas and to receive a few compliments yourself. When your team has finished the task, make a drawing or diagram of the device.

3. Imagine that your research team is at an international conference. As a group, present your device to the other "scientists"(your classmates) assembled in the main conference hall. Use the diagram your team developed to help explain the principles of the device. After each group has presented its work, be sure to compliment them on their presentation.

7 **Giving Insincere Compliments.** Try this activity for fun! Take turns "buttering each other up," that is, giving an excessive number of compliments because you want something very much and don't want to be refused. You may want to role-play one or more of the following small-group situations, or you may choose just to be yourselves.

Situations

1. a Hollywood party with producers, directors, and actors
2. a company Christmas party
3. a reception for a famous visiting physicist
4. a reception at the White House
5. a dinner party with your future in-laws

Focus on Testing

You will hear a short presentation. After the presentation, you will be asked some questions. Circle the letter of the best answer to each question.

Question 1
a. in the 1930s
b. in the 1950s
c. March 14, 1879
d. April 18, 1933

Question 2
a. because Einstein had reached the age of 15
b. because Einstein had not completed secondary school
c. because Einstein was failing his exams
d. because the family business failed

Question 3
a. electrical engineer
b. patent office clerk
c. secondary school teacher
d. mathematician

Question 4
a. wrote scientific papers
b. read a lot of books on physics
c. talked to other physicists
d. taught mathematics and physics

Question 5
a. the Kaiser-Wilhelm Gesellschaft in Berlin
b. the German University of Prague
c. the University of Zurich
d. the University of Bern

Question 6
a. in the United States
b. in Germany
c. in Switzerland
d. in Italy

Video Activities: Advances in Medicine

Before You Watch. Discuss these questions in small groups.

1. What do you think happens if the nerves that control your muscles die? Do you know the name of the disease that kills these nerves?

2. Have you ever known anyone who had a disease that affected his or her movement? How did this disease affect his/her life?

Watch. Circle the correct answers.

1. The main idea of this video segment is that _____.
   a. ALS is a very difficult disease to have
   b. a cure will soon be found for ALS
   c. there is hope for people with ALS

2. Jerry Lineberger controls his wheelchair and his computer by moving his _____.
   a. legs and arms   b. hands and feet   c. head and eyes

3. Dr. Jeffrey Rosenfeld's treatment _____.
   a. has cured some people
   b. may help some people live longer
   c. is dangerous and difficult

Watch Again. Write answers to these questions.

1. How long has Jerry Lineberger had ALS? _____

2. What are the initials of the protein that Dr. Rosenfeld uses in his treatment? _____

3. Use the words below to complete the description of Dr. Rosenfeld's treatment.

   | abdomen | catheter | implanted | inserted |
   | pump | release | spinal fluid | vertebra |

A _____ the size of a hockey puck is _____ in the _____.
A _____ is _____ between two _____. Tiny holes continuously _____ the drug into the _____.

4. *Diagnosed* is a verb. The noun is _____.

5. *Optimistically* is an adverb. The adjective is _____.

6. Listen and write words that have these meanings.
   a. incredible _____
   b. a doctor who specializes in the nervous system _____
   c. to increase the amount of time _____
   d. unproved theory _____

After You Watch. Discuss these questions with your class.

1. Although Jerry Lineberg's life is very difficult, he is still able to enjoy life. Have you ever known or read about anyone with a serious illness who did not give up?

2. Have you heard or read about any other medical breakthroughs in the treatment of terminal diseases? What are they?

Chapter 9

Art and Entertainment

Did You Know?

■ Elvis Presley spent the most weeks on the U.S. singles charts with 1,586 weeks. The Beatles were listed for 629 weeks.

■ The biggest selling album of all time is *Thriller* by Michael Jackson. This record sold over 45 million copies from 1982 when it was first released until 2001. It continues to sell today.

■ The Beatles have had the most gold albums (albums that sell over 500,000 copies) with 40; the Rolling Stones are second with 37 gold albums. Aretha Franklin has 13 gold albums.

PART 1

Getting Started

Sharing Your Experience

1   As a class or in small groups, discuss the following questions.

1.   What kinds of music are popular among your friends?

2.   What are your favorite types of music and who are your favorite performers?

3.   How often do you listen to music at home? Do you listen to music while you study? Cook? Clean? Exercise?

4.   Have you ever attended a live concert or show? If so, describe who you heard and where you went.

5.   Do you like rock 'n' roll? Why or why not?

6.   Do you play any musical instruments? If so, describe what type of music you like to play and why. If not, discuss what you would like to learn to play and why.

Vocabulary Preview

2   **Crossword Puzzle.** The following vocabulary words have been taken from the radio program in this chapter. Complete the crossword puzzle with the correct forms of the words on the list. Check your answers in the appendix on page 194.

Rock 'n' Roll Crossword Puzzle

accompaniment

acoustic

blues

to boo

cellist

censorship

to enhance

harmonies

hillbilly

indifferent

musicologist

nostalgically

outrageous

to reaffirm

segregation

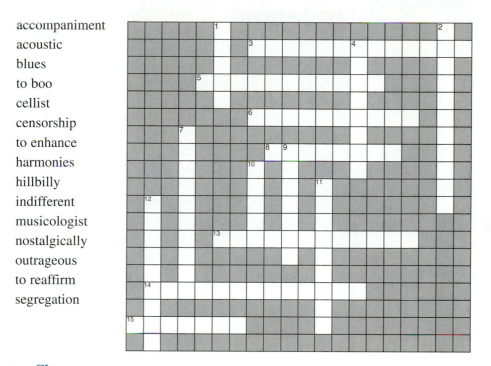

Across Clues

3. music that is played while the principal singer sings
5. the separation of one group from another based on race, class, or ethnic origin
6. the removal of offensive material from communications
8. state with confidence
13. one who studies music from a historical and scientific standpoint
14. in a manner that shows longing for something out of the past
15. one who plays the cello, the next-to-largest member of the violin family

Down Clues

1. shouted disapproval or contempt
2. having no preference; not interested in anything
4. of or relating to sound; natural sound, not electronic
7. extremely unusual; fantastic
9. make more valuable, beautiful, desirable; upgrade
10. a style of music characterized by sadness
11. a person from a mountainous backwoods area
12. pleasant or congruent arrangements of parts, such as musical chords

PART 2

Distinguishing between Fact and Opinion

Imagine this: A friend of yours made $10,000 in two years by buying old records and reselling them. You like music, and you decide to try to make some money, too. You go to a record trade show and find an old recording of "She Loves You" by the Beatles. It is an unusual recording because it was made without drummer Ringo Starr. The salesperson offers to sell it for $2,290 and tells you that the recording will triple in value in the next year and that if you are smart, you will buy it now and resell it when the value goes up. Is this a fact or only the salesperson's opinion? How do you know?

Some statements about the future are facts. For example:

The sun will rise in the east tomorrow.

Some statements about the future are merely opinions. For example:

This record will triple in value next year.

In everyday life and in academic life, it is important to distinguish fact from opinion. Facts, however, can be "slippery." A rare recording of "She Loves You" may be of great value today, but if someone finds a warehouse with 200,000 copies of this "rare" recording tomorrow, it won't be so valuable.

Sometimes people say things very strongly to make them sound like facts. If, for example, someone said with great confidence, "Elvis Presley was the first rock 'n' roll singer," that would sound like a fact. But it's not a fact. This statement is not true. If you don't know the fact yourself, it would be wise to check it for accuracy.

An opinion is someone's feeling, belief, or judgment about someone or something. It is not objective. Personal feelings, biases, and attitudes influence opinions. In the radio program in this chapter, there are many personal opinions that may sound like facts.

How to Distinguish Opinions from Facts

1. Look/listen for words and phrases that may signal an opinion:

I believe	often
I feel	personally
In my opinion	personally speaking
I think	probably
It seems to me	sometimes
Occasionally	usually

2. Look/listen for adjectives that express value judgments:

good	bad
safe	dangerous
pretty	ugly
extraordinary	outrageous

3. Question the expertise of the speakers. Are they reliable sources? Are they well-known and respected authorities in their fields?

4. Question the sources the speakers use. How reliable are those sources?

5. Most important, try to form a contrasting point of view. Is this contrasting point of view as reasonable and acceptable as the speaker's? If so, the speaker may be presenting only opinions and not facts.

Before You Listen

1 **Sharing Your Knowledge.**   In small groups, answer the following questions based on the knowledge you already have. Then share your answers with the rest of the class to expand your shared knowledge of this topic.

1. What is rock 'n' roll?
2. What is the origin of the term *rock and roll*?
3. What is rockabilly music?
4. Who is Elvis Presley?
5. What kind of music did Bob Dylan write and sing?
6. Who were the most popular rock musicians in the 1960s?
7. What is soul music?

Listen

2   **Listening for Facts and Opinions.** Listen to the radio program once all the way through. Then read the following statements and listen to the radio program again. This time stop the tape as necessary so that you can answer the questions that follow each statement. For each item, mark whether the statement is a fact or an opinion and then tell why. If you decide a statement is an opinion, indicate whether you agree or disagree with this opinion and explain why. Two examples have been provided.

Example A: Music is a universal phenomenon.

__x__ Fact   _____ Opinion   Why? _____

Because musicologists are probably reliable sources.
_____

_____ Agree   _____ Disagree   Why? _____

_____
_____

Elvis Presley in concert, Tampa, Florida, 1956

Example B: Music has the most meaning for the people from the culture in which it was created.

_____ Fact   __x__ Opinion   Why? _____

Because speaker said "I think" and "it seems to me."
_____

__x__ Agree   _____ Disagree   Why? _____

Personal experience; I don't fully understand music from other countries.
_____

1. The name *rock 'n' roll* comes from Alan Freed.

_____ Fact   _____ Opinion   Why? _____

_____

_____

_____ Agree   _____ Disagree   Why? _____

_____

_____

Bill Haley and the Comets

2. The actual beginning of rock 'n' roll music was on April 12, 1954, in New York City when Bill Haley and the Comets recorded "Rock around the Clock."

_____ Fact   _____ Opinion   Why? _____

_____

_____

_____ Agree   _____ Disagree   Why? _____

_____

_____

3. Rockabilly is a mixture of the blues harmonies of black music and the hillbilly country sounds of white music.

_____ Fact   _____ Opinion   Why? _____

_____

_____

_____ Agree   _____ Disagree   Why? _____

_____

_____

4.   The '50s generation was eager to grow up.

_____ Fact   _____ Opinion   Why? _____

_____

_____ Agree   _____ Disagree   Why? _____

_____

_____

5.   Teenagers in every society have rebelled against or resisted their parents in some way.

_____ Fact   _____ Opinion   Why? _____

_____

_____

_____ Agree   _____ Disagree   Why? _____

_____

_____

6.   In the '60s there was a mood of confusion and instability.

_____ Fact   _____ Opinion   Why? _____

_____

_____

_____ Agree   _____ Disagree   Why? _____

_____

_____

7.   Bob Dylan was more a poet than a songwriter.

_____ Fact   _____ Opinion   Why? _____

_____

_____

_____ Agree   _____ Disagree   Why? _____

_____

_____

The young Bob Dylan

8. Protest-rock condemned the evils of our society.

_____ Fact _____ Opinion Why? _____

_____

_____

_____ Agree _____ Disagree Why? _____

_____

_____

9. The Beatles appeared respectable to adults.

_____ Fact _____ Opinion Why? _____

_____

_____ Agree _____ Disagree Why? _____

_____

_____

10. The Beatles had a good sense of humor.

_____ Fact _____ Opinion Why? _____

_____

_____

_____ Agree _____ Disagree Why? _____

_____

11. The Rolling Stones were outrageous compared to the Beatles.

_____ Fact _____ Opinion Why? _____

_____

_____

_____ Agree _____ Disagree Why? _____

_____

_____

Soul singer Aretha Franklin

12. Soul music is an expression of black pride.

_____ Fact   _____ Opinion

Why? _____

_____

_____

_____ Agree   _____ Disagree

Why? _____

_____

_____

After You Listen

3 **Comparing Judgments.** In groups of three, compare your answers with your class-mates. Which strategies did you use to decide which items were fact and which were opinions? Which strategy did you think was the most useful?

Talk It Over

4 **Role-Playing the Part of a Critic.**   For this activity, you will be a critic of the arts.

1. Choose one of the arts that interests you, such as painting, architecture, dance, music, sculpture, or theater.

2. Find a visual example of the type of art you've chosen. For example, you might find a postcard with a reproduction of a painting, a picture from a book on architecture, or a newspaper ad for a movie, play, dance performance, or opera.

3. Gather as much factual information as you can from the visual example you selected. For example, who painted the picture, wrote the script, or did the choreography? Where is the event taking place? What time? What materials did the artist use?

4. Now pretend you have actually seen this artwork or performance and critique it. Evaluate it and decide whether you like it or not, whether you will give it a favorable review or an unfavorable one.

5. Prepare and present a two-minute review of the work to your classmates. Try to include as many facts and opinions about the work as you can. Your classmates' job is to remember at least three facts and three opinions from your presentation.

6. After each presentation, discuss the various facts and opinions. Which do you and your classmates usually find most interesting, facts or opinions? Why?

PART 3	# Expressing Doubt or Disbelief

People sometimes present statements as facts when actually these so-called facts have either not been proven or are only opinions. When people do this, you may want to express doubt or disbelief. If you express doubt or disbelief too formally, you will never be considered rude. However, if you speak too informally, you take the chance of offending some people.

Expressions for Expressing Doubt or Disbelief

Formal

Are you sure that's (it's) correct?
Are you sure that's (it's) okay?
Are you sure that's (it's) right?
Could he (she) really do that?

Could he (she, they) really think (believe) that?
Do you really believe that?
I find that hard to believe.

Informal

Are you serious?
Don't give me that!
Get out of here!
Get real!
That can't be true!
I'll believe it (that) when I see it.
No way!

Oh, sure!
Really?
Seriously?
I doubt it (that).
You're kidding!
You've got to be kidding!
Oh, come on!

Note: You may wonder why "I don't believe it!" is not on this list. This is because when you use the expression "I don't believe it!" in this context, usually placing strong emphasis on the word *believe,* it shows surprise without disbelief. It really means "I believe you, but I'm very surprised."

1   **Listening for Expressions of Doubt.**   You will hear four conversations in which people's responses range from very formal to very informal. After listening to each one, answer the questions in the spaces provided. When you are finished, compare your answers in small groups.

Conversation 1

Carl discusses a project with Professor Johnson.

1. What expression does Carl use to express doubt? _____

2. Why do you think he uses that expression? _____

    _____

    _____

3. Professor Johnson expresses disbelief twice in this conversation. Is he polite to Carl? _____

4. The first time he expresses disbelief through intonation alone. What words does he use? _____

5. What expression does he use the second time? _____

    _____

Conversation 2

Mr. Jones chats with Mr. Smith about his son's band.

1. Is this conversation formal or informal? _____

2. When the second speaker says, "Get outta here," does he sound amused or angry?

    _____

3. How does the second speaker sound when he says, "Oh, sure!"?_____

    _____

4. When the second speaker says "Yeah, right, and I'm Mick Jagger," does he sound rude? _____

5. Why do you think the second speaker expresses disbelief this way?_____

    _____

    _____

Ballet dancer Rudolf Nureyev

Conversation 3

Jenny and Al talk about dancing.

1. Are Jenny's expressions of disbelief formal or informal?

   _____

2. Is she polite or rude? _____

3. What are some expressions Jenny uses?

   _____

   _____

Conversation 4

Rachel attends Professor Starr's music appreciation class.

1. Are Rachel's expressions of disbelief formal or informal? _____

2. Is she polite or rude? _____

3. Does the professor seem impatient with Rachel? _____

4. What are some expressions Rachel uses? _____

   _____

2 Listening for Opinions. When you listened to the radio program and did the activities in Part 2, you answered questions about some of the facts and opinions you heard. Listen to the radio program again.

1. This time listen for additional statements that you think are not proven facts. When you hear one, ask the teacher to stop the tape and replay the statement.
2. Copy the statement onto the lines provided here.
3. After each statement, add a response that expresses your doubt or disbelief about it.
4. Share your responses with your classmates.

1. Statement: _____

   _____

   Response: _____

   _____

2. Statement: _____

   _____

   Response: _____

   _____

3. Statement: _____

_____

Response: _____

_____

4. Statement: _____

_____

Response: _____

_____

5. Statement: _____

_____

Response: _____

_____

6. Statement: _____

_____

Response: _____

_____

3   **Completing Conversations.**

1. Choose a partner and complete these conversations together using expressions of doubt or disbelief. A sample is provided for Conversation 1.

2. If you wish, you can create some original conversations using the sample as a model.

3. Choose one conversation (either one from the book or an original one) and present it to the rest of the class.

Conversation 1

A: I went to a terrific concert last night.

B: Oh, which one?

A: It was a John Cage concert, and a woman played the cello underwater.

B: No way!

A: Not only that, but the piano player was underwater, too.

B: Get out of here!

A: Really! John Cage concerts are always experimental.

B: Yeah, I know, but I'll believe it when I see it!

Conversation 2

Christo, the artist, wrapped two islands in pink plastic

A: Do you remember the contemporary artist, Christo, who wrapped the coast of Australia in canvas and an entire island in pink plastic?

B: Yeah, why?

A: Because his latest project is wrapping the Eiffel Tower in blue silk.

B: _____

A: _____

B: _____

Etc.

Conversation 3

A: What a disaster at the theater tonight!

B: Why? What happened?

A: We were trying to rehearse, and first the lights went out, then the scenery fell over, then the leading man was taken to the hospital, and as if that weren't enough, we put out a fire in a trash can just in time! I think someone is trying to keep the play from opening.

B: _____

A: _____

B: _____

Etc.

Conversation 4

A: Did you hear what your friend David did?

B: No, what?

A: He had a singer come into the room where he and 300 others were taking their law exams and sing "Happy Birthday" to his girlfriend.

B: _____

A: _____

B: _____

Etc.

Talk It Over

4 Presenting Facts and Expressing Doubts.   This game is one that you win by fooling your friends.

1. Divide into two teams and share interesting or unusual facts about your life that have to do with the arts. These events do not have to involve you directly, but you must be connected to them in some way. For example:

■ One of my drawings is on display in the city hall in my hometown.

■ My father-in-law is a famous actor.

■ I once got a standing ovation for my dancing at a folk dance festival.

■ When I was 17, I won third prize in a whistling contest.

■ My brother is a well-known graffiti artist.

2. Make up some events that did not actually happen and share these with your teammates, too.

3. With your team, choose some of the real and imaginary events to tell the other team about. Each person can present facts about himself or herself, or about other team members.

4. Take turns presenting these facts to the team. They can choose to believe what you say and respond, "OK, I believe that" or they can respond with expressions of doubt or disbelief.

5. Each time a team is correct in distinguishing fact from opinion, it gets a point.

PART 4

Focus on Testing

You will hear a short review of a music festival. After the review, you will be asked some questions. Circle the letter of the best answer to each question.

Question 1

a. It was a large "happening."

b. It was an important sociological event.

c. It was an important political event.

d. All of the above.

Question 2

a. Aquarian Exposition

b. Woodstock

c. Music and Art Fair

d. The Happening

Question 3

a.   as many as one million

b.   between 16 and 30

c.   more than 400,000

d.   thousands

Question 4

a.   between 16 and 30

b.   between 30 and 60

c.   between 13 and 60

d.   between 16 and 40

Question 5

a.   because they happened to get stuck in a traffic jam in Bethel

b.   because they wanted to go on a pilgrimage to Bethel

c.   because they wanted to reject traditional values and goals

d.   because they wanted to see the cast of top rock stars

Question 6

a.   an inadequate sound system

b.   an inadequate sanitation system

c.   an inadequate amount of food

d.   an inadequate amount of dry ground

Video Activities: Women in Jazz

Before You Watch.   Discuss these questions in small groups.

1.   Which of these musicians played jazz?
     a. Billie Holiday   b. the Beatles   c. Luciano Pavarotti

2.   Do you ever listen to jazz? Do you know any other famous jazz musicians?

Watch.   Circle the correct answers.

1.   What kind of music does Rosetta Records publish?
     a. songs by modern female jazz musicians
     b. songs from early jazz musicians
     c. early songs by female jazz musicians

2.   According to Rosetta Weitz most people today do not realize that women _____.
     a. sang with jazz bands
     b. had a powerful influence on jazz
     c. were better jazz musicians than men

3. Successful female jazz musicians had _____.
   a. wealth and power
   b. everything but power
   c. to depend on men

4. What did early female jazz singers sing about?
   a. love   c. pride   e. poverty
   b. war   d. abandonment

Watch Again. Answer these questions in small groups.

1. Complete the names of these jazz musicians. Put a check mark (√) next to the women.

Jazz Musicians	Women?
a. _____ Cox	
b. _____ McKinney	
c. Maxine _____	
d. Lester _____	
e. _____ Calloway	
f. _____ Ellington	
g. _____ Basie	
h. _____ Humes	

2. *Impact* means the same as _____.
   a. destruction   b. influence   c. connection

3. Something that is *quintessential* is _____.
   a. a perfect example   b. necessary   c. successful

4. *Alongside* means the same as _____.
   a. near   b. with   c. instead of

After You Watch. Discuss these questions with your class.

1. Why do you think the importance of female jazz musicians has been downplayed?

2. What is your favorite kind of music? Who are the most popular musicians? Are they male or female?

Chapter 10

Conflict and Resolution

Did You Know?

- If we keep following the idea of an eye for an eye and a tooth for a tooth, we will end up in an eyeless toothless world. - *Gandhi*

- He that cannot forgive others breaks the bridge over which he must pass himself, for every man has need to be forgiven.- *Lord Herbert*

- American industrialist Henry Ford once stated, "Thinking is the hardest work there is, which is the probable reason so few people engage in it." Conflict resolution is probably the second-hardest work there is, and it requires thinking, which is the probable reason why so many conflicts remain unresolved. - *Bheki Sibiya, a human resources director*

- When angry, count to ten before you speak; if very angry, count to a hundred. – *Thomas Jefferson*

- When angry, count to four; when very angry, swear. – *Mark Twain*

PART 1

Getting Started

Sharing Your Experience

1   In small groups discuss the following questions:

1. What conflicts did you have as a child? How did you resolve them?

2. What conflicts did you have as an adolescent? How were they different from the ones you had as a child? How did you resolve them?

Vocabulary Preview

2   **Breaking a Secret Code.**   Discover the secret code!

1. Study the list of words and phrases. Then use clues a through l to fill in the corresponding blanks (a—l) with the correct forms of the vocabulary words. The first one has been completed for you.

1.	arousal state	a.	extreme anger
2.	big picture	b.	to become calm (slang)
3.	chill out	c.	to become calm (slang)
4.	contingency	d.	to cause, create, produce
5.	cool off	e.	excited state
6.	generate	f.	to go back and forth with ideas; compromise in negotiation
7.	give-and-take	g.	old information, something you already know
8.	to honor	h.	well-meaning, having the plan to help, not hurt
9.	old hat	i.	to respect
10.	rage	j.	entire idea, or a complete sense of a situation
11.	trial balloon	k.	a test case used to judge whether to continue with something or not
12.	well intentioned	l.	unforeseen event, unexpected situation

a. $\underset{1}{\underline{r}}$ $\underset{2}{\underline{a}}$ $\underset{3}{\underline{g}}$ $\underset{4}{\underline{e}}$

b. $\underline{}_{5}$ $\underline{}_{6}$ $\underline{}_{7}$ $\underline{}_{8}$ $\underline{}_{8}$ $\underline{}_{9}$ $\underline{}_{10}$ $\underline{}_{11}$

c. $\underline{}_{5}$ $\underline{}_{9}$ $\underline{}_{9}$ $\underline{}_{8}$ $\underline{}_{9}$ $\underline{}_{12}$ $\underline{}_{12}$

d. $\underline{}_{3}$ $\underline{}_{4}$ $\underline{}_{13}$ $\underline{}_{4}$ $\underline{}_{1}$ $\underline{}_{2}$ $\underline{}_{11}$ $\underline{}_{4}$

e. $\underline{}_{2}$ $\underline{}_{12}$ $\underline{}_{9}$ $\underline{}_{10}$ $\underline{}_{14}$ $\underline{}_{2}$ $\underline{}_{8}$ $\underline{}_{14}$ $\underline{}_{11}$ $\underline{}_{2}$ $\underline{}_{11}$ $\underline{}_{4}$

f. $\underline{}_{3}$ $\underline{}_{7}$ $\underline{}_{15}$ $\underline{}_{4}$ - $\underline{}_{2}$ $\underline{}_{13}$ $\underline{}_{16}$ - $\underline{}_{11}$ $\underline{}_{2}$ $\underline{}_{17}$ $\underline{}_{4}$

g. $\underline{}_{9}$ $\underline{}_{8}$ $\underline{}_{16}$ $\underline{}_{6}$ $\underline{}_{2}$ $\underline{}_{11}$

h. $\underline{}_{18}$ $\underline{}_{4}$ $\underline{}_{8}$ $\underline{}_{8}$ $\underline{}_{7}$ $\underline{}_{13}$ $\underline{}_{11}$ $\underline{}_{4}$ $\underline{}_{13}$ $\underline{}_{11}$ $\underline{}_{7}$ $\underline{}_{9}$ $\underline{}_{13}$ $\underline{}_{4}$ $\underline{}_{16}$

i. $\underline{}_{11}$ $\underline{}_{9}$ $\underline{}_{6}$ $\underline{}_{9}$ $\underline{}_{13}$ $\underline{}_{9}$ $\underline{}_{1}$

j. $\underline{}_{19}$ $\underline{}_{7}$ $\underline{}_{3}$ $\underline{}_{20}$ $\underline{}_{7}$ $\underline{}_{5}$ $\underline{}_{11}$ $\underline{}_{10}$ $\underline{}_{1}$ $\underline{}_{4}$

k. $\underline{}_{11}$ $\underline{}_{1}$ $\underline{}_{7}$ $\underline{}_{2}$ $\underline{}_{8}$ $\underline{}_{19}$ $\underline{}_{2}$ $\underline{}_{8}$ $\underline{}_{8}$ $\underline{}_{9}$ $\underline{}_{9}$ $\underline{}_{13}$

l. $\underline{}_{5}$ $\underline{}_{9}$ $\underline{}_{13}$ $\underline{}_{11}$ $\underline{}_{7}$ $\underline{}_{13}$ $\underline{}_{3}$ $\underline{}_{4}$ $\underline{}_{13}$ $\underline{}_{5}$ $\underline{}_{21}$

2. Now decode the secret phrases! To fill in the letters of the secret phrases, match the number under each letter blank with the corresponding number under the blanks from Step 1. Note that not all of the letters from the vocabulary above are used, and *m* and *q* are given.

A. $\underline{}_{18}$ $\underline{}_{4}$ $\underline{}_{6}$ $\underline{}_{2}$ $\underline{}_{15}$ $\underline{}_{4}$ $\underset{4}{\underline{m}}$ $\underline{}_{11}$ $\underline{}_{11}$ $\underline{}_{6}$ $\underline{}_{4}$

$\underline{}_{4}$ $\underline{}_{13}$ $\underline{}_{4}$ $\underset{21}{\underline{m}}$ $\underline{}_{2}$ $\underline{}_{13}$ $\underline{}_{16}$ $\underline{}_{6}$ $\underline{}_{4}$ $\underline{}_{7}$ $\underline{}_{14}$ $\underline{}_{10}$ $\underline{}_{14}$.

—*Walt Kelley*

B.

$\overline{17}$ $\overline{4}$ $\overline{4}$ $\overline{20}$ $\overline{5}$ $\overline{9}$ $\overline{9}$ $\overline{8}$ $\overline{2}$ $\overline{13}$ $\overline{16}$ $\overline{21}$ $\overline{0}$ $\overline{10}$

$\overline{5}$ $\overline{9}$ $\overline{\overset{m}{}}$ $\overline{\overset{m}{}}$ $\overline{2}$ $\overline{13}$ $\overline{16}$ $\overline{4}$ $\overline{15}$ $\overline{4}$ $\overline{1}$ $\overline{21}$ $\overline{19}$ $\overline{9}$ $\overline{16}$ $\overline{21}$.

—*St. Just*

C.

$\overline{18}$ $\overline{6}$ $\overline{4}$ $\overline{13}$ $\overline{2}$ $\overline{13}$ $\overline{3}$ $\overline{4}$ $\overline{1}$ $\overline{2}$ $\overline{1}$ $\overline{7}$ $\overline{14}$ $\overline{4}$ $\overline{14}$

$\overline{11}$ $\overline{6}$ $\overline{7}$ $\overline{13}$ $\overline{17}$ $\overline{9}$ $\overline{12}$ $\overline{11}$ $\overline{6}$ $\overline{4}$

$\overline{5}$ $\overline{9}$ $\overline{13}$ $\overline{14}$ $\overline{4}$ $\overline{\overset{q}{}}$ $\overline{10}$ $\overline{4}$ $\overline{13}$ $\overline{5}$ $\overline{4}$ $\overline{14}$.

—*Confucius*

D.

$\overline{7}$ $\overline{18}$ $\overline{2}$ $\overline{14}$ $\overline{2}$ $\overline{13}$ $\overline{3}$ $\overline{1}$ $\overline{21}$ $\overline{18}$ $\overline{7}$ $\overline{11}$ $\overline{6}$

$\overline{\overset{m}{21}}$ $\overline{12}$ $\overline{1}$ $\overline{7}$ $\overline{4}$ $\overline{13}$ $\overline{16}$:

$\overline{7}$ $\overline{11}$ $\overline{9}$ $\overline{8}$ $\overline{16}$ $\overline{\overset{m}{21}}$ $\overline{18}$ $\overline{1}$ $\overline{2}$ $\overline{11}$ $\overline{6}$,

$\overline{\overset{m}{21}}$ $\overline{18}$ $\overline{1}$ $\overline{2}$ $\overline{11}$ $\overline{6}$ $\overline{16}$ $\overline{7}$ $\overline{16}$ $\overline{4}$ $\overline{13}$ $\overline{16}$.

$\overline{7}$ $\overline{18}$ $\overline{2}$ $\overline{14}$ $\overline{2}$ $\overline{13}$ $\overline{3}$ $\overline{1}$ $\overline{21}$ $\overline{18}$ $\overline{7}$ $\overline{11}$ $\overline{6}$

$\overline{\overset{m}{21}}$ $\overline{12}$ $\overline{9}$ $\overline{4}$:

$\overline{7}$ $\overline{11}$ $\overline{9}$ $\overline{8}$ $\overline{16}$ $\overline{7}$ $\overline{11}$ $\overline{13}$ $\overline{9}$ $\overline{11}$,

$\overline{\overset{m}{21}}$ $\overline{18}$ $\overline{1}$ $\overline{2}$ $\overline{11}$ $\overline{6}$ $\overline{16}$ $\overline{7}$ $\overline{16}$ $\overline{3}$ $\overline{1}$ $\overline{9}$ $\overline{18}$.

—*William Blake*

Predicting Exam Questions

Most students want to get good grades. One strategy for getting good grades is to predict which questions an instructor will ask on an exam.

Information Likely to Be on Exams

1. Any point the instructor tells you will be on the exam or anything the instructor says would make a good exam question.
2. Information that the instructor repeats directly from the textbook or class readings.
3. Things stated more slowly or more loudly than other things. (Instructors often slow down or speak louder when they want to point out something important.)
4. Key facts.

Examples:
For a course about the history of civil rights conflicts:
   Who was Martin Luther King?
For a business management course:
   What should you say if you don't want to recommend someone for a job and do want to avoid a lawsuit?

5. Information about recent research, especially the instructor's own research. (Instructors want to make sure their students are up-to-date. Also, asking questions about data that cannot yet be found in the library is a good way to find out if students have been attending class.)
6. Information on handouts

Before You Listen

1 **Considering the Context.**   The lecture in this chapter is for a training course for resident advisors (RAs). Resident advisors are students living in dormitories (dorms) who receive special training and then are paid to assist new students. They answer questions students may have about campus life and help resolve conflicts in the dorms. In small groups discuss the following questions:

1. Would you like to live in a dorm? Why or why not?

2. What questions do you think a resident advisor needs to be able to answer?

3. What kinds of conflicts do you think people might have in dorms? How would you handle these conflicts?

Listen

2 **Listening to Predict Exam Questions.**   As you listen to the resident advisor's lecture, "Dealing with Conflicts," imagine that you are one of the new resident advisors. Listen and use the handout to take notes of the important points the resident advisor makes. Put an asterisk next to any point on the handout that you think will be likely to be an exam question.

Seven Strategies for Dealing with Conflicts

1. Cool off, chill out.

2. Talk and listen to each other.

3. Be clear about needs.

4. Brainstorm solutions.

5. Evaluate the solutions.

6. Choose one solution, or use a combination of solutions.

7. Agree on contingencies, monitoring, and reevaluating.

After You Listen

3   Evaluating Possible Exam Questions.   For each of the following questions, circle Yes or No to indicate whether you think the head resident advisor would include this question on the exam. Note in the spaces provided your reasons for circling *Yes* or *No*.

Question	Good exam question?
Example: Conflict resolution is an important skill for a resident advisor to have.	Yes (No) Reason: *too easy* _____ _____
1. When did Dale Carnegie write *How to Win Friends and Influence People*?	Yes No Reason: _____ _____ _____
2. What are three ways to get angry people to cool down?	Yes No Reason: _____ _____ _____
3. What are some ways to restate what a speaker is saying?	Yes No Reason: _____ _____ _____
4. What did Jack Benny say to the thief?	Yes No Reason: _____ _____ _____
5. Why is it important to provide for contingencies?	Yes No Reason: _____ _____ _____

4   Comparing Notes and Predictions.   With a partner compare the notes you made on the handout and which points you predicted would be included on an exam. Share some of the similarities and differences with the whole class.

Talk It Over

5   **Discussing Types of Exam Questions.**   In small groups, discuss the types of questions that appear on tests, such as true-false, multiple choice, short answer, and essay. Discuss how the subject matter of the course (math, literature, business, etc.) influences the types of questions the instructor chooses. For instance, when might a literature instructor choose to ask a true-false question? When might a mathematics instructor choose to ask an essay question?

In your discussion, consider the kinds of questions that would be asked in courses such as those in the following list. Add to the list any additional courses that are of interest to you.

biology	English
philosophy	sociology
chemistry	history
computer science	marketing
statistics	engineering
operations research	urban planning

6   **Asking and Answering Exam Questions.**   Using your lecture notes to refer to, complete the following activity with a partner.

1.   Make a list of five to ten questions you think might appear on an exam that covers the lecture.
2.   Ask a partner your exam questions.
3.   After your partner has answered your questions, answer his or her questions.
4.   Change partners and try the activity again. If time permits, do this several more times.
5.   As a class, discuss the variety of types of questions you and your classmates predicted would be on the exam.

Acquiescing and Expressing Reservations

Whether you are having an informal discussion with a friend or engaging in a formal business negotiation, there will be times when you will have doubts or reservations about what the other person is suggesting. If so, you should express them. If the person presents a logical, well-supported argument for his or her point of view, you will probably be convinced of, or acquiesce to, the other person's point of view. However, if the person is very aggressive in expressing his or her opinions, you may be tempted to "give in" or acquiesce and not express your reservations whether the person makes a convincing argument or not.

Useful Expressions for Acquiescing and Expressing Reservations

Acquiescing

Do whatever you think is best.

I suppose you must know best.

I trust you completely.

If you think that's best.

I'm putting myself completely in your hands.

I'm willing to go along this once.

OK, I'll go along with you this time.

Whatever you say.

Expressing reservations

How long do I have to think it over?

I'd like to get a second opinion.

I have some reservations about …

I'm not sure.

I'm not sure that will work for me.

Let me think it over.

One concern I have is …

One drawback is …

Possibly, but …

Yes, but the question really is …

What bothers me is …

What I'm afraid of is …

1   **Listening for Acquiescence and Reservations.**   Listen to the conversation between a resident advisor and students in her dorm, in which they acquiesce or express reservations. Answer the questions you hear after the conversation. When you are finished, compare your answers in small groups.

1. Why does the resident advisor allow Mohammed to speak first? _____ _____ _____ _____

2. What expression does James use to acquiesce? _____

_____

_____

3. What is the problem? _____

_____

_____

4. What expression does James use to express reservations?_____

_____

_____

5. What do James and Mohammed agree to try? _____

_____

_____

6. What expressions do they use to show that they have acquiesced? _____

_____

_____

2 **Listening for Suggestions about Conflict Resolution.**   In the lecture, the head resident advisor suggests three ways to help people cool down when they are angry.
Listen to that part of the lecture again. Write the suggestions and decide how you
would react to each one. Would you acquiesce, or would you express reservations?
Write the expression that feels most appropriate for you. Discuss your responses with
your classmates.

1. Suggestion: _____

_____

Your response: _____

_____

2. Suggestion: _____

_____

Your response: _____

_____

3. Suggestion: _____

_____

Your response: _____

_____

3   **Listening for Ways to Express Reservations.**   In the lecture, the head resident advisor suggests ways to get people to talk and listen to each other by restating the problem using ways of expressing reservations. Listen to this part of the lecture again and write down the suggested ways for expressing reservations. Discuss your answer with your classmates.

Talk It Over

4   **Acquiescing and Expressing Reservations.**

1.   Divide into groups according to the number of characters for each situation. Role-play the following conflicts using appropriate expressions to acquiesce and express reservations. Stay "in character" as you express the opinions of the character that you are role-playing. You may add characters of your own or make up another situation.

2.   Perform your role-play for the class.

Situation 1

Tony, Ming, Ruth, Larry, and Masa are sitting in a dorm room at 9:00 A.M. planning their Sunday. They want to have a picnic, rehearse for a play they are in, and study for an exam the next day.

Characters

- Tony, who lives to play sports and be outdoors
- Ming, who would like to be an actor after she graduates
- Ruth, who wants to get all As so that she can get into graduate school
- Larry, who hates to stay up late and doesn't want to "pull an all-nighter" studying for the exam
- Masa, who is enjoying college and just wants to see a compromise that will work for everyone

Situation 2

The office workers in a computer company are planning an office party. They cannot agree on a theme, the kind of food, or a location.

Characters

- An administrative assistant in human resources
- A computer programmer
- A young manager who hopes to date the assistant in human resources
- A 40-year old manager who is a single parent and hopes to bring his kids to the party
- A 35-year-old supervisor who is a single parent and hopes to leave her kids with a baby-sitter
- A young receptionist who is working and going to school and wants to make sure that the party doesn't conflict with final exams

Situation 3

Marcia, 20, is a premed student. She has just gotten back her chemistry midterm exam with a grade of C+ on it. She looks over the exam and realizes that the professor did not see page three of her six-page exam. This professor, however, had announced on the first day of class that he never changes a grade. Grades are important to Marcia, and she decides to speak to the professor about her exam anyway.

Characters

■ Marcia

■ Professor Thomas

Situation 4

Five students are looking for a house to rent. They know they would like to live together, but have different ideas about what makes a good living space.

Characters

■ Daniel, who wants a large house with an extra room for parties and to study in

■ Alan, who wants a "eat-in" kitchen so they can all have breakfast together

■ Pat, who wants a computer room so they don't have to keep the computers in their bedrooms

■ Sandy, who wants to make sure that no one has to share a bedroom

■ Norm, who wants to have a backyard so he can keep his dog

Situation 5

Edward and Paul are roommates in the dorm. They are having problems because Edward wants to keep the dorm room door open and Paul likes to play loud music, so other students complain. Edward is an early riser and Paul likes to sleep late. Also Edward is very messy and Paul is neat.

Characters

■ Edward

■ Paul

5 **Discussing Conflicts and Resolutions.**   Discuss the following questions in small groups or as a whole class.

1. Describe a conflict you've had with someone in the last six months. How did you resolve the conflict? Which of the steps for conflict resolution mentioned in the lecture did you use?

2. Describe a time when you helped someone resolve a conflict. What steps did you take? What expressions of acquiescing or expressing reservations did you use?

| **PART 4** | # Focus on Testing |

Listen to Professor Taylor and some students discuss an upcoming exam. Then listen to the questions. Circle the letter of the best answer to each question.

Question 1

a.   the conflicts in the Middle East

b.   the conflicts in Northern Ireland

c.   the conflicts in Africa

d.   A and B above

Question 2

a.   material covered in the video shown in class

b.   material covered in the discussion section

c.   material covered in lecture

d.   student presentations

Question 3

a.   short answer

b   true/false

c.   essay

d.   B and C above

Question 4

a.   true/false

b.   open-book

c.   short answer

d.   take home

Question 5

a.   Take the weekend off.

b.   Wait and see what the next exam is like.

c.   Analyze the concepts studied so far.

d.   Study hard over the weekend.

Video Activities: A Strike

Before You Watch.   Discuss these questions in small groups.

1.   Why do workers go on strike?

2.   Are government workers allowed to go on strike?

Watch.   Circle the correct answers.

1.   What have the unionized workers of the country of Los Angeles decided to do?
     a. go back to work   b. go on strike   c. go to court

2.   How much of a pay increase is the union asking for?
     a. 15.5% over three years   b. 15% over three years   c. 5% in one year

3.   How much of a pay increase is the county offering the union?
     a. 19% over five years   b. 9% over three years   c. 11% over two years

Watch Again.   Answer these questions in small groups.

1.   Check the employees that are mentioned in the video segment.
     _____ a. librarians   _____ d. teachers   _____ f. typists
     _____ b. nurses   _____ e. cooks   _____ g. cashiers
     _____ c. building maintenance workers

2.   Which of the employees above are going back to work tomorrow? _____

3.   According to the woman in the video, which two of these problems do the nurses have?
     a. too little pay   b. too much work   c. poor working conditions

4.   *Principal* means _____.
     a. the most important   b. the smallest   c. the leader

5.   When something is *booming,* it is _____.
     a. just starting   b. growing rapidly   c. declining

6.   If something is *critical,* it is _____.
     a. dangerous   b. expensive   c. necessary

After You Watch.   Discuss these questions with your class.

1.   Do you think that people in critical jobs (such as nurses) should be allowed to go on strike? Why or why not?

2.   What are the advantages and disadvantages of belonging to a union?

Chapter 11

Medicine and Science

Did You Know?

- The first heart transplant took place in Cape Town, South Africa, in 1967 and was performed by Christiaan Barnard. The patient, Louis Washkansky, lived for only 18 days after the surgery.

- 74,000 Americans are waiting for a transplant. A new name is added to the waiting list every 18 minutes.

- 261 medical institutions in the United States operate organ transplant programs.

- 25 different organs and tissues can be transplanted including heart, lungs, kidney, liver, corneas, bone, and cartilage.

- 90% of American say they support the concept of organ donation, but urgently needed organs are actually donated only 1/3 of the time.

- One donor can provide organs, bone, and tissue for 50 people.

- More than 60% of all organ recipients are between the ages of 18 and 49.

PART 1

Getting Started

Sharing Your Experience

1 Discuss the following questions as a class or in small groups.

1. The choices of several famous men and women are described here. What are the advantages and disadvantages of these decisions? In similar circumstances, would you have made the same choices?

Buddha

Socrates

a. Buddha left his family and gave up all his worldly possessions; he vowed to sit in meditation until he achieved enlightenment for the sake of all human beings.

b. Socrates chose to accept his unjust punishment of drinking poison rather than escape from prison and live in hiding.

Harry S. Truman   Joan of Arc

c. Harry Truman chose to drop the atomic bomb and face worldwide criticism because he thought that even more people would die if World War II continued.

d. Joan of Arc chose to be burned to death rather than deny her belief that her actions were directly guided by God.

2. Choose someone you know who had to face a difficult ethical choice and describe it to the class. It may be a famous person, a friend, an acquaintance, or someone you have heard about.

3. What principles do you live by? How did you develop them? Do you ever go against any of them?
   Examples:
   a. Do unto others as you would have them do unto you.
   b. Never lie.
   c. Honor your father and mother.
   d. Never kill.
   e. Never steal.
   f. Do whatever you want, but harm no other person.

4. What would you sacrifice to maintain your principles?

Vocabulary Preview

2 **Prefixes, Roots, and Suffixes.**   One way to determine the meaning of a word you don't know is to break it down into parts. You can look at prefixes, roots, and suffixes.

For example, the word *transportable* can be broken down into these parts:

trans   a root that means "across"
port   a root that means "carry"
able   a suffix that means "can be done"

Therefore you can figure out that the word *transportable* describes something that can be carried from one place to another. With a partner, practice figuring out the meanings of words by looking at their prefixes, roots, and suffixes.

1. Fill in the meanings of each prefix, suffix, and root. (Some meanings have been filled in for you.)
2. Try writing a short definition of the meaning of the whole word.
3. When you are finished, compare your answers with those of your classmates.
4. Use a dictionary to check the meaning of a word part or a whole word to fill in anything the class could not complete.

1. *a(d)-*   = *to* _____

   loc(are) = *place* _____

   -at(e)   makes the word   *a verb* _____

   -ion   makes the word   *a noun* _____

   allocation = _____

2. *commod(us)* = _____

   -ity   makes the word _____

   commodity = _____

3. *com-*   = _____

   pati   = _____

   -ible   makes the word _____

   compatible = _____

4. *de-*   = _____

   gener   = _____

   -ative   makes the word _____

   degenerative = _____

5. *discrimin (discrimen)* = _____

   -ate   makes the noun a _____

   to discriminate   = _____

6. *humane*   = _____

   -ness   makes the word _____

   humaneness = _____

7. *immuno-* = _____

    su(b) = _____

    press = _____

    -io   makes the word a _____

    immunosuppression = _____

8. *in-* = _____

    cur(e) = _____

    -able   makes the word a _____

    incurable = _____

9. *ir-* = _____

    re- = _____

    verse = _____

    -ible = _____

    irreversible = _____

10. *pro-* = _____

    gnosis = _____

    prognosis = _____

11. *recipi(ens)* = _____

    -ent = _____

    recipient = _____

3 **Using Prefixes, Roots, and Suffixes.** Work in small groups.

1. Choose several prefixes, roots, or suffixes and see how many words you can list with each. Compare lists with your classmates.

2. Make a list of other prefixes, roots, and suffixes that you know the meanings of. Pass your list to another group and have that group list words that use your prefixes, roots, and suffixes. See which group makes the longest list.

3. Make a circle. Each person in the circle creates a made-up word using a known prefix, root, or suffix. He or she must also think of a "true" definition for the made-up word. Go around the circle, with each person saying his or her made-up word, and the person on his or her left guessing its definition.

4. Go around the circle again, this time giving the "true" definition of the made-up words. For example, the made-up word is "brunner". The person on the left guesses "a new kind of broom that sweeps rugs and floors and ceilings" while the "true" definition is "when you only have time for one meal – a combination of breakfast, lunch, and dinner."

Cohesion and Reference

For a paragraph to make sense, the individual sentences must fit together. Likewise, for a series of paragraphs to make sense, they must also be connected in a logical manner. When sentences or paragraphs are well connected, we say that they *cohere*, that they are *cohesive*. This means literally that they stick together.

> *co* (the prefix) = together   *here* (the root) = to stick

How is cohesion maintained in both spoken and written language? One of the ways is called *reference*. Reference is the use of nonspecific words to refer back to a specific noun or idea. There are several ways to make sure that the reference is clear.

Option 1: Creating Dependent Relationships

Consider the following sentences:

1. The doctor had to make a choice.
2. The doctor had to decide which of the accident victims to treat first.

These sentences are *independent*. They seem to be related to the same topic, but the meaning of one sentence does not depend on the meaning of the other.

To create a *dependent* relationship between two sentences, connect them so that together they have meaning and that one of the sentences alone is ambiguous. For example:

3. The doctor decided to treat the little boy first.
4. He hoped that he had made the right choice.

Sentence 3 establishes that we are talking about the doctor. In sentence 4, *he* refers to the doctor, but this reference would not be clear without sentence 3. Sentence 3 and sentence 4 are dependent and cohesive.

Option 2: Using Personal Pronouns to Create Cohesion

Every language has words that refer to other words. You are already familiar with the use of personal pronouns.

Personal Pronouns

Subject and Object Pronouns	Possessive Pronouns	Possessive Adjectives
I, me	mine	my
you	yours	your
we, us	ours	our
he, him	his	his
she, her	hers	her
they, them	theirs	their
it	its (rarely used)	its

The use of the word *it* deserves special attention. This pronoun can refer to an idea or concept expressed by a phrase, a whole sentence, a paragraph, or perhaps even an entire conversation. For example:

5. The doctor cleaned up the wounds on the little boy's face, ordered some X-rays of his head, and told the nurses to get the operating room ready while the medical assistant checked the rest of the boy's body for other injuries.
6. So far, it was going well.

In sentence 6, *it* refers to the treatment described by all of sentence 5 and perhaps even to the ethical choice the doctor had to make that was described in sentences 1 through 4.

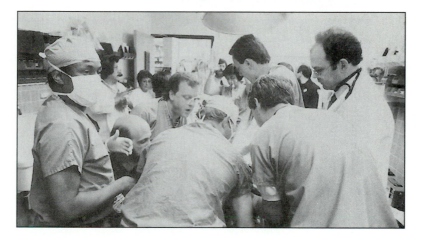

Option 3: Using Demonstrative Pronouns to Create Cohesion

The words *this*, *that*, *these*, and *those* often help create cohesion between sentences. However, it can be difficult to understand exactly what these demonstrative pronouns refer to when they are used to describe something that cannot be named in one or two words. Consider the following sentences:

7. The surgery was taking a long time; the doctor felt tired, hungry, and worried about the other accident victims who still needed to be treated.
8. That was the way it went some days in the emergency room.

Notice that the word *that* in sentence 8 refers to a particular circumstance described and feeling conveyed by sentence 7. However, the word it in sentence 8 refers to daily life in general.

Option 4: Demonstrative Pronouns that Come before their Referent

Sometimes a demonstrative pronoun may come before rather than after the sentence it refers to. For example:

9. This was going to be hard.
10. He never enjoyed making life-or-death decisions.

In this case, the word *this* in sentence 9 does not refer back to something already mentioned. Instead, *this* refers ahead to "making life-or-death decisions," which is mentioned in sentence 10.

A Final Note

Although reference words allow you to avoid repetition, they can be ambiguous and confusing if not properly used. Consider the following:

11. The little boy smiled at the doctor as he opened his eyes.

Whose eyes are they? Most likely they are the little boy's. However, what if sentence 9 had been this:

12. This was going to be hard; the weary doctor closed his eyes for a moment.

In this case, we could not be certain whose eyes opened, the doctor's or the little boy's.

Ways to Avoid Confusing References

When speaking or writing:
- Do not overuse reference words.
- Restate exactly who or what you are talking about periodically.

When listening or reading:
- For all reference words, ask yourself: Who? Whose? What? When? Where? Immediately try to connect the reference word with its referent.
- If you do become confused, stop the speaker at an appropriate time and ask for clarification, or put a question mark in the margin of your book or notes and ask for clarification from an instructor or friend later.

Before You Listen

1 **Discussing Medical Resources.**

1. Medical resources such as doctors, nurses, hospital beds, expensive drugs, and highly advanced medical machines are scarce. In your opinion, should these resources be given to the most needy or to those who can afford them? If too many people need one item, should the person who will receive that item be chosen by lottery, by judges, or by some other method?

2. Do you think people should be allowed to sell their own organs on the Internet? Why or why not?

Listen

2 **Listening for Cohesive Devices.**   Listen to the discussion once all the way through. Then listen again and fill in the blanks in each of the following items with the appropriate information. Note that:

- In items 1- 5, the "clue" question has been provided, and you simply answer it.
- In items 6-20, you must write both the "clue" question and the answer.
- In items 1- 10, the reference words are italicized.
- In items 11-20, you must first find the reference words before completing the rest of the item.

Example: Try to imagine *this* situation.

Question: <u>What situation?</u>

Answer: <u>The entire story about David needing a transplant and finally getting one.</u>

1. *They* had been told that David's only hope was a liver transplant.

    Question: Who had been told?

    Answer: _____

2. So anyway, *this* boy's parents hoped that their son's liver could help.

    Question: Which boy's parents?

    Answer: _____

3. The patients needing organs vastly outnumber donors, *those* who can give organs.

    Question: Those what?

    Answer: _____

4. Because of *this*, each year, thousands of people who could be saved by a routine transplant die.

    Question: Because of what?

    Answer: _____

5. I heard *it* once, but I've forgotten *it*. How does *it* go again?

    Question: Heard what once?

    Answer: _____

    Question: How does what go?

    Answer: _____

6. As the sea becomes rougher, *it* is clear to all of you in the boat . . .

    Question: _____

    Answer: _____

7. If so, do you trust *his* or *her* fairness in making the decision?

    Question: _____

    Answer: _____

8. In *that* case, the only fair method of decision would be some sort of lottery.

    Question: _____

    Answer: _____

9. In other situations like this where the public welfare is affected so dramatically, the government *here* has always intervened.

    Question: _____

    Answer: _____

10. I thought that recently, laws have been proposed that would make *this* a crime.

    Question: _____

    Answer: _____

11. And that these laws would place the allocation of this precious commodity entirely in the hands of the federal government.

    Question: _____

    Answer: _____

    Question: _____

    Answer: _____

Organs often must be rapidly delivered to needy recipients.

12. ...doctors in that hospital would keep their organs alive artificially until they are needed.

    Question: _____

    Answer: _____

    Question: _____

    Answer: _____

13. I suppose this would be something like harvesting the dead, though.

    Question: _____

    Answer: _____

14. The response to that argument has often been that few people, if any, have the wisdom to see what the social good is now.

    Question: _____

    Answer: _____

15. Nor can they see what it will be in the future.

    Question: _____

    Answer: _____

    Question: _____

    Answer: _____

16. The problem with this position is still the shortage of organs and the large number of needy people.

    Question: _____

    Answer: _____

17. What if three people are in immediate danger of dying from kidney failure, but there is only one kidney? Then this solution does not help.

    Question: _____

    Answer: _____

18. Should we discriminate against them and put them last on the list?

    Question: _____

    Answer: _____

19. At least they would know that no one discriminated against them for any reason.

    Question: _____

    Answer: _____

20. It's really overwhelming to realize that certain ethical choices can mean that one person will live and others will probably die.

    Question: _____

    Answer: _____

After You Listen

3   **Discussing the Lecture.**   As a class or in small groups, discuss the following questions. As you discuss, listen for the reference words. Ask for clarification of references as necessary.

1. Do you think the lifeboat analogy is a good one? Why or why not?
2. Do you think an organ transplant lottery is a good idea? Why or why not?
3. Do you think the government should regulate organ transplants? Why or why not?
4. Do you think facilities should be set up that make it easier to obtain the organs of the dead? Why or why not?
5. What do you think is the best solution to the organ shortage problem? Why?
6. Would you want to be a person who decides who gets an available organ and who doesn't? Why or why not?

The family of Nicholas Green, who was killed in a robbery attempt in Italy and whose organs were donated for transplant.

Talk It Over

4   **Understanding and Using Reference Words.**   Find a brief article in a magazine or newspaper that deals with some type of ethical choice and bring it to class.

1. In small groups, take turns reading your articles aloud.
2. Whenever those who are listening hear a reference word, they should call out the appropriate question to clarify the reference. Several people may call out similar questions at the same time.
3. Someone in the group who did not ask the question should answer it.
4. Then continue reading the article.

5   **Identifying Reference Words.**

1. Listen to friends, TV and radio commentators, and other English speakers, or look in magazines or newspapers and try to pick out:
- examples of reference words
- examples of ambiguous references
- examples of extended references in which the thing referred to is described in a whole sentence or paragraph, not just one word

2. Write down examples and discuss them with your classmates. Consider the following questions:

- How or why was the reference ambiguous?
- How could the ambiguity be avoided?
- What happened because of the ambiguity? Was there a misunderstanding?
- Were the examples of extended reference hard to find? Why or why not?
- What did most referents refer to? Things? People? Places? Ideas?

| PART 3 |

Taking and Keeping the Floor

In conversation, people take turns listening and speaking. Smooth "turn taking" is a critical part of any conversation.

However, turn taking does not always occur smoothly—even among native speakers of the same language. For instance, there are many times when what you have to say may be ignored unless you assert your right to say it. More important, people may interpret silence as agreement, or they may assume that you have nothing to say if you do not claim a right to say it.

Taking the Floor

Asserting yourself and speaking out is called *taking the floor*. As with other functions in English, there are appropriate ways to take the floor in both formal and informal situations.

Formal Situations

1. Unless you are specifically asked to save questions until after the speaker is through, you may interrupt in order to:
   - Ask for clarification or repetition
   - Add pertinent information
   - Challenge a point

2. When you interrupt, stick to the immediate topic. Do not raise issues from previous lectures or sources unless they are relevant. If you do, you risk interrupting the speaker's train of thought and annoying other listeners as well as the speaker.

Informal Situations

Interruption and overlap are acceptable. The limits depend entirely on the individuals involved and their relationship as well as their cultural backgrounds.

Expressions and Cues for Taking the Floor

Polite (Verbal)

Excuse me for interrupting, but . . .

If I could interrupt . . .

May (Can, Could) I interrupt?

That's true, but . . .

Can (Could, May) I just say (add) something here?

I don't think so.

If I could just come in here . . .

That reminds me . . .

Yes, but . . .

Polite (Nonverbal), depending on the situation, relative status of speaker, and listener

Clear your throat.

Move closer to the speaker.

Raise your hand or index finger.

Take an audible breath.

Impolite (Verbal), except among close friends

Enough about ...

Hold on there.

Wait a minute.

What about . . . ?

Yeah, but . . .

Impolite (Verbal), even among close friends

No, you're wrong!

That's ridiculous!

What a stupid idea!

Impolite (Nonverbal)

Any threatening gesture

Derisive laughter

Fidgeting

Rolling your eyes

Keeping the Floor

Refusing to give up a turn is called *keeping the floor*. The rules for keeping the floor in both formal and informal situations are similar to the rules for taking the floor. You can use expressions and nonverbal cues that enable you to let the listener know that you want to finish what you are saying. Be sure to allow people to interrupt you when necessary.

Expressions and Cues for Keeping the Floor

Polite (Verbal)

I don't want to lose my train of thought.   Just a minute (second), please.

Let me just finish what I was saying.   Let me just say this (one more thing).

Let me just tell you . . .   Please don't interrupt just now, OK?

Can (May, Could) I please just get
through (saying) this?

Polite (Nonverbal), depending on the situation, relative status of speaker, and listener

Signal "stop" with hand.   Talk louder.

Talk faster, keeping pauses to   Any combination of the three.
a minimum.

Impolite (Verbal)

Don't interrupt me!   (Shut up and) let me finish!
Let me handle this!

Impolite (Nonverbal)

Any threatening gesture   Derisive laughter

1   **Listening for Expressions for Taking and Keeping the Floor.**   You will hear two conversations in which people take and keep the floor. After listening to each one, answer the questions in the spaces provided. When you are finished, compare your answers in small groups.

Conversation 1

Erik and Sylvia are talking in the cafeteria after class.

1. What nonverbal cue might Erik have used when he said, "That's true, but…"?

_____

_____

_____

_____

_____

_____

2. What nonverbal cue might Erik have used when he said, "Yes, but ..."?

_____

_____

3. What nonverbal cue might Sylvia have used when she said, "Let me just tell you the main point he made"? _____

_____

4. What nonverbal cue might Sylvia have used when she said, "Let me finish what I was saying"? _____

_____

Conversation 2

A teaching assistant and some students are in class.

1. Was Sally's interruption about youth in Asia polite or impolite? _____

_____

Why? _____

_____

2. Was Gina's interruption about states allowing for extenuating circumstances polite or impolite? _____ Why? _____

_____

3. Was Fred's interruption about research for a term paper polite or impolite? _____ Why? _____

_____

2 **Listening for Opportunities to Take the Floor.** Listen to the discussion on organ transplants again. As you listen:

1. Pretend that Susan and Richard have invited you home with them for the weekend and that you are sitting at the breakfast table with them.
2. Signal that you wish to interrupt by raising your hand. The teacher will stop the tape. Then use appropriate verbal and nonverbal cues to take the floor and make your point.
3. You might wish to interrupt to:
   - explain how you feel about an issue
   - ask for clarification or repetition
   - add pertinent information
   - challenge a point

Talk It Over

3   **Presenting Your Point of View.**   In this activity, you will have a chance to "stand on a soapbox" and give a two- to -three-minute speech on what you think about a particular ethical question.

1. Select a topic from the following suggestions.
2. Organize your thoughts before you begin.
3. Give your opinions in small groups. Later you may want to share them with the whole class.
4. When you are the speaker, it will be your task to keep the floor as much as possible. You may, however, want to give the floor to someone who has pertinent questions or information.
5. When you are listening, it will be your task to interrupt the speaker as many times as possible. Since this activity is only a game, you may play the role of a rude person if you wish. But no more than one or two people in the group should work at interrupting any speaker.
6. During this activity, practice using a variety of verbal and nonverbal cues for taking and keeping the floor.

Topics

1. using live animals for research
2. declaring someone officially dead when the brain stops rather than when the heart stops
3. buying and selling organs
4. pleading insanity for murder
5. euthanasia
6. appropriate versus inappropriate uses of technology (for instance, nuclear fission)

7. genetic engineering (for instance, changing existing organisms or developing entirely new ones)

8. shortening sentences of prison inmates for participating in potentially dangerous medical research

9. respecting the wishes of the dead (wills, informal requests)

10. taking away licenses or putting people in jail for drunk driving

11. placing the elderly in nursing homes

12. using ridicule as a punishment for crime (for example, forcing a person to wear a sign that says, "I stole $50 worth of groceries")

13. forcing people with contagious diseases to live apart from everyone else

---

PART 4   Focus on Testing

You will hear a short human interest story. After the story, you will be asked some questions. Circle the letter of the best answer to each question.

Question 1

a. from Marissa's hip

b. from the medical team

c. from Marissa's parents

d. from the older sister Anissa

Question 2

a. one out of seven

b. seventeen out of one hundred

c. seven out of ten

d. three out of ten

Question 3

a. The Ayalas could have aborted the fetus if it wasn't a match for Anissa.

b. A body part was harvested from a living body.

c. The baby gave a part of her body without her consent.

d. All of the above.

Question 4

a. in order to receive a bone marrow transplant

b. in order to receive a heart-lung transplant

c. in order to receive a liver in exchange

d. in order to receive a kidney in exchange

Question 5

a.   the United States

b.   China

c.   India

d.   North America

Video Activities: Stealth Surgery

Before You Watch.   Answer these questions in small groups.

1.   What kinds of pictures does an X-ray machine take? Have you ever had an X-ray?

2.   Do you know the name of any other machines that can take pictures of the inside of a body? What are they? How are they different from X-rays?

Watch.   Answer these questions in small groups.

1.   What is Leonard Novak's favorite free time activity? Why is it unusual?

   _____

   _____

2.   What health problem did Leonard Novak have recently?
   a. eye problems
   b. bad headaches
   c. a cancerous tumor

3.   What is the name of the new treatment that Novak received? _____

4.   Why is this treatment better than traditional surgery? _____

   _____

Watch Again.   Answer these questions in small groups.

1.   Use the words below to complete the description of the new treatment.

anatomical	converted	creates	CT
images	MRI	placed	scans

   Two hundred or more _____ and _____ _____ of the patient's head are fed into the computer and _____ into 3D _____. Then a band _____ on the patient's head _____ an _____ map.

2. He was *benched* means that he _____.
    a. couldn't play   b. was hit with a bench   c. got sick

3. She *threw him a curve ball* means that she _____.
    a. hit him   b. pitched the ball to him   c. surprised him

4. The word *invasive* is an adjective related to _____.
    a. invalid   b. invasion   c. invent

5. The *skull* is the _____.
    a. bone of the head   b. the nose   c. the neck bone

6. *Stealth* refers to the action of moving _____.
    a. quickly   b. secretly   c. carefully

After You Watch.   Discuss these questions with your class.

1. Do you know any elderly people who are very active? How old are they? What activities do they do?

2. Do you know anyone who has ever had surgery? How long were they in the hospital? How long did it take them to recover?

Chapter 12

The Future

Did You Know?

- Nothing is certain but death and taxes. - *Benjamin Franklin, famous American inventor and politician*
- Prediction is very hard, especially when it's about the future. - *Yogi Berra, a former New York Yankees baseball player and manager, famous for his comic misuse of the English language*
- People bury time capsules with objects of what life is like today so that future generations can learn about how we lived. These capsules contain newspapers, photographs, and other documents. It is estimated that there are over 10,000 time capsules in the world. If you want one already made, you can buy one online.
- I have seen the future, and it does not work. - *Philip Toynbee, historian*
- The future is like heaven. Everyone exalts it, but no one wants to go there now. – *James Baldwin, African American writer*
- It is bad enough to know the past; it would be intolerable to know the future. - *W. Somerset Maugham, British writer*
- I like men who have a future and women who have a past. - *Oscar Wilde, British playwright*
- We do not inherit the land from our fathers; we are borrowing it from our children. - *David Brower, American environmentalist*

Getting Started

Sharing Your Experience

1 **Visualizing the Future.**   Imagine for the next few moments that it is now the year 2050. For you, it is an ideal world; all your hopes for yourself and humanity have been realized. Take a moment to let this image of an ideal world sink in. Then, as a class or in small groups, share your responses to these questions.

1. How old are you?
2. What kind of job do you have?
3. Where do you live?
4. What do you see when you look out the window at home? At work?
5. Is there romance in your life?
6. What do you do during your leisure time?
7. What do you do on vacations?
8. In what ways are you involved in community or government affairs?
9. What are your friends like?
10. What is a typical day like for you?

Think about the following questions and then share your responses as a class or in small groups.

1. Do you think that the ideal world you described is really a possibility? Why or why not?
2. Do you think that the future will basically be good, or do you fear a dark future?
3. What are some of your worst fears about the future?
4. How did these fears arise? For instance, is the source of one of your fears a program you saw on TV? A movie? An article in a newspaper? Is the source something a friend, acquaintance, or family member said?
5. Are your fears reasonable? Are they based on hard evidence such as statistics or scientific surveys, or are they based on things such as feelings, opinions, or gossip?
6. Do you think you have enough hard evidence about any one of your fears to help persuade a government body to do something?

Vocabulary Preview

2   **Vocabulary in Context.**   The definitions of the words in this list reflect the ways in which they are used in the discussion in this chapter. Then choose the word or phrase that best completes each of the following analogies. Compare your answers with your classmates.

apathy	*indifference; lack of care, interest, or emotion*
bleak	*gloomy, cheerless*
to commission	*to authorize, command, empower*
to deplete	*to use up*
extinct	*no longer existing (refers to a group or class, not to an individual)*
to implement	*to put into action*
to replenish	*to replace or restore*
scarcity	*shortage*
to have strings attached	*to have obligations, often not formalized, beyond a basic agreement*

Example: have strings attached : _____ :: be in hot water : be in trouble

Have strings attached is to *be obligated* as *be in hot water* is to *be in trouble*.

1. add : subtract :: replenish : _____deplete_____
2. present : absent :: excitement : _____apathy_____
3. fish in the sea : plenty :: bald eagles : _____scares_____
4. polar bear : living :: dinosaur : _____extinct_____
5. make : recipe :: _____to implement_____ : plan of action
6. black : white :: use up : _____replenish_____
7. ask : request :: authorize : _____to commission_____
8. cheerful : pleasant :: cheerless : _____bleak_____

| PART 2 | # Critical Thinking |

Critical thinking involves evaluating facts, concepts, and opinions and then making your own decisions. However, making accurate analyses is not always easy. Effective critical thinking involves thinking carefully, making judgments, and stepping back to view things objectively.

Throughout this book you have been introduced to learning strategies that can help you develop your ability to think critically. For example:

1. As you consider a speaker's ideas you can compare and contrast your (or someone else's) ideas with the speaker's ideas (Chapter 6).
2. Seeing cause-and-effect relationships (Chapter 7) may help you break down complicated ideas into a simpler sequence of causal events and their results.
3. Critical thinking (and listening) also requires you to distinguish facts and opinions (Chapter 9). Here are some suggestions to help you think critically.

Facts and Opinions

As you refine your critical thinking ability, you will find that the ideas you encounter generally fall into one of three categories:

1. **Facts**—Facts can be proven either right or wrong by comparing them with data known to be accurate.
2. **Questionable concepts**—Explanations of vague terms and abstract ideas can be evaluated by comparing them to other more concrete or explicit explanations.
3. **Opinions**—Personal judgments, beliefs, values and tastes, that is, can be evaluated in light of your own personal preferences and by asking yourself the following questions:
   - Is the speaker using emotions rather than logic to persuade me?
   - Is an issue oversimplified?
   - Is the issue misunderstood?
   - Is the information presented relevant to the main issue?
   - Is the speaker basing his or her ideas on valid theory?

Guide for Critical Thinking

1. Don't believe everything you hear. Be skeptical.
2. As you look for questionable concepts, question not only the controversial, but the reasonable concepts as well.
3. Find out the speaker's attitude and purpose. Does the speaker have a prejudice? Is he or she being paid to support a specific concept? Are important points of an argument left out in order to make one argument appear stronger?
4. Look for inconsistencies so that you are not fooled by arguments based on poor reasoning.
5. Examine data to be sure that the speaker has presented it accurately and that you are interpreting it correctly.

Before You Listen

1 **Listening Warm-Up.** Read along as your instructor reads aloud this passage about what life might be like in a space colony. Answer the questions that follow. Then compare your responses with those of your classmates.

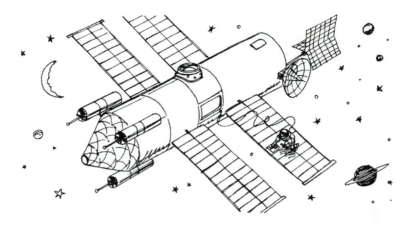

Gerard O'Neill, author and scientist, has seriously considered the idea of colonies in space. He believes that by the year 2010 it will be technically feasible to build a space city in the shape of a cylinder that would rotate through space. O'Neill is convinced that such colonies would provide an adequate alternative to life on earth for our ever-expanding population. Fiberoptic light would duplicate the passing of the sun overhead, so people would continue to function in the daytime and nighttime they are used to. These space citizens would live in a cylinder, and their view up would be of other people and buildings standing upside down. I think this would be the most serious drawback: the sky would be missing.

1. What are the facts in the passage? _____

    _____

    _____

    _____

2. What are the questionable concepts? (Hint: How are the key terms defined and who is defining them?) _____

    _____

    _____

    _____

    _____

    _____

    _____

3.   What are the opinions of Mr. O'Neill? _____

      _____

      _____

      _____

      _____

4.   Do you agree with Mr. O'Neill? _____ Why or why not? (Use the suggestions
in the boxes on page 180 to guide your evaluation.) _____

      _____

      _____

      _____

5.   What is the opinion of the speaker? _____

      _____

      _____

      Do you agree? _____ Why or why not? _____

      _____

      _____

Listen

2   **Listening Critically.**   In the year 2050, will our planet be able to accommodate a population that seems to be increasing geometrically? You will hear a father and his two college-age children, Jenny and Ted, as they discuss an old paper that the father wrote while he was in college.

In the year 2025, will our planet be able to accommodate a population that seems to be increasing geometrically?

1.   Listen to the discussion once all the way through.

2.   Listen once or twice more and list the facts, questionable concepts, and opinions expressed in the conversation.

Facts

1. _____
   _____

2. _____
   _____

3. _____
   _____

4. _____
   _____

Irrigated farmland

Drought-stricken farmland

Family planning awareness

Questionable concepts

1. _____
   _____
   _____

2. _____
   _____
   _____

Opinions

1. _____
   _____
   _____

2. _____
   _____
   _____

3. _____
   _____
   _____

4. _____
   _____
   _____

After You Listen

3   **Thinking Critically.**   Analyze your responses in Activity 2 according to the suggestions for critical thinking on page 180 and answer these questions.

1. Do you think the statements of fact hold up on closer examination? _____

    Why or why not?_____

    _____

    _____

    _____

    _____

2. Do you agree with the ways in which the dad uses terms in the statements of concepts? _____ Why or why not? _____

    _____

    _____

    _____

    _____

    _____

3. Do you agree with the dad's opinions? _____ Why or why not? _____

    _____

    _____

    _____

    _____

    _____

4. Do you think that the dad is trying to persuade his children to accept a particular point of view? _____ If so, what are the techniques he uses to do this?_____

    _____

    _____

    _____

    _____

    _____

4   Critically Evaluating Proposals.

1. Listen to the part of the discussion again in which the father makes proposals to remedy the world's problems. Take notes if you have not already done so.

2. Share your list of proposals with your classmates.

3. In pairs or small groups, evaluate the proposals using the criteria suggested on page 180.

Talk It Over

5   Gathering and Reporting Research.

1. Work in groups of three. Each person should choose one of the following methods of gathering information about the future.

2. Group members complete their individual assignments, taking notes on what they find out.

3. Share with your group what you learned from your interviews, readings, and investigations of photographs and advertisements. Be sure to distinguish fact from opinion in your reports.

Method 1

1. Design a questionnaire that includes five to ten questions such as:
   - What do you think life will be like in the year 2075? You may wish to consider specific topics such as health, education, environment, energy, religion, population, food supply, transportation, or communication.
   - Do you think the future will be better than the present?

2. Administer the questionnaire (interview) to two or three people.

Method 2

Explore some new viewpoints by reading newspaper articles, magazine articles, and material in books that deal with life in the future. (Hint: The study of the future may be called *futurology* in your bookstore or library.)

Method 3

Find an interesting photograph or advertisement intended to depict life in the future. Make notes on your ideas about what the item is trying to say about the future, whether or not you agree with this statement, and why you think the photo or ad was displayed where it was.

6   Evaluating Statements.

1. To further practice critical thinking, read the following statements and decide if you agree with each one and why or why not.
2. Discuss your opinions with your classmates.
    - Do you agree with your classmates about the validity of each statement?
    - Do you agree on the definition of terms in each statement?
    - In particular, do you agree on definitions of the more abstract terms?

Statements

1. All people are born equal.
2. Better late than never.
3. The United States was a democracy before women were allowed to vote.
4. Other animals can learn language.
5. Morality is not important to someone living alone on an island.
6. Virtue is its own reward.
7. Thirteen is an unlucky number.
8. Blondes have more fun.
9. Where there's a will to do something, there's a way to do it.
10. Someday all countries will live peacefully with one another.
11. Truth is stranger than fiction.

Washoe the chimp asks Greg for bread in sign language.

PART 3

Speculating about the Future; Reminiscing about the Past

Speculating

Most of us cannot see exactly what will happen in the future. In order to prepare ourselves for unknown future events, we often *speculate* about various possibilities. The following expressions are used to introduce all types of speculations, whether they are about globally significant issues such as life on earth in the 21st century, or about more local daily events such as the chance of rain.

Expressions to Introduce Speculations

. . . is bound to . . .
I can only guess that . . .
I estimate that . . .
If you ask me, I'd say that . . .
I have a hunch that . . .
I predict that . . .
I speculate that . . .
I wouldn't be surprised if . . .
I'd forecast that . . .
I'd guess that . . .
I'll bet that . . .
It is doubtful that . . .
It is inevitable that . . .
It seems that . . .
My guess is that . . .
My projection is that . . .
My forecast is that . . .
There's a good chance that . . .
There's no chance that . . .
There's not much chance that . . .

Reminiscing

Inevitably, some possibilities of the future become events of the past. When someone asks you a question or says something that reminds you about a past event and you want to share your recollections, your *reminiscences*, the following expressions will be useful.

Expressions to Introduce Reminiscences

As I recall . . .
As I remember it . . .
(Do you) Remember the time? . . .
I remember the days when . . .
I remember when . . .
I'll never forget the time . . .
In my day . . .
In those days . . .
My recollection is that . . .
That reminds me of the time . . .
That takes me back to when . . .

1   **Listening for Expressions of Speculation and Reminiscence.**   Listen to this conversation in which two speakers are speculating and reminiscing. Answer the questions you hear after the conversation, and then compare your answers in small groups.

1.   Who are the two speakers? _____

2.   What are they doing? _____

3.   What is their relationship? _____

4.   What topics do the speakers speculate about, and what expressions do they use to introduce their speculations?

	Topics	**Expressions**
Speaker A		
Speaker B		

5.   What topics do the speakers reminisce about, and what expressions do they use to introduce their reminiscences?

	Topics	**Expressions**
Speaker A		
Speaker B		

6.   Why does Speaker A want Speaker B to stop reminiscing?

_____

_____

2 Listening for Speculations and Opinions.   The family discussion in this chapter contains many speculations about what the world would be like during the 21st century. Some of the speculations are from the study commissioned by President Carter in 1975. Some of the speculations are personal opinions of the speakers.

1. Listen to the presentation.
2. Each time a statement is introduced by one of the expressions used for speculating, write down the expression used.
3. In response to the speculations, make a few speculations of your own.
4. The following speculations have been paraphrased from the lecture to get you started. Add as many more as you can. Then compare your answers and speculations with those of your classmates.

Expressions	Speculations	Your speculations
1. _____	The number of poor and hungry will rapidly increase.	Do you agree? _____ Explain. _____ _____ _____
2. _____	Food and farmland will rapidly decrease.	Do you agree? _____ Explain. _____ _____ _____
3. _____	100 million people will be born each year.	Is this certain? _____ Why or why not? _____ _____ _____
4. _____	The gap between the wealthy industrialized countries and the developing countries will widen.	Do you agree? _____ Explain. _____ _____ _____ _____
5. _____	The industrialized countries will use too much of the world's resources.	Why might this be so? _____ _____ _____ _____
6. _____	Forests will be depleted because of the increase in population.	How will this change planet Earth? _____ _____ _____ _____

Expressions	Speculations	Your speculations
7. _____	For many countries, starvation will become the greatest problem.	Do you believe this? _____ Explain. _____ _____ _____
8. _____	The United States might lead a global program of providing food.	Is this realistic? _____ Why or why not? _____ _____ _____
9. _____	Exports should be priced according to the incomes of the consumer nations.	Why won't this happen? _____ _____ _____
10. _____	The only thing that will make people change is disaster.	What does this mean? _____ _____ _____

Talk It Over

3 **Predicting the Future.**   Are you wondering what the future will bring? Why not visit your local psychic or fortuneteller?

1. In groups of three to five, take turns playing the role of a psychic or fortuneteller, who "sees all, knows all, and tells all."
2. Let your classmates ask you whatever questions they wish about future global or personal events.
3. As you answer each of their questions, use an expression listed on page 187 to introduce your speculation about the future.

4 **Role-Playing Reunions.** Reunions are popular in many cultures. There are family reunions, class reunions, and team reunions, to name a few. In fact, any gathering of people who have not seen each other for a long time can be called a reunion.

A Class Reunion

1. Imagine that it is 25 years from now, and you and your classmates have decided to come back together for a reunion.
2. At a party, get reacquainted in small groups by sharing what has happened in the last 25 years, reminiscing about the past, and speculating about the future.
3. Throughout the activity, try to stay in character as you move from group to group as at a party. Play yourself as you might be 25 years from now.
4. If possible, include some refreshments at your reunion party to get you into the mood.

A Family Reunion in the 21st Century

1. Divide the class into four groups to represent four generations of a family, which will include parents, children, grandparents, and grandchildren.
2. Decide what your individual roles and relationships will be.

3. Choose a characteristic for your person (e.g., very kind, greedy, funny, thoughtful, tired, happy).

4. Staying in character, imagine that you are all attending a family reunion. It's like most other family reunions, except for one thing— it takes place in the year 2076.

5. Circulate at the party and chat with various family members. Share your reminiscences and speculations about the future.

6. Afterward, speculate about which characteristic each person was trying to role-play. As you guess, use expressions to introduce speculations

---

PART 4   # Focus on Testing

You will hear a short presentation. After the presentation, you will be asked some questions. Circle the letter of the best answer to each question.

Question 1

a. seers
b. forecasters
c. futurologists
d. all of the above

Question 2

a. in 1950
b. in 1915
c. in 1903
d. in 1890

Question 3

a. because oil and gas stoves were developed
b. because unexpected things keep happening
c. because being popular doesn't make you right
d. because not everyone can write a best-seller

Question 4

a. the rise in the number of people who watch a lot of TV
b. the rise in the number of people who work at home
c. the rise in the number of women who work outside the home
d. the rise in the number of marriages for each person

Question 5

a. pessimistic
b. optimistic
c. backward
d. gentle

Question 6

a. because Boston had a lot of crime
b. because high-tech inventions create slave societies
c. because they had dark and haunting visions in 1984
d. because scientists had produced better weapons

Video Activities: Concept Cars

Before You Watch.   Answer these questions in small groups.

1. What does the word *concept* mean?
   a. beginning   b. idea   c. imagination

2. Describe the kind of car that you would like to own. You can describe one that exists, or use your imagination.

Watch.   Answer these questions in small groups.

1. Which of these statements is true?
   a. All concept cars become production cars.
   b. Car manufacturers use concept cars to "try out" new ideas.
   c. Concept cars are too expensive to build.

2. Which of these concept cars did not become production cars?
   a. the Avalanche   b. the Lacrosse   c. the PT Cruiser   d. the Prowler

3. Write the name of the concept car next to the correct description.
   _____ a. video monitors and voice-activated lights and turn signals
   _____ b. a popular design
   _____ c. a combination of a truck and an SUV

Watch Again.   Circle the correct answers.

1. Which of these car companies are mentioned in the video segment?
   a. Ford   c. Chrysler-Daimler   e. Toyota
   b. Mercedes   d. Chevrolet (Chevy)   f. Buick

2. It's a real *eye-popper* means it looks _____.
   a. great   b. dangerous   c. terrible

3. *I'm a Ford man* means _____.
   a. He works for Ford.   b. He buys Ford cars.   c. His name is Ford.

4. "The club *just got its motor running* last December" means that it just _____.
   a. bought a car   b. fixed an engine   c. started

After You Watch.   Discuss these questions with your class.

1. Cars are extremely important in American society. Are they as important in other countries? Why or why not?

2. Do you think that the government should encourage the automobile industry to do more to promote public transportation?

Appendix

Answers

Chapter 2 Part 3 Talk It Over. Pages 25–27.

QUESTION	STRONG YES	WEAK YES	MAYBE	WEAK NO	STRONG NO
1.	4	3	2	1	0
2.	6	5	3	2	1
3.	5	4	3	2	1
4.	6	5	3	2	1
5.	7	6	4	2	1
6.	2	1	5	0	0
7.	3	2	1	.5	0
8.	6	5	3	2	1
9.	7	6	4	2	1
10.	7	6	4	2	1
11.	9	8	6	4	2
12.	7	6	4	2	1
13.	10	9	8	4	2
14.	8	7	5	3	1
15.	10	9	8	4	2
16.	10	9	8	4	2
17.	5	4	2	1	0
18.	4	3	2	1	0
19.	5	4	2	1	0
20.	9	8	6	4	2
21.	8	7	5	3	1
22.	7	6	4	2	1
23.	3	2	1	.5	0
24.	2	1	.5	0	0
25.	7	6	4	2	1

Chapter 9 Part 1 Vocabulary Preview. Page 126–127.

Tapescript

Chapter 1 | Language and Learning

PART 2 | Understanding the Main Ideas

Lecture: To School or Not to School

Lecturer: Good afternoon. Welcome to the first lecture of your teaching methods course. Before we begin the practical part of this course, that is, the actual methods you will use as teachers in the classroom, I would like to ask you a few questions. When future great artists and scientists are in your classrooms, will you recognize them and know how to encourage them? When someone asks the next Picasso or Marie Curie who was important in his or her schooling, will he or she name you? Do you think that teachers, in general, are able to help scientific or artistic geniuses develop their gifts? These questions are very important ones for you as future teachers to consider.

Stop 1

First of all, to help us answer these questions, I think we have to separate the arts and the sciences. Why do you think I want to do this? Amy?

Amy: Well, the stereotype is that artists are moody and nonconformist and that they don't like to follow rules.

Lecturer: Is that different from the rest of us?

Amy: Well, yes. I think so. They seem different because they often must "get away from it all," go off to their workrooms or studios to be creative. You know, you read about opera stars and actors that have to be handled *very carefully*, so they won't get angry and walk off the job.

Lecturer: Right, Amy. And because they are nonconformists, we might not expect these students to do well in school. In school environments, students are expected to follow the rules.

Of course, rules are not the only reasons why artistic people may not do well in school. Many gifted writers, actors, painters, and dancers have not been enthusiastic about their early education. In his famous books *Huckleberry Finn* and *Tom Sawyer*, Mark Twain writes about boys who constantly play tricks in class or don't go to school because they think it is so boring. Like Huck and Tom, Twain was bored by school, and he was beaten by his teachers again and again because he refused to obey the rules and complete his assignments.

Yes, Peter.

Peter: Didn't Charlie Chaplin, the comic genius of old movies, also hate school?

Lecturer: You're right, Peter. He was not interested in school subjects at all, except for plays he could watch or act in.

Here's another example of an artist who hated school. Vincent van Gogh, the Dutch impressionist artist, loved being outside watching the light and colors of the countryside as the seasons passed. He only wanted to draw and paint what he saw outdoors and did not want to study with the other students. At eleven years old, he already acted like an artist. Yup! You guessed it. He was moody, and his classmates didn't like him very much.

Mark Twain, Charlie Chaplin, and Vincent van Gogh are examples of what we expect to find:

Stop 2

that is, that schools don't help the artist very much. But there are exceptions to this rule. Martha Graham, the dancer and choreographer who totally changed the art of dance in America, did her schoolwork so quickly and well that her teachers sent her to the library to read during her free time. And Maria Tallchief, one of the greatest ballerinas of her time, was not a nonconformist. She was an obedient child who tried to please her parents and teachers and did well in every subject she studied. The famous British poet William Wordsworth was also happy at school as a child. He did well in math, history, and literature courses and felt he had a free and happy life at school.

Stop 3

And now what about great scientists? How well did they do in school? Did their teachers see the greatness in them? In general, as with many great artists, the answer to this question is no. Let's take Thomas Edison as our first example. He was a truly great inventor. He is credited with 1,099 inventions in his lifetime, including the lightbulb, the phonograph, and the motion picture projector. His elementary school teachers, however, thought he was very strange. He always asked a lot of questions, and this made his teachers feel uncomfortable. So Edison's mother decided to teach him at home. By the time he was nine, he had read most of the English classics, including Gibbon's *Decline and Fall of the Roman Empire*, a book that covers thirteen centuries of Roman history. He was a curious person who read all the time and loved doing experiments.

Yes, Susan.

Susan: Didn't Edison once set fire to his father's barn in order to "see what would happen"?

Lecturer: He sure did. He also built a chemistry laboratory in the basement of his parents' house. Instead of going to school, he worked to earn money to finance his experiments.

Charles Darwin, the scientist who developed the theory of evolution, was another curious, creative thinker. And he didn't do any better in school than Edison did. Darwin's grades ranged from average to poor. And Darwin, unlike Edison, did *not* read the classics, even though they were required reading in his British school. Instead, he preferred to study natural history. He continuously collected insects, plants, and rocks. Like Edison, however, he did conduct lots of experiments.

Perhaps the most well-known scientist of modern times is Albert Einstein, and our discussion would not be complete without considering his school experiences. Although he did fairly well in school, he didn't like it at all. In fact, he once said, "I hate school. It's like being a soldier. School is like a barracks, the teachers are like officers who tell the soldier what to do. If you don't learn your lessons by heart, they scold or beat you. Even if you don't understand what the books say. They are angry when you ask questions, and I like to ask questions."

But there is another side to this story. Even though these scientific giants experienced conflicts between the demands of school and the development of their own minds, we should not jump to conclusions.

Stop 4

There are other examples of scientists who performed well in school and considered it to be a good place to prepare for their careers. Marie Curie, who discovered the element radium and invented radiation therapy, was a star pupil in all subjects. In fact, while most of her classmates were having difficulty learning because of the excessive strictness of her Polish school, she *refused* to fail. She worked very hard and succeeded in spite of the poor teaching methods.

Another example of success in school is Lillian Moller Gilbreth, one of the founders of industrial engineering. Because of her shyness, Gilbreth did not attend school until the age of nine, when she entered the fourth grade and was an excellent student. And Alexander Fleming, who discovered penicillin, loved the one-room schoolhouse he attended in Scotland. He passed his medical school entrance examinations with higher marks than any other student.

Stop 5

So what can we learn from these examples of famous people and their experiences at school? Yes, Sasha.

Sasha: Well, they were very curious.

Lecturer: Yes! They asked questions. And the traditional teachers did not accept their questions. Part of your job as future teachers is to encourage your students to ask questions. You may have the next great artists or scientists in your classes. How can you tell which ones they are? They are the ones who will ask you more than you know.

Students: (laughter)

Lecturer: Well, that's it for today. See you next time.

Requesting the Main Point

1 Listening for Appropriate Expressions and Tone of Voice. Page 8.

Conversation 1

Randy tries to tell Sandy some interesting news.

Randy: Did you see the seven o'clock news last night?

Sandy: No, what about it?

Randy: Well, they showed the Save the Rainforest March that I participated in with my ecology class. You know, the one where we went to the state capitol building and we protested and there were some people dressed up as trees and plants and stuff, and anyway, I was really surprised at the way the newscaster handled it. Remember I told you it was raining really hard that day and some people were even throwing things at us and I forgot my umbrella – most people did – and we all got drenched, absolutely soaking wet. Well, the march was picked up by the major news networks, and boy, did their reports surprise me! I didn't think the march was so controversial. It didn't feel like a very daring thing to do at the time.

Sandy: Get to the point, would you? How did the networks handle it?

Question 1: Was this conversation friendly or unfriendly?
Question 2: Was it formal or informal?
Question 3: Was Sandy polite or impolite?

Conversation 2

Professor Draper is talking about the midterm exam.

Professor Draper: Well, students, I want to reorganize our schedule and change the date of the midterm. You know, we had scheduled the readings of Jones and Tomkins for the sixteenth and the readings by Rockford and Pebble for the fourteenth and those by McVey and Gill for the twelfth. Well, I want to move McVey and Gill to the fourteenth, the midterm to the twelfth, Rockford and Pebble to the sixteenth, and Jones and Tomkins to the nineteenth.

Student: So, what are you driving at? I don't get it. Are you trying to tell us that we only have two more days until the midterm?

Question 1: Was the student's request for the main point polite or impolite?
Question 2: What would you have said in the same situation?

Conversation 3

Professor Werner and Richard discuss an upcoming field trip.

Professor Werner: Okay, now students, let me explain how we'll organize this plant-hunting expedition. You'll want to have a buddy and to keep your buddy with you at all times. You are to search for the various plants of the genus Rhus, but remember many of them are quite poisonous, so make sure your arms and legs are well covered and wear plastic gloves when you pick the plants. Of course, you will be free to wander wherever you like, but the terrain changes quickly and is unmarked. We did have a problem with students getting lost two years ago, and one of them broke her leg.

Student: Excuse me, Professor Werner, I don't quite understand what you're getting at.

Professor Werner: Well, Richard, the point is this trip could be dangerous if you don't follow all the rules carefully.

Question 1: Did Richard handle the situation well?
Question 2: Was he polite or impolite?

2 Requesting the Main Point. Page 9.

Lecture: To School or Not to School

Lecturer: Good afternoon. Welcome to the first lecture of your teaching methods course. Before we begin the practical part of this course, that is, the actual methods you will use as teachers in the classroom, I would like to ask you a few questions. When future great artists and scientists are in your classrooms, will you recognize them and know how to encourage them? When someone asks the next Picasso or Marie Curie who was important in his or her schooling, will he or she name you? Do you think that teachers, in general, are able to help scientific or artistic geniuses develop their gifts? These questions are very important ones for you as future teachers to consider.

First of all, to help us answer these questions, I think we have to separate the arts and the sciences. Why do you think I want to do this? Amy?

Amy: Well, the stereotype is that artists are moody and nonconformist and that they don't like to follow rules.

Lecturer: Is that different from the rest of us?

Amy: Well, yes. I think so. They seem different because they often must "get away from it all," go off to their workrooms or studios to be creative. You know, you read about opera stars and actors that have to be handled *very carefully,* so they won't get angry and walk off the job.

Lecturer: Right, Amy. They are nonconformists.

Stop 1. Request the main point.

Of course, rules are not the only reasons why artistic people may not do well in school. Many gifted writers, actors, painters, and dancers have not been enthusiastic about their early education. In his famous books *Huckleberry Finn* and *Tom Sawyer*, Mark Twain writes about boys who constantly play tricks in class or don't go to school because they think it is so boring. Like Huck and Tom, Twain was bored by school, and he was beaten by his teachers again and again because he refused to obey the rules and complete his assignments.

Yes, Peter.

Peter: Didn't Charlie Chaplin, the comic genius of old movies, also hate school?

Lecturer: You're right, Peter. He was not interested in school subjects at all, except for plays he could watch or act in.

Here's another example of an artist who hated school. Vincent van Gogh, the Dutch impressionist artist, loved being outside watching the light and colors of the countryside as the seasons passed. He only wanted to draw and paint what he saw outdoors and did not want to study with the other students. At eleven years old, he already acted like an artist. Yup! You guessed it. He was moody, and his classmates didn't like him very much.

Stop 2. Request the main point.

Mark Twain, Charlie Chaplin, and Vincent van Gogh are examples of what we expect to find. Martha Graham, the dancer and choreographer who totally changed the art of dance in America, did her schoolwork so quickly and well that her teachers sent her to the library to read during her free time. And Maria Tallchief, one of the greatest ballerinas of her time, was not a nonconformist. She was an obedient child who tried to please her parents and teachers and did well in every subject she studied. The famous British poet William Wordsworth was also happy at school as a child. He did well in math, history, and literature courses and felt he had a free and happy life at school.

Stop 3. Request the main point.

And now what about great scientists? How well did they do in school? Did their teachers see the greatness in them? Let's take Thomas Edison as our first example. He was a truly great inventor. He is credited with 1,099 inventions in his lifetime, including the lightbulb, the phonograph, and the motion picture projector. His elementary school teachers, however, thought he was very strange. He always asked a lot of questions, and this made his teachers feel uncomfortable. So Edison's mother decided to teach him at home. By the time he was nine, he had read most of the English classics, including Gibbon's *Decline and Fall of the Roman Empire,* a book that covers thirteen centuries of Roman history. He was a curious person who read all the time and loved doing experiments.

Stop 4. Request the main point.

Yes, Susan.

Susan: Didn't Edison once set fire to his father's barn in order to "see what would happen"?

Lecturer: He sure did. He also built a chemistry laboratory in the basement of his parents' house. Instead of going to school, he worked to earn money to finance his experiments.

Charles Darwin, the scientist who developed the theory of evolution, was another curious, creative thinker. And he didn't do any better in school than Edison did. Darwin's grades ranged from average to poor. And Darwin, unlike Edison, did *not* read the classics, even though they were required reading in his British school. Instead, he preferred to study natural history. He continuously collected insects, plants, and rocks. Like Edison, however, he did conduct lots of experiments.

Stop 5. Request the main point.

Perhaps the most well-known scientist of modern times is Albert Einstein, and our discussion would not be complete without considering his school experiences. Although he did fairly well in school, he didn't like it at all. In fact, he once said, "I hate school. It's like being a soldier. School is like a barracks, the teachers are like officers who tell the soldier what to do. If you don't learn your lessons by heart, they scold or beat you. Even if you don't understand what the books say. They are angry when you ask questions, and I like to ask questions."

Stop 6. Request the main point.

But there is another side to this story. Marie Curie, who discovered the element radium and invented radiation therapy, was a star pupil in all subjects. In fact, while most of her classmates were having difficulty learning because of the excessive strictness of her Polish school, she *refused* to fail. She worked very hard and succeeded in spite of the poor teaching methods.

Stop 7. Request the main point.

Another example of success in school is Lillian Moller Gilbreth, one of the founders of industrial engineering. Because of her shyness, Gilbreth did not attend school until the age of nine, when she entered the fourth grade and was an excellent student. And Alexander Fleming, who discovered penicillin, loved the one-room schoolhouse he attended in Scotland. He passed his medical school entrance examinations with higher marks than any other student.

So what can we learn from these examples of famous people and their experiences at school? Yes, Sasha.

Stop 8. Request the main point.

Sasha: Well.

Lecturer: Yes! They asked questions. And the traditional teachers did not accept their questions. It's part of your job as future teachers.

Stop 9. Request the main point.

You may have the next great artists or scientists in your classes. How can you tell which ones they are?

Stop 10. Request the main point.

Students: (laughter)

Lecturer: Well, that's it for today. See you next time.

Focus on Testing. Page 11.

You will hear a short presentation. After the speaker finishes talking, you will hear a series of questions. Circle the letter of the best answer to each question.

Presentation

Artificial intelligence, or AI, is the ability of a machine to exhibit intelligent behavior. Artificial intelligence systems are modeled after the human brain. Like the brain, an AI system receives information, processes it, and then produces an appropriate action or response. Since the 1940s, many specialists, including computer scientists, mathematicians, philosophers, and electrical engineers, have tried to make a machine as intelligent as the human brain, but so far no computer has come close.

AI, however, has proved to be better than the human brain for answering certain types of questions. For example, AI seems to be better, and certainly faster, than the human brain for problem solving when you must remember and process a large amount of information. However, AI is still not capable of any type of adaptable or truly intelligent behavior. So far, AI programs are quite primitive when compared to the kinds of reasoning, language, and learning the human brain can do.

Although the fastest computers are able to perform about 10 billion calculations per second, AI systems still cannot recognize or produce natural language as well as the human brain can. Also, all knowledge contained in AI systems is based on logical rules. Intuition does not come into it. Someday, when scientists completely understand the mysteries of human language and learning, they may be able to create an AI system as good as or even better than the human brain.

Question 1: What is the main topic of the presentation?

Question 2: What is the model for artificial intelligence systems?

Question 3: When is an artificial intelligence system better than the human brain?

Question 4: What is all knowledge contained in artificial intelligence systems based on?

Chapter 2　Danger and Daring

PART 2　Noting Specific Details

Lecture:　Hooked on Thrills

Professor:　Good morning.

Students:　Good morning.

Professor:　Did you know that the towers of the World Trade Center in New York were a challenge to a variety of stuntmen and women? These twin towers, which were two of the world's tallest buildings, used to be irresistible to a variety of daredevils. Does anyone know what a 27-year-old French high-wire artist named Philippe Petit did on August 17, 1974?

Student A:　I think he was mentioned in the article you gave us for homework. Didn't he disguise himself as a construction worker to get past the building guards? And then didn't he put a cable between the two towers?

Professor:　Yes! He did! Then he did something I'd never do in a million years!

Student A:　Me neither! I believe the article said that Petit balanced on that cable—around 1,300 feet above the street—for 45 minutes!

Professor:　Right. And what did the article say about an unemployed construction worker named Owen Quinn?

Student B:　He was the guy who jumped off the roof of one of the towers, wasn't he?

Professor:　Yes, that's true. But you left out a very important part. He was wearing a parachute.

Professor:　A few years later, another parachutist pulled off an even more amazing stunt: he jumped from an airplane and landed on the roof of the South Tower.

Students:　Scary. Amazing. Wow!

Professor:　But the most famous of all the stunts performed on the World Trade Center towers was the one performed by George Willig. He was a 27-year-old toy maker who had already been nicknamed "the human fly." Between 6:30 and 10:10 in the morning on May 26, 1977, using only ropes and clips, he climbed the smooth vertical face of the North Tower all the way to the top, 110 stories.

Students:　Wow! Incredible! Awesome!

Professor:　In addition to the reporters waiting to question George on the roof, there were several New York City police officers. They handcuffed him and charged him with the crimes of trespassing, disorderly conduct, and criminal endangerment.

Students:　Really? That doesn't seem fair. What for?

Professor:　Then they handed him a notice saying that he was being sued for $250,000, because the city government wanted to discourage anyone else from doing another daredevil stunt like this one.

Students:　Awwwww!

Professor:	But to the thousands of people on the street and the millions who watched his stunt on TV, George Willig was not a criminal. He was a hero. On his way to jail, women kissed him, reporters cheered, and even the police officers who arrested him asked for his autograph. By the following morning, Willig had so many fans that the mayor himself attended a ceremony honoring Willig, and he reduced Willig's fine from $250,000 to $1.10, just a penny for each floor of the tower.
Students:	(cheer and laugh)
Professor:	What motivates daredevils like Philippe Petit and George Willig to risk criminal prosecution, injury, and even death by performing such dangerous stunts? Is it the hope of gaining fame and fortune, the desire for headlines and business deals? This may be true of some, but certainly not of Willig. He said he was "amazed at the hullabaloo" he created and insisted that his motives were pleasure, not profit, and increased self-esteem, not glory. He told a reporter that "far above the streets I was very much alone with myself and at peace with myself. . . . It was a personal challenge; I just wanted the prize of getting to the top."

Psychologists who study what motivates people to take up these kinds of risks agree with Willig. They have categorized stunts such as Willig's as "thrill and adventure seeking"—a subdivision of the larger class of activities called "sensation seeking." According to Marvin Zuckerman, a leading researcher in this field, sensation seeking is a basic human characteristic. That is, sensation seeking is part of the human nervous system, passed on from one generation to the next and encouraged by the social community. He claims that sensation seeking is a major factor that can be used to determine and classify personality types. It was not the desire for fame or fortune that led George Willig to the top of the World Trade Center. Instead, it was a need for the intense sensation of a risky activity. Zuckerman and his colleagues theorize that we all seek different levels of sensation. Some people are most comfortable with a low level of sensation and don't like risky situations. Others require higher levels of sensation to be happy, and without it they become anxious or bored. And others require unusually high levels of stimulation to be happy. These are the thrill and adventure seekers, the ones who take up extreme sports such as skysurfing, bungee jumping, and rock climbing.

Researchers distinguish four types of high-level sensation seekers. The first type is the thrill and adventure seeker. This type includes people who love activities that involve speed and danger. These physical conditions stimulate intense sensations in the tissues and nerves of the body.

The second type of sensation seeker is called the experience seeker. This type includes people who search for powerful and unusual mental rather than physical activities. Experience seekers may travel to exotic places, listen to the most experimental music, and use mind-altering drugs such as LSD. Occasionally, experience seekers may rebel against established authority. Zuckerman has nicknamed this kind of sensation seeking the "hippie factor," because many of these behaviors were characteristic of the hippies of the 1960s and 1970s.

A third type of sensation seeker is the disinhibitor. The form of sensation seeking at work here is called disinhibition and is nicknamed the "swinger factor." Disinhibitors find their optimal sensation level in activities such as heavy social drinking, frequent sexual encounters, wild parties, and gambling.

The fourth type of sensation seeker is the boredom avoider. Boredom avoiders dislike repetition, routine work, and people who are predictable and unexciting. They frequently feel restless and generally prefer variety over sameness.

To determine whether people are higher-level or lower-level sensation seekers in each of the four categories, Zuckerman and his colleagues developed a questionnaire called the "Sensation Seeking Survey," or SSS. The survey requires yes or no responses to statements such as these:

1. I like to ride in open convertibles.
2. I sometimes like to do crazy things just to see the effects on others.
3. A person should have a lot of sexual experience before marriage.
4. The worst social sin is to be a bore.

"Yes" responses to all these items on the questionnaire indicate a person who seeks higher levels of sensation. "No" responses indicate someone who is happy at a much lower stimulation level.

Using the SSS as a tool, researchers have discovered several patterns. First, who do you think are higher-level sensation seekers, men or women?

Students:	Men! No, no I think women are! No way. It's *got* to be men! Why does it have to be that way?
Professor:	OK, OK. Let me tell you. Men tend to be higher-level sensation seekers than women, particularly in the first and third subcategories— the thrill and adventure seeker, and the disinhibitor. I suppose that's not too surprising considering when this research was done, but somehow I think we might get different results if we surveyed *this* class.
Students:	(laugh)
Professor:	And what do you all think the results might be according to age?
Student B:	I'd bet people our age tend to take the most risks.
Student C:	Well, could be. But it could also be teenagers.
Professor:	Well, you're *both* right! Adolescents and college students have the highest number of high-level sensation seekers. Sensation seeking tends to decrease steadily as people get older, and very young children do not seem to be high-level sensation seekers.

However, excessive and dangerous sensation-seeking behavior in 10 to 12-year-olds and teenagers is a serious problem. For example, two teenage boys jumped off the Brooklyn Bridge. One of them was killed instantly, but the other boy survived. When authorities asked him if he and his friend had understood how foolish this stunt was, he replied that they realized the danger involved but they jumped anyway, "just to see what it felt like." By recognizing the creative functions of sensation seeking, doctors are helping children and parents find ways to decrease the self-destructive aspects of sensation-seeking behavior and to increase the self-expressive and creative ones.

Well, that's all we have time for today. Finish reading Chapter 17 and we'll go on with this discussion next time.

PART 3

Saying Yes and No

1

Listening for *Yes* and *No* Expressions. Page 22.

Conversation 1

Ted and Paul are discussing their plans for the weekend.

Ted:	I'm going white-water rafting this weekend, Paul, and one of my buddies, Phil– you know Phil, don't you?
Paul:	Uh-huh.
Ted:	Well, Phil can't go because he sprained his back playing soccer, so there's room for one more. You want to go with us?
Paul:	Are you kidding? I've never gone white-water rafting.
Ted:	Aw, come on. There's a minicourse being given by the Explorers' Club Wednesday night this week. Take it and you'll be ready to go with us.
Paul:	No way! I'll never learn enough in two hours to go on a trip for a whole weekend!
Ted:	Sure you can! The instructor is great. I know of lots of people who've done it.
Paul:	Well, it's probably not such a good idea, but how much does it cost?
Ted:	Well, the trip'll cost you about $150 with everything— food, equipment, everything. The course is only 20 bucks.
Paul:	That's not too bad. I'll think about it.
Ted:	Don't just think about it; do it! You've got the money, don't you?
Paul:	I think so.
Ted:	Well, then, it's settled. Let's go over to the student union, get something to drink, and then sign you up.

Conversation 2

Terry and Lynn are discussing vacation possibilities.

Terry:	Hey Lynn, I saw the greatest trip advertised in this travel magazine I get. It's a mountain-climbing trip in Nepal— you know, in the Himalayas. We'd go all the way to the base camp on Annapurna. That means we'd follow in the footsteps of the women's expedition that climbed Annapurna in 1978! Wouldn't that be great? Let's go!

Lynn:	Not on your life! You won't get me up there! I don't even like riding in those glass elevators that go up and down the outside of fancy hotels.
Terry:	Come on! Think about it a bit. There's a month-long training program and then the trip is three weeks. Think how strong and brave you'll feel at the end.
Lynn:	You may feel strong and brave after a month, but not me! Never in a million years!
Terry:	Oh, don't be like that. It's important to overcome your fears. You'll be a better person for it!
Lynn:	I won't climb a mountain! Not for all the tea in China, and that's that! Find someone else to go with you.
Terry:	But I want you to go. You're my best friend. Besides, there won't be any technical climbing with ropes and all that, just some high-altitude hiking, really! Come on! It'll be fun. We'll have a good time!
Lynn:	I like having a good time, but my idea of a good time is seeing a movie, going out to dinner, or watching a baseball game on TV. Wanna go out to dinner?
Terry:	Definitely! Maybe I'll even convince you by the time we order dessert.

PART 4

Focus on Testing. Page 27.

Listen to the short news program. After the news feature, you will be asked some questions. Circle the letter of the best answer to each question.

News Feature

Bungee jumping is a popular sport among the young, particularly in California, New Zealand, and France. Bungee jumping was once done only by a handful of sky divers, mountain climbers, and other daredevils. Recently, however, dozens of bungee adventure clubs have opened. One club, Bungee Adventures in California, has already sent more than 10,000 thrill seekers over the edge. There have been no fatal accidents so far in the United States, but two French jumpers fell to their deaths when their bungee cords severed. The cords just snapped apart as they were stretched to the limit. A third jumper died when he bounced off the jump tower.

Bungee jumpers claim that the thrills are greater than the risks. Jumpers leap headfirst from bridges, towers, cranes, and even hot-air balloons. They leap from 90 to 300 feet above the ground, with only the long nylon and rubber bungee cord to break their fall. The bungee cord is a lot like a giant rubber band. Tied around the ankles or the body, the cord is only long enough to allow a few seconds of free fall before it stretches to the limit, stopping the jumper just a few feet short of the land or water below. The jumper is then thrown skyward as the cord snaps back to its original length. Bungee jumping does not require any special physical training or ability. The strength required is only psychological.

Bungee jumping is based on a ritual practiced by the villagers of Pentecost Island in the South Pacific. Every spring the villagers collect vines and wind them into long cords or ropes. Then young men climb high wooden towers, tie the vines around their ankles and jump. A successful jump is considered to be a demonstration of courage and a sign that there will be a plentiful yam harvest.

Question 1: What kind of a sport is bungee jumping?
Question 2: What do bungee jumpers do?
Question 3: What equipment must bungee jumpers use?
Question 4: Why do the Pentecost Islanders leap from the towers?

Chapter 3 Sex and Gender

PART 2 Abbreviating—When and How

Lecture: Becoming a Man, Becoming a Woman

Students:	Hi. Nice haircut. Can I borrow a pen? When's the midterm?
Lecturer:	Good morning. Today's lecture is about rites of passage. What are rites of passage? Randy?
Randy:	Aren't they the ceremonies that take place when people go from one stage in life to another?
Lecturer:	That's right. Rites of passage are the ceremonies and rituals that take place in every society in the world as people go from one stage in life to another. They mark the transition from infancy to childhood, from childhood to adolescence, adolescence to adulthood, adulthood to maturity, maturity to old age, and finally, old age to death. What ceremonies and rituals mark these transitions in the United States? Get into groups of three and quickly write down what ceremonies mark these stages and how old people are at each stage.

Note to instructor: Stop the tape at this point and discuss the answers to the lecturer's questions in small groups.

Lecturer:	OK. Group 1. What did you get for the transition from infancy to childhood?
Student from Group 1:	Graduation from kindergarten or entrance into first grade in elementary school at 5 or 6.
Lecturer:	Good. Group 2, the change from childhood to adolescence?
Student from Group 2:	Confirmations at church; graduation from elementary school; and starting middle school or junior high school, around age 13.
Lecturer:	Good. What about adolescence to adulthood, Group 3?
Student from Group 3:	Graduation from high school or college, or maybe getting a real job, from 18 to 20.
Students:	(laugh nervously)
Lecturer:	Yes, that's right. What about old age, Group 4?
Student from Group 4:	How about a retirement party, you know, like people have when they retire at 65?
Marti:	or 70. And at that age they get the title "senior citizen."

Lecturer:	That's right, Marti. And funerals, of course, mark death. These transitions from one stage of life to another involve changes that might be difficult. For example, children starting school no longer can play all day long. Newly retired people no longer have work to do. Instead, they have free time all day long. Such changes may be extremely stressful. Anthropologists believe that the ceremonies and rituals help relieve some of the stress that comes with the changes. Rites of passage are celebrations of the "passage," or transformation, of people from one social identity or role in society to another as they grow older. The rites may also signify a transformation of the mind of an individual, that is, a deepening of the understanding of the meaning of life.
	Today we will focus on tribal rites that mark the change of girls into women and boys into men in their society. These rites of passage, rites of becoming a man or a woman, are called puberty rites.
	Puberty rites are often very dramatic rites of passage. The passage to womanhood or manhood is based on two things: (1) physical maturation and (2) the emergence of secondary sexual characteristics. For girls, it is obvious when the ceremony should take place. It depends on when a girl gets her first menstrual period. With boys, it's not so obvious, but usually their voices change and body hair begins to grow
	Although the first menstruation is the obvious occasion for a girl's initiation, in some societies— for instance, the Bimin Kuskusmin of New Guinea— the change from child to adult takes place over a period of years. This is also true of the Carrier Indians of British Columbia. They have the adolescent girls live for three or four years all alone, in complete isolation, after their first menstruation.
Students:	Wow! No kidding? All alone?
Lecturer:	Yes. Now in other societies, the transition from child to adult is celebrated on a single occasion.
	All tribal rites of passage, whether they take a long time or a short time, have three stages. The first stage is the rite of separation. In this stage, the person going through the transformation— the initiate, as he or she is called— is removed from his or her previous surroundings. For example, among the Bimin Kuskusmin of New Guinea and the Kurnai of Australia, a boy is suddenly taken from his mother's house and the company of all the women who raised him and never allowed to return.
Randy:	Imagine that! No more home-cooked meals.
Students:	(laugh)
Lecturer:	Furthermore, all sports and games of boyhood are forbidden from that time on.
	Now, the second stage is the rite of transition. This rite involves either a physical or symbolic journey to a place outside normal time and space. The journey usually begins with an ordeal involving one or more of the following: fasting, isolation, humiliation, or intense physical pain. Among the Omaha and Ojibway Indians of the Great Plains, the child and all his relatives are taken to a sacred hut. The child is attached to a board and acts lifeless during the entire

ceremony. The other participants are then symbolically murdered by medicine men. This ceremony represents the death of the childlike person and the beginning of a new life as a man. The child can now identify with the adult males. He has been made one of them. He will now be thought of as an adult member of the society. All those who participate with him in the ceremony develop a feeling of closeness, or solidarity. Perhaps you have had this feeling?

Marti: Yes, I really felt that when my friends and I climbed Mount Fuji. Boy, did that feel great!

Rene: I know it's not the same as climbing a mountain, but a group of us really felt that solidarity after we stayed up all night together to study for your last exam.

Students: (laugh)

Lecturer: That's great, Rene. It's just this sort of solidarity that holds any society together. After an experience like this, the members of the group have a renewed feeling of closeness to each other.

Here's another example: During the puberty rites of certain tribes in the lower Congo, the young man must speak a special language and wear no clothes. In this way, all his previous self-concepts, all his ideas about himself and images of himself, are removed. The idea is that he must face his own true nature and, by doing this, come to understand the nature of God.

OK, now, the third stage is the rite of incorporation. The initiate is healed, welcomed back to the ordinary world, and given a new social status. For example, the Omaha and Ojibway Indians end the ritual with a great feast where they exchange gifts and the initiate receives his new adult name. In both North American Indian and Australian aboriginal societies, these rites of incorporation include showing sacred objects such as masks that the child has never been permitted to see before.

So far, the examples of puberty rites that I've mentioned involve young men. Now I'd like to present a couple of examples of female puberty rites. In Nigeria, a girl who is a member of the Tiv tribe lies quietly on the ground next to her mother while an old man cuts the skin of her stomach with a razor. He inscribes three circles around her navel and a vertical line to her chest. Other lines branch outward to both sides and downward. These lines signify the structure of time. They symbolically place the girl at the point where past and future generations meet. The old man rubs charcoal into the cuts. In three days, the cuts will become infected. Then the girl will bathe and cover the cuts with palm oil. When the cuts have healed, they leave scars. A suitor will kill a chicken and present it to her as a gift. Then she can make fun of all the younger, unmarked girls of her society, who do not have suitors.

In New Mexico, in the United States, there's a very different kind of ceremony. A Navajo Indian girl is dressed in many layers of colorful clothing. Then she spends four days and nights in isolation in her family house. After the four days and nights, her relatives sing and dance to celebrate the arrival of her first menstrual period. She chants a series of traditional verses to identify herself as the daughter of the mythical goddess, Changing Woman. Then the older women of the tribe give her a vigorous massage, symbolically rubbing away the old identity. Now she is considered to be a re-formed person, capable of having children and helping the human race to continue.

Although all the ceremonies I've mentioned are somewhat different, they do have one important similarity. The person who goes through the puberty ritual changes from a receiver of the culture to a giver of the culture. The lengthy preparation periods, the chanting and the singing of ritual songs during the rites provide formal education both in the social customs and in the sacred traditions of the society. In fact, as I said before, many puberty rites symbolize the death of the old self and the birth of the new.

Rene: Excuse me, but some of these rites seem really painful and difficult. I don't see why this is necessary.

Lecturer: Well, you're certainly not the only one who feels that way! Researchers who observe the tribal rites of passage often have trouble viewing them. On the one hand, many of the ordeals seem unnecessarily painful and oppressive. On the other hand, anthropologists understand that if outsiders change or threaten these rites, it also threatens the life and equilibrium of the society as a whole. But whatever judgment you make about these rites, the fact remains that rites of passage are one of the important ways that human beings give meaning to the changes that occur in life.

OK, that's enough for today. See you next week. Good night, class.

Students: Good night, Professor. See you tomorrow. Bye-bye.

PART 3

Extending Congratulations and Condolences

1   Listening for Sincere and Insincere Congratulations. Page 38.

Conversation 1
A: Guess what! I'm getting married next month!
B: Oh! Terrific! I'm so happy for you.

Conversation 2
A: Guess what! Louise and I are engaged!
B: Congratulations. I'm so happy for you.

Conversation 3
A: Hey! I've got some news! I got a promotion at work.
B: Congratulations! I'm so pleased for you.

Conversation 4

A: Hey, listen to this! I got a raise this week.

B: No kidding! Congratulations! I'm thrilled.

Conversation 5

A: It's my 90th birthday today!

B: Congratulations! May you have many more!

Conversation 6

A: Guess what! I'm 25 years old today!

B: Congratulations! Many happy returns!

2 Listening for Expressions of Congratulations. Page 39.

A: Boy! The traffic downtown sure was terrible today.

B: Yeah— sure was. Are you still having trouble with your car over-heating in heavy traffic?

A: Oh, no! I finally got a new car.

B: Congratulations! What kind of car did you get?

A: A blue Toyota with all the extras.

B: Great! Does it get good mileage?

A: Sure does! It's so much better than my old car!

B: Well, I'm really glad to hear that! Use it in the best of health!

A: Thanks! I will!

3 Listening for Expressions of Condolences. Page 39.

A: What have you been up to lately?

B: Not much – just work, work, and then a little more work. But things will look brighter when we get this project finished in December.

A: Are you still driving to Los Angeles every week to take care of your mother?

B: No, I'm not doing that anymore. She died in September.

A: Oh! I'm so sorry. Is there anything I can do?

B: No, I don't think so. Everything's under control now. My father had a rough time for a while, but he's doing much better now.

A: I just can't tell you how sorry I am.

B: Oh, no, you mustn't be! It was for the best. She was suffering so much.

A: Yes, I suppose so. Well, please give my condolences to the rest of your family.

B: Yes, I will. Thanks so much.

Focus on Testing. Page 41.

You will hear a short conversation. After the conversation you will be asked some questions. Circle the letter of the best answer to each question.

Conversation

Patty: Jacobson's class is pretty interesting, don't you think? I especially enjoyed the lecture yesterday on puberty rites. How 'bout you, Alphonso?

Alphonso: Yeah, really! Some of that stuff was pretty strange though, right? I mean, going on a vision quest, climbing a mountain, and meditating for a while sounds kinda neat, but some of that other stuff was too much.

Patty: What do you mean?

Alphonso: Well, I can't exactly see myself sacrificing an animal or anything, can you?

Patty: No way!

Alphonso: Right! And how about scarification? Could you sit there while they carved sacred designs into your body?

Patty: Oooh. I don't think so. I see what you mean now. But it's all based on your cultural perspective, isn't it?

Alphonso: Huh?

Patty: I mean, what seems okay, what seems normal in terms of these kinds of rituals is all a matter of what you're used to. You know, what the cultural norms are. In fact, I wonder what people in tribal cultures think of some of our rites of passage. Or for that matter, I wonder what people in the year 3000 will think of the things we do to mark becoming a man or a woman in our society.

Alphonso: You're right! I hadn't quite thought of it like that. I wonder if getting your driver's license will be as big a deal then as it is now?

Patty: I swear, all you ever think about is cars! How about when we went out on our first date? Wasn't that a big moment for you?

Alphonso: Of course it was, Patty. But are you saying that our first date was a rite of passage? You know, my first date with *you* wasn't exactly my first date.

Patty: Is that so? Well, you could have fooled me.

Patty and Alphonso: (both laugh)

Question 1: Who is Jacobson?
Question 2: What does Alphonso think about vision quests?
Question 3: Which statement about cultural norms is not true?
Question 4: What does Patty say Alphonso thinks about most?

Lecture: The Origins of Our Solar System

Student 1: This stuff is just like what I'm learning in my philosophy class!

Student 2: Yeah, and my physics professor talked about similar stuff too!

Professor: Good evening, class. I'm happy to inform you that the astronomy texts for this class are in the bookstore.

Students: (cheers and applause)

Professor: So. . . . no more excuses for not doing the reading, right?

Students: (groans and laughter)

Professor: Okay. Now. . . . tonight we're going to look at some of the most important ideas about the origin of the solar system. As we said last time, we will really be talking about our ignorance. When you get right down to it, the bottom line is we just don't know much about the origin of the solar system. Last time we had just started talking about Descartes. Do you remember what century we were talking about? Larry?

Larry: I'm sorry, but I can't remember.

Students: Thirteenth century. Fifteenth! No, I think it was the 1400s. That's the same thing, silly. OK, then seventeenth century. How about the eighteenth? I have no idea.

Professor: Well, it was in the seventeenth century, 1644 to be exact, that the French philosopher and mathematician, René Descartes, proposed a theory, called the vortices theory, that is still accepted by some scientists. According to this theory, at the very beginning there was only a cloud of dust and hot gases. Descartes hypothesized that this cloud of dust and gases looked and moved just like the whirling winds in tornadoes. As the cloud cooled, these whirling winds came together somehow to form a large central body and other smaller bodies revolving around it.

Yes. . . . Toni?

Toni: Did Descartes work on that theory for many years or did the idea come to him all of a sudden in 1644?

Professor: That's a good question, but I'm afraid I don't know the answer. Sorry. Let's see, now where was I? Oh, yes. During the late eighteenth century, the German philosopher Immanuel Kant and the French astronomer Pierre-Simon Laplace further developed Descartes's hypothesis about the origin of our solar system. They combined Descartes's ideas with Sir Isaac Newton's new theory of gravitation.

Kant and Laplace developed a theory known as the "nebular hypothesis." According to this theory, after the sun was formed, a disk-shaped cloud of dust and gas was pulled toward the sun by the sun's gravity. As this dust cloud revolved around the sun, lumps within the cloud became smaller centers of gravity. Do you know what this process led to? Jonathan, do you know?

Jonathan: I'm very sorry, I have no idea.

Professor: That's OK. I just wanted to see if anyone had any background in this. Well, this process of gravitational attraction led to the formation of a series of concentric rings. Eventually this led to the formation of dense, round planets. So you see, according to the nebular hypothesis, the formation of planets is a natural result of the existence of stars. Therefore, solar systems like our own could very possibly be found throughout the universe.

At the beginning of the twentieth century, however, the British astronomers James Jeans and Harold Jeffries proposed another hypothesis. They suggested that our solar system was the only one like it in the universe, and that the formation of our solar system was the result of an accident. They suggested that millions and millions of years ago another star passed very close to the sun and that the gravitational attraction between the two stars caused lines of dense matter to break off from the surface of the sun. But this matter was still affected by the sun's gravity, and so it remained trapped in orbit around the sun. As the matter cooled, it condensed – that is, it got smaller and smaller – and eventually formed the planets.

By 1920— less than twenty years later— new discoveries led to even newer theories. James Clerk Maxwell and some other scientists demonstrated that a newly discovered principle, the law of conservation of angular momentum, makes both Descartes's model and the nebular hypothesis impossible. Does anyone know what the law of conservation of angular momentum states? Margaret, how about you this time?

Margaret: I'm sorry. I don't know.

Professor: Anyone else? No? Well, don't worry about this; you'll go over this again in the discussion sessions. Just bear in mind that the law of conservation of angular momentum states that the amount of circular movement within a closed system must remain constant. That is, the amount of movement cannot change.

So if the sun and the planets were produced when the large clouds of matter condensed and got smaller, each of these bodies would have picked up speed, just as a whirling skater who pulls in his or her arms picks up speed. Furthermore, the sun and the planets would now have to be spinning faster than the speed of light, and we know that they don't spin that fast.

Astronomers were confused by this paradox until the late 1950s. That's when discoveries were made about the nature of plasmas. Plasmas are the gases that make up the clouds between the stars. Astronomers discovered some interesting interactions between these plasmas and electromagnetic fields. These discoveries helped a Swedish physicist named Hannes Alfven to develop a new hypothesis about the origin of the universe. Does anyone know what Alfven's hypothesis is called? Frank, do you know?

Frank: I'm not certain, but I'll guess. Is it the plasma-nebular hypothesis?

Professor: Yes, Alfven's hypothesis is quite naturally called the plasma-nebular hypothesis. According to this hypothesis, our solar system appeared between 4½ and 5 billion years ago, and our sun began as a protostar. A protostar is a very dense cloud of hydrogen and helium, with some smaller quantities of heavier elements such as mercury. The protostar measured about a light year in diameter. Our sun was formed as the cloud condensed. As it turned faster and faster, it built up enough electromagnetic energy, heat, and light to set off a permanent thermonuclear reaction— the kind of reaction that powers true stars and also hydrogen bombs. The center of this cloud came together into a dense, explosive sphere, and the outer sections of the cloud came together into a disk-shaped mass of gas. This gaseous mass was held solidly by spokes of magnetic force radiating from the dense center— much like the spokes of a wheel – as you can see in the picture on your handout. At first, the disk turned much more slowly than the sphere. Later the disk gained speed until it was turning much faster than the sphere.

Now, as the central sphere cooled, the cloud around it began to condense like the way rain and snow condense from a storm cloud. But instead of drops of rain or snowflakes, sphere-shaped grains of matter were formed. Then these round grains of matter bumped into each other and stuck together, forming lumps. Evidence of these lumps has been found in meteors and— anyone know where else? Eloise?

Eloise: I'm afraid I don't remember for sure, but I think it might be in rocks from the moon and maybe from Venus.

Professor: Well, good, you're half right. Evidence of these lumps has been found in rock samples from the moon and from Mars. Then gravity caused the lumps to accumulate into larger and larger bodies, with the larger bodies swallowing the smaller ones. In this way, the planets and their moons were formed. Well, according to this theory anyway.

Also according to this theory, the chemical composition of the lumps varied according to the temperature. Close to the sun, where the heat was greater, only the heavier, denser chemical compounds like metals and silicates condensed. And since there wasn't very much of these compounds, the planets close to the sun remained small. Farther out, away from the sun, where temperatures were much lower, the lighter substances like hydrogen, helium, and methane condensed. Since there were a lot of these compounds, the larger planets like Jupiter and Saturn were formed.

The plasma-nebular hypothesis accounts for the chemical composition and sizes of Mercury, Venus, Earth, Jupiter, and Saturn. However, this hypothesis does not explain why Mars is smaller than the earth, nor does it in any way account for the sizes and compositions of the outer planets: Uranus, Neptune, and Pluto.

So, as you can see, we really don't know exactly how the solar system originated. Physicists and astronomers hope that all the information that comes from developing technology will soon reveal a complete and understandable explanation. But it is also possible, as has happened before, that more data will only complicate rather than clarify this issue.

Roberto: Excuse me, professor, do you have any ideas about what the next theories might be?

Lecturer: I'm afraid as of now, Roberto, I couldn't even begin to guess.

PART 3 # Admitting a Lack of Knowledge

1 **Listening for Formal and Informal Expressions. Page 53.**

Conversation 1

Woman: Excuse me, sir, could you give me directions to the Statue of Liberty?

Man: I'm sorry, I don't know. I'm not from around here myself.

Conversation 2

Samantha: Professor Hill, what did the ancient Egyptians believe about the origin of the universe?

Professor Hill: I'm afraid I don't remember the answer to that anymore, Samantha, but almost any text on ancient Egyptian history should tell you.

Conversation 3

Phil: When is the next space shuttle supposed to take off?

Bob: Beats me. I haven't a clue.

Conversation 4

Carmine: How long does it take to get from Kyoto to Tokyo?

Dorothy: Don't ask me. I haven't any idea.

Conversation 5

Gary: When were the temples at Machu Picchu built?

Sarah: I'm sure I don't know!

PART 4 # Focus on Testing. Page 55.

You will hear a short American Indian folktale. After the folktale, you will be asked some questions. Circle the letter of the best answer to each question.

Folktale

Once upon a time, Silver Fox was the only one living. There was no earth. There was no water. Only fog. Silver Fox walked along through the fog feeling lonely. So she began to sing:

I want to meet someone.

I wish I would meet someone.

I want to meet someone.

I really want to know someone else.

She sang this song over and over as she walked along. Soon she met Coyote.

"I just knew I was going to meet someone," Silver Fox said. "Why are *you* traveling?"

"I don't know," Coyote said. "Why are *you* traveling?"

"I am traveling because I am lonely," Silver Fox said.

"Me, too," Coyote said. "So, why don't we travel together?"

Then, as they traveled, Silver Fox spoke. "I know what we should do. Let's make the world!"

"How will we do that?" Coyote said.

And Silver Fox answered, "We will sing the world." So the two of them began to sing and to dance. They danced around and around in a circle and sang and sang. Soon a small lump formed in the fog below their feet.

"Look down, Coyote. Do you see something?" Silver Fox said.

"I see something, but it is very small," Coyote said.

"Oh, then let's close our eyes and keep dancing and singing," Silver Fox said. And that's what they did. They sang and danced and danced and sang until the earth took shape beneath them.

"Look down now," Silver Fox said.

"I see it! It's big enough now!" Coyote said.

Then the two of them jumped down onto the earth. They sang and danced until they made everything on earth with their footsteps and their song. They jumped up and down and made the valleys and the mountains. They skipped up and down and made the lakes and the rivers. They sang all the songs of the trees, the birds, the fish, and the animals. And then they danced the dance and sang the song of the people.

Question 1:   Who was traveling?
Question 2:   What did Coyote and Silver Fox decide to do?
Question 3:   How did they do it?
Question 4:   What is the best title for this tale?

Chapter 5   Transitions

PART 2   Understanding and Using Figurative Language

Radio Program: The Stages of Life – A View from Shakespeare

Grace George: In some ways life is like a giant puzzle. To construct a puzzle you have to gather and put together the parts. Similarly, we gather and piece together our life experiences as we learn and grow and change.

Hello. This is Grace George and welcome to Transformations, the show that talks about change—in ourselves and in our society. Tonight we are pleased to have with us the distinguished professor of English literature, Francis Black, who will speak about Shakespeare's view of the stages of life.

We hope you'll enjoy the program. We'll have a call-in discussion afterward as usual. Our newsletter has a speech from Shakespeare's play, *As You Like It* in the latest issue. Professor Black will be referring to this speech in today's presentation.

And now, Professor Black.

Prof. Black: Most people look forward to changes in the future. We hope that these changes will bring good fortune, yet we also know that not all changes are good. We want to see time and change as positive, but let's face it – we also see time and change as negative because they always bring our decline and eventual death.

In my view the ways people react to change are more important than what actually happens to them. Frankly, I think that some people waste time worrying about what they weren't able to do or what they didn't become. Other people take a more positive view and learn to accept and take pleasure in what is – in what they *were* able to do and in what they *did* become. For example, if they've lived an ethical life and been kind to others, they don't worry about the fact that they've never sailed around the world, earned a million dollars, or won a Nobel Prize.

Of course, there are people who have positive feelings toward humanity. They believe that a lifetime is a period in which we must work hard to develop and perfect ourselves. On the other hand, other people aren't as optimistic about the intelligence and goodness of people. Those who believe that humankind is not worthy of trust, and therefore not worth caring about, are known as misanthropes.

There are many ways to view people and the stages that they go through in life. A Buddhist would probably see transformation or change as an opportunity for spiritual growth. A business executive might only be concerned with the financial aspects of change. And there are, of course, as many ways to deal with the transformations in our lives as there are points of view. In Western civilization, we seem to be afraid that all our planning and struggling for success are simply meaningless moves in a game that can't be won. We fear that our efforts will produce, as Shakespeare wrote, merely "sound and fury, signifying nothing." One of the most disturbing visions is the idea that we are just actors playing out roles created for us by genetics, the choices our families made, or any number of other circumstances. Or even worse, what if we are just puppets whose strings are pulled by forces beyond our control? I'm sorry to tell you that if this is the case, we do not have any freedom. Each and every moment, every move, every gesture, and every thought is decided for us.

Of course, when we are young, we don't like the idea of being puppets, because this limits our freedom. As we grow older, though, we are often willing to settle for less freedom. We agree to play roles that are predetermined by our own characters and society's expectations of us. These roles sometimes make us feel that we're in a rut— stuck in a boring, repetitive world— but for some reason, we do not rebel. Eventually, we might even become cynics - people who do not believe in free choice and who distrust human nature and people's motives. Cynics believe that most people basically are selfish. And when the cynics describe our failures, we listen eagerly. Why? Well, perhaps the cynics' view of humanity reassures those people who are weak. You see, if that's the way humanity is, then the weak just can't help themselves. They have the best possible excuse for their behavior: That's simply the way all people are. Cynics also criticize authority in society, because people, especially those in power, always make a mess of everything. The cynics, however, offer nothing constructive, no positive suggestions or solutions. They merely whine and complain about the poor condition of the world and how it's all our own fault.

Because we are so aware of the fact that we will all die eventually, the dark visions of the cynics and even darker visions of the misanthropes can be fascinating to us. One of the most famous speeches in literature about the stages in life that we all pass through is the one given by Jacques in Shakespeare's play, *As You Like It*.

Let me tell you a little about Jacques. Jacques is one of the lords serving the duke in the play. He also presents himself as a philosopher who wanders from place to place, has no connections with other people, and no desire for them. At the drop of a hat, though, he will comment freely to anyone and everyone about the state of the world.

As I read the speech, you can decide for yourselves whether you think Jacques is a cynic, a misanthrope, or someone who sees things as they really are. Now please follow along on your handout:

All the world's a stage,
And all the men and women merely players.
They have their exits and their entrances,
And one man in his time plays many parts,
His acts being seven ages.

So, Jacques says that we are all simply actors going through our lives as if they were real, when actually we are only playing roles already determined for us. He says the seven stages of life are like acts in a play. In the next few lines, he describes the first two stages:

At first the infant,
Mewling and puking in the nurse's arms,
Then whining schoolboy, with his satchel
And shining morning face, creeping like a snail
Unwillingly to school.

Jacques is so cynical that all he has to say about the sweet, innocent baby in the first act of life's drama is that he cries (that's the "mewling") and he spits up his milk, or "pukes." And the next 12 years don't get any better. The child is sent off to school with his face washed and his books in his "satchel," in his bag. He does nothing of importance but continues to whine and complain as he goes unwillingly to school. The only choice he makes is to go to school slowly, "creeping like a snail." Soon he reaches adolescence– his teenage years– and his interest in girls grows quickly:

And then the lover,
Sighing like a furnace, with a woeful ballad
Made to his mistress' eyebrow. Then a soldier,
Full of strange oaths, and bearded like a pard,
Jealous in honor, sudden and quick in quarrel,
Seeking the bubble reputation
Even in the cannon's mouth.

So, now, in this third stage of life, our hero burns with desire ("sighing like a furnace") and not much else. He becomes possessed by the passion he feels for his sweetheart. Jacques makes the youth seem foolish by having him write a poem about the beauty of his girlfriend's eyebrow. That is certainly silly stuff, but it is all the lover has to say.

The next stage of his life, however, is not as amusing nor perhaps as understandable. The youth soon grows beyond love and sexual desire into anger, jealousy, and the most forceful emotion: ambition. And to him, fulfilling the ambition of becoming a man means becoming a soldier. His language changes. It becomes coarser; to put it bluntly, he swears a lot. He begins to hate his enemies more than he loved his sweetheart— his "mistress." He grows a beard, hoping to look as fierce as a "pard," that is, leopard. He does this to intimidate his enemies. He fights "quarrels," in order to make a name for himself, to improve his reputation. He is so driven by his ambition for recognition that he doesn't care if it endangers his life. That is, he pursues the "bubble of reputation" even into "the cannon's mouth," even if someone is about to shoot him. He ignores the fact that he is mortal and puts glory and reputation before reason and thought.

If the youth manages to survive these years, he will achieve the fifth stage, making a career and accumulating things and ideas. He will shift from liberal to conservative, from adventurous to cautious, from passionate to self-controlled. Listen:

And then the justice,
In fair round belly with good capon lined,
With eyes severe and beard of formal cut,
Full of wise saws and modern instances,
And so he plays his part.

So, you see, now our young man has become a justice – a court judge. He has become fat from eating chicken (that is, lining his belly with "capon") and other tasty foods. His beard is no longer bushy and fierce-looking but is well trimmed. Furthermore, he is full of sayings and examples. Not to beat around the bush, he's boring. If this were the last stage, he might be quite content, but there are still two more stages. And the next stage brings the trouble of aging:

The sixth age shifts
Into the lean and slippered Pantaloon,
With spectacles on nose and pouch on side,
His youthful hose, well saved, a world too wide
For his shrunk shank, and his big manly voice,
Turning again toward childish treble, pipes
And whistles in his sound.

Here our man puts on the clothes of old age: loose comfortable pants and warm slippers. His eyes are weak, and he wears glasses on his nose. He carries his tobacco and perhaps his money, too, in a pouch or purse at his side. There it will be easier for an old man to reach and to guard. The colorful stockings that he once wore on his strong, youthful legs are too large to fit his small thin legs now. He no longer has the clear voice of lover, soldier, and judge, but speaks in a high, childlike voice, often whining like Scottish bagpipes. To add insult to injury, his missing teeth give a whistling sound to his words. His life has almost come full circle, and the next stage ends the play:

Last scene of all,
That ends this strange eventful history,
Is second childishness and mere oblivion,
Sans teeth, sans eyes, sans taste, sans everything.

And so he returns, without teeth, without sight, without taste, without any of the senses, to the emptiness from which he first came into the world.

We all travel the same path. Sometimes our lives are disappointing, even tragic; sometimes delightful; sometimes they are merely routine. We might be glad to be alive, or uncertain of life's value. In any case, only when we die is our role in the play completed.

And let's face it, whether we are simply actors in a play that we have not written or are in control of our own fates is a fascinating question. If you found the answer, would it make a difference in the way you lead your life? I'll leave you with that question.

Grace George: Hello again, listeners. This is Grace George. Professor Black's question seems like a good place to start the call-in segment of our program. Our phone lines are now open. If you knew for certain whether or not you could control your own fate, would it make a difference in the way you live your life? Go ahead, Salim in Milwaukee, you're on the air.

Making Negative Statements or Comments Politely

1   **Listening for Appropriate Tone of Voice. Page 65.**

Conversation 1A

Mickey: Gloria, have you seen my Uncle Ted lately?

Gloria: Yeah, I saw him last week at the club meeting.

Mickey: Oh, really? How was he?

Gloria: Well, to be honest with you, I don't think he looked very good. He seemed so thin and pale and . . . well, just old.

Mickey: Well, he's been working very hard, and let's face it, he's no youngster anymore. I've been trying to persuade him to retire, but he just won't do it.

Question 1:   Is Gloria really concerned about Ted? Is Mickey?
Question 2:   How do you know?
Question 3:   How would Ted feel if he overheard this conversation?

Conversation 1B

Mickey: Gloria, have you seen my Uncle Ted lately?

Gloria: Yeah, I saw him last week at the club meeting.

Mickey: Oh, really? How was he?

Gloria: Well, to be honest with you, I don't think he looked very good. He seemed so thin and pale and . . . well, just old.

Mickey: Well, he's been working very hard, and let's face it, he's no youngster anymore. I've been trying to persuade him to retire, but he just won't do it.

Question 1:   Is Gloria really concerned about Ted now? Is Mickey?
Question 2:   How do you know?
Question 3:   How would Ted feel if he overheard this conversation?

Conversation 2A

Miranda: Dad, I've something to tell you.

Dad: Well, what is it, sweetheart?

Miranda: Jeremy asked me to marry him.

Dad: And?

Miranda: And I said yes. We'd like to be married right away. What date this month would be best for you?

Dad: To tell the truth, if you go ahead with this plan, you'll have to get married without me.

Question 1:   How does the father feel about not going to his daughter's wedding?
Question 2:   How do you know?
Question 3:   What reason might he have for not going?

Conversation 2B

Miranda: Dad, I've something to tell you.

Dad: What is it, sweetheart?

Miranda: Jeremy asked me to marry him.

Dad: And?

Miranda: And I said yes. We'd like to be married right away. What date this month would be best for you?

Dad: To tell the truth, if you go ahead with this plan, you'll have to get married without me.

Question 1: How does the father feel about not going to his daughter's wedding?
Question 2: How do you know?
Question 3: What reason might he have for not going?

Conversation 3A

Paul: Well, how do you like it? I know it's not professional quality yet. I've only taken one course. But what do you think? Should I quit my job and become a photographer?

Jane: To tell the truth, I can't make out what it is.

Paul: It's a bird soaring over a rainbow. See the little point here? That's the beak. Well, what do you think?

Jane: Well, not to beat around the bush—don't quit your job just yet.

Question 1: Does Jane like Paul's artwork?
Question 2: How can you tell?
Question 3: Does Jane like Paul?
Question 4: How can you tell?

Conversation 3B

Paul: Well, how do you like it? I know it's not professional quality yet. I've only taken one course. But what do you think? Should I quit my job and become a photographer?

Jane: To tell the truth, I can't make out what it is.

Paul: It's a bird soaring over a rainbow. See the little point here? That's the beak. Well, what do you think?

Jane: Well, not to beat around the bush—don't quit your job just yet.

Question 1: Does Jane like Paul's artwork?
Question 2: How can you tell?
Question 3: Does Jane like Paul?
Question 4: How can you tell?

Focus on Testing. Page 69.

You will hear a short presentation. After the presentation you will be asked some questions. Circle the letter of the best answer to each question.

Presentation

Nearly 85% of the population of India is classified as Hindu. Unlike most other religions, Hinduism, which began to develop about 4,000 years ago, has no single founder or creed. It consists of a vast variety of beliefs and practices and has no centralized organization or leadership. Hinduism does, however, suggest a commitment to or respect for an ideal way of life, known as Dharma.

Hinduism divides Dharma, or the ideal way of life, into four stages. In each stage there are different duties. The first stage is studentship, or Brahmacarya, which lasts from initiation into the Hindu community at five to eight years of age until marriage. During the second stage of the ideal life, Grihasthya, one marries, raises a family, and takes part in society. Vanaprasthya is the third stage. It is during this stage, after one's children have grown up, that the Hindu leaves the household and prepares for the spiritual search or quest. The fourth and final stage is Samnyasa, renunciation. This is when one gives up attachment to all worldly things and seeks spiritual liberation.

The ideal stages of life and their duties encompass males only. The position of women in Hinduism has always been highly ambiguous. They are, on the one hand, venerated as a symbol of the divine. On the other hand, women are often treated as inferior beings. Women are traditionally expected to serve their husbands and to have no independent interests.

Question 1: What percentage of the Indian population is Hindu?
Question 2: During which of the four stages of Dharma is the ideal time for a Hindu man to marry and raise a family?
Question 3: Which of the statements is *not* true?,
Question 4: What is the Hindu ideal way of life called?

Chapter 6 The Mind

Listening for Comparisons and Contrasts

1 Listening for Comparison and Contrast in Informal Conversations. Page 76.

Conversation 1
Otto and Henry

> *Otto:* I really like that German restaurant on Second Street, Henry. You know, the one with the giant beer stein on the roof?
>
> Henry: I don't think I've ever been there, Otto. Why do you like it?
>
> Otto: They cook the food the same way my mother did. It makes me daydream about my childhood.

Conversation 2
Judy and Paula

Judy: Paula, do you think we should drive or take the train to the concert in Chicago? I can't decide. There are advantages and disadvantages to both.

Paula: Well, let's see. Driving means that we can leave whenever we want. On the other hand, Judy, taking the train means we don't have to worry about parking and we can both sleep on the way home.

Conversation 3
A teaching assistant and students

TA: I've talked with Professor Thornton and there's going to be some changes this week. What do you want first - the good news or the bad news?

Students: Oh no - What?

TA: Well - the good news is we're not going to have a quiz today.

Students: Really? That's great! No kidding?

TA: And the bad news is that this means that next week we'll have two quizzes – one on the mind on Wednesday, and one on dreams and the dream state on Friday.

Students: Oh, no. Great!

Lecture: Dreams and Reality

Professor: Hello, everyone. Well . . .how did you do with the reading for this week? Any problems?

Student 1: Oh, yes. I thought that the textbook was really hard to understand.

Student 2: Yeah, me too. I thought I knew something about the topic for this week, you know, "Dreams and Reality", until I started doing the reading.

Student 3: I agree. I finally went to the library and got another book on the subject.

Professor: Okay. How many others had problems? Yes, well, it looks like about half of you had some difficulty. So let's not use the textbook today. Instead, let's talk about some ideas from a science fiction book that are good examples of the concepts in the textbook.

Last summer I read a science fiction book called *The Lathe of Heaven.* My lecture is based on some of the ideas in this book. And I'm very interested to hear your reactions. So let me just share a few ideas with you, then we'll open it up for discussion. Okay?

Students: Sure. Yeah. Great. Sounds good.

Professor: Most of us have had intense dreams. While we are sleeping, these dreams seem very real, but after we wake up, the dream images break up and become much less intense, perhaps like photographs of something way off in the distance.   Even though the dream images have become much less intense, they still stay with us as we go about our daily activities. We may be only partly aware of these images and only partly aware of the changes in perception that they may cause. But our dreams can affect our lives during the day without our conscious awareness. This is because our dreams influence our decisions and choices even though we don't realize it.

Often, however, our dreams seem trivial and useless. On the other hand, many breakthroughs in science and in the arts come during dreams. In the sciences, for example, a German chemist, F. A. Kebule von Stradonitz, dreamed about a snake with its tail in its mouth. He said that this dream led him to visualize the benzene molecule. The dream helped him to conceptualize a model of this molecule.

Samuel Taylor Coleridge wrote a poem titled Kubla Khan. Coleridge said that he created the poem during a dream and that the minute he woke up, he began to write it down. While he was doing this, a visitor came to see him and interrupted his writing. Later, when he tried to finish the poem, he couldn't. He had forgotten the end of it. That's sad but, on the bright side, critics still consider it one of his best poems, even though it is not finished.

So dreams can be very important. My dreams, however, do seem pretty silly. For example, the other night I dreamed about buying a suit, something I had actually done that day. And one night last week I dreamed about hot dogs piled up on a bridge— no useful images for scientific discoveries or artistic creations there that I can figure out. But at least I do dream. And we know that dreaming, any kind of dreaming, is necessary for both physical and mental health.

So the mind can create two basic types of dreams: On the one hand, the powerful and intense images that can change our lives, and, on the other hand, the fleeting, chaotic, meaningless images that contain no important messages.

Ursula LeGuin, a popular and highly respected science fiction writer, explores the world of dreams in *The Lathe of Heaven*. In this book, she looks at the relationship between dreams and reality in a fascinating way. Let me briefly summarize the story for you.

George Orr, the main character in the story, has a problem. When he has certain kinds of dreams, the world changes according to his dream. So he frequently awakens to a different world from the one that existed when he fell asleep.

Student 2: Wow! That would be neat.

Student 3: Yeah! Cool!

Professor: Yes, that's quite an extraordinary power. But as you can imagine, it frightens him because he doesn't believe that it is right to use his dreams to change reality. His fear grows bigger when he realizes that no one else knows that he is changing the entire world night after night. Everyone else changes completely to become a part of the new world that George creates in his dream. Every time George dreams a new reality, each person has a new set of memories to fit this new reality. They remember nothing of the old reality that existed the night before.

Student 1:	That sounds awful!
Student 2:	Yes it does, but just think of the power he has to change the world!
Professor:	Right, and it's interesting that you should point that out. You see, George is extremely upset. He is afraid to go to sleep and dream, so he goes to a psychiatrist named Haber. Fortunately, Dr. Haber believes George and does not think he is insane. However, Dr. Haber wants to use George's power for his own purposes, so at first he does not tell George that he knows that the dreams really change things. But in the end someone else finds out that George can actually change reality through his dreams, and Dr. Haber is forced to admit that he is not trying to cure George of his fear of dreaming. Instead, Dr. Haber is trying to use George's dreams to change the world.
	The upside of this is that the doctor wants to change the world into a "better" place. He wants to do good things for the world by controlling George's dreams.
Student 4:	That sounds OK, but I bet there's a downside, right?
Professor:	Right. Dr. Haber builds a special machine that records George's dreams, so that he can transfer George's brainwave patterns during dreams to his own dreams. Dr. Haber thinks that this machine will give him the power to change the world by himself, through his own dreams, without George.
	This technique works, sort of. Dr. Haber does, in fact, gain some power to change reality through his own dreams. But he fails to understand what is real and what is unreal. Because he sees only the concrete, material world as real, his dreams produce nightmarish realities with no flexibility. For example, Dr. Haber decides that he wants complete equality in the world. He wants all people to be absolutely equal in all ways. So he dreams, and when he wakes up, everything is gray. People's skin, their clothes, the houses, the trees, the animals— everything!
Students:	Oh, no!
Professor:	Everything is certainly equal, but only in a material sense. But things could be worse. Just imagine if Dr. Haber were an evil person rather than a basically good man. Eventually Dr. Haber goes mad from the stress of never getting it quite right.
Students:	(laugh)
Professor:	Well, now. What's the point that LeGuin is trying to make in this story? One clue is in the title, *The Lathe of Heaven*. A lathe is a machine on which objects are turned and shaped into new forms. If the wood or the metal is not flexible, it will crack when it is shaped by the machine. The same thing happens with the lathe of heaven. If a person is not flexible and accepts only one part of the mind—the rational, logical part—he or she will be destroyed by the lathe.
	In this novel, Dr. Haber represents the inflexible, rational, materialistic person who thinks that he can control nature, that he can bend nature to serve himself. His mind is never still, never quiet. Instead, his mind is always active, looking for new ways to change reality. George, on the other hand, is mentally quiet. He never thinks of

manipulating reality. His dreams are powerful not because he wants power but because he is in tune with nature.

But LeGuin suggests that George, even though he is in harmony with reality, will still suffer. Imagine what it would be like to wake up to a new world with a new history every few days and to be the only one who can remember the old world.

Likewise, the lathe of heaven forms and re-forms the world and plays with time like a child playing with a tape recorder. Time is moved forward or backward like fast forwarding or rewinding a tape.

LeGuin asks us to let go of our concept of time, which is the idea that time continuously moves forward, inch by inch, as on a ruler. Instead, she wants us to see time in relation to a central point. George represents that central point and all of time depends on him. Perhaps LeGuin wants us to see that change cannot be pushed from behind along a straight course, but only exists in relation to a stable central point.

Uh-oh. I can see there are mixed reactions to this idea. So. . .let's take a short break and then open it up for discussion. I'm really anxious to hear what *you* think.

Expressing the Positive View

1 **Listening for the Positive View. Page 82.**

Conversation 1
Gary and Julius

Gary:	Hi, Julius. How's it going?
Julius:	Hi, Gary. I'm really tired. I didn't sleep much last night because I had this terrible dream. I dreamed that I got the second-to-lowest grade on the history final.
Gary:	Oh, yeah? And who got the *lowest* grade?
Julius:	Henry Mitchell. Wow, what a horrible dream!
Gary:	Oh, yeah! But it could have been worse!
Julius:	Yeah? How?
Gary:	Well, you could have woken up and discovered *you* were Henry Mitchell.

Question 1:   What expression does Gary use to help Julius "look at the bright side"?
Question 2:   Is Gary's suggestion amusing? Why or why not?

Conversation 2
Christine and Eric

Christine:	Oh, shoot, Eric! It's raining again, and I was looking forward to going to the soccer team picnic.

Eric:	Yeah— too bad— but look at it this way. Now we'll have time to go see that therapist I was telling you about.
Christine:	Oh, well– maybe . . .
Eric:	Now come on, Christine. You said you wanted to stop smoking, didn't you?

Question 1: What does Eric suggest doing instead of going to the picnic?
Question 2: What expression does he use to introduce this suggestion?
Question 3: Do you think Eric was glad the picnic was rained out? Why or why not?

Conversation 3
Clara and Joyce

Clara:	Hi, Joyce. What's up?
Joyce:	Hi, Clara. I'm on my way over to my study skills class. We're starting a unit on speed reading, and I'm not looking forward to it.
Clara:	Really? Why not?
Joyce:	Well, I'm afraid that those speed-reading techniques might interfere with my reading comprehension. And I already have so much trouble understanding a lot of the material in my classes.
Clara:	Oh, but just think. You'll learn to read everything so quickly that you'll at least read everything once. You *were* having trouble completing all the reading assignments on time, weren't you?
Joyce:	Yes, but remember what the comedian Woody Allen said a speed-reading course did for him?
Clara:	No— what?
Joyce:	He said: "Well, after the speed-reading course I really improved. I was able to read Tolstoy's *War and Peace* in five minutes . . . Yes, uh huh—it's about war."

Question 1: What is Joyce's complaint?
Question 2: What does Clara suggest?
Question 3: What expression does Clara use to introduce her suggestion?
Question 4: Was Clara able to convince Joyce to see the bright side? How do you know this?

PART 4

Focus on Testing. Page 87.

You will hear a short conversation. After the conversation you will be asked some questions. Circle the letter of the best answer to each question.

Conversation

Kelly:	Hi, Brian. What's up?
Brian:	Uh? What? What?
Kelly:	Oh, sorry. I didn't mean to startle you. Am I interrupting anything?

Brian:	Oh, Kelly. It's you. No, no, you're not interrupting anything. I was just dreaming. Or at least I *think* I was dreaming.
Kelly:	What do you mean *think*?
Brian:	Well, I'm so tired, I may be losing touch with reality. You know, I've been studying for final exams and it's really important that I get all As and Bs this semester. Anyway, I've been up about three nights in a row now. And just before you came in I was reading this psychology book and I guess I sort of drifted off. Only I didn't realize it until you came in.
Kelly:	What do you mean? What happened?
Brian:	Well, I thought I was awake and then this girl came in and she said that I needed to rest and that I should go with her to the garden and sit there and she would bring me some refreshments.
Kelly:	Refreshments? Nobody uses that word any more. Sounds to me like you just fell asleep for a few minutes and you were dreaming.
Brian:	But it seemed so real. She took my hand in hers and it was so soft. I followed her and sat at the table in the garden. She left for a minute. I leaned over to smell the roses and I picked a really beautiful pink one. Then she came back and gave me a cup of tea and the most delicious cookies I've ever tasted. I was eating the cookies and just about to ask her name when. . .well, I guess that's when you came in.
Kelly:	I don't know who she was, Brian, but these cookies are really good. Where did you get them?
Brian:	What? What cookies? I didn't have any cookies here a few minutes ago!
Kelly:	Relax, Brian. I'm just teasing. I brought you the cookies. You're not losing touch with reality. You were just dreaming.
Brian:	Yeah, I guess you're right. It sure was a great dream, though.
Kelly:	Sounds like wishful thinking. You know, that's what Freud said about dreams— that they can represent what we hope for or what we need.
Brian:	Well, after this dream, I'm sure Freud was right. A lovely lady to share some tea and cookies with me is exactly what I need right now.
Kelly:	Well, here I am.

Question 1: What was Brian doing when Kelly arrived?
Question 2: Why is Brian so tired?
Question 3: What did the girl in the dream do?
Question 4: Why was Brian surprised and a little anxious about the cookies?
Question 5: What does Brian think he needs right now?

Chapter 7 | Working

Persuading and Giving In

Webcast: Japanese and American Business Management

Technician: Phil, you're on in ten seconds.

Phil: OK, thanks. Are we ready, everybody? Here we go.

Technician: Five, four, three, two, one. You're on the air.

Phil: Good evening. I'm Philip Grant, and I will be your moderator for tonight's Downlink Discussion. As usual we have a live audience here in our broadcast studio.

Audience: (applauds)

Phil: Tonight's discussion is "Japanese and American Business Management." And we are fortunate to have two very knowledgeable people on this topic here— Laura Gordon and Brian Mani. Laura and Brian are management consultants and have worked for over 15 years with corporations in Japan and America.

First, Ms. Gordon and Mr. Mani will give us some background information and then we will open up the discussion to participants from our studio audience and all the Downlink sites. So, without further delay, Laura Gordon and Brian Mani.

Laura: Good evening. Let me begin by saying a few familiar, well-loved words: Nikon, Honda, Mitsubishi, Sony . . .

Audience: (laughs)

Laura: Yes, these names are household words to Americans. They demonstrate the success of Japanese goods in the American marketplace.

From cars to cameras, from video recorders to violins, we are surrounding ourselves with more and more products "Made in Japan." We choose them because they are easy to get, well made, and not too expensive. Consequently, the demand for Japanese goods has cut deeply into the sales of American companies, and they are losing a great deal of business.

In response to this situation, some leaders in business, labor, and government want to have protective taxes and import quotas on Japanese products. Other leaders, however, have suggested a different approach. They say that instead of trying to keep the Japanese out, we should learn from them by studying and using Japanese methods for producing better goods at lower cost.

What are these methods? What are the differences between Japanese management techniques and our own? Before I answer these questions, let me ask you a few. Take a look at the blue handout in your study packet. It says "Audience Survey" at the top. And the title is "How Would *You* Run a Doorbell Company?"

OK. Everybody got it? Good. Look at the handout. As you read it, imagine that you are the manager of a large corporation that is setting up a new electronic doorbell assembly factory. For each item, decide which of the choices, *a* or *b*, you would use to increase productivity at your company. On your handout, mark *a* or *b*, depending on which choice you think is better.

We'll give you a few minutes to complete this survey, and then Brian will go over the handout with you.

Brian: OK. It looks like everybody is just about finished. So, if you haven't figured it out already, let me explain what we've got here.

The *A*s and *B*s describe the two systems of management, Japanese and American. All the *A*s describe one system, and all the *B*s describe the other system. Which is which? Do you know? How many of you think that the as describe the American system of management?

Well, you are right. If you chose mostly *A*s you picked the American management system. And, of course, if you chose mostly *B*s, you picked the Japanese management system.

Let's look at the *A*s first, the statements that describe typical American management. If you are a typical American manager, you encourage and reward individual initiative. Therefore, you separate the people who are moving up in a company from those who aren't.

On the other hand, if you are a typical Japanese manager, illustrated in the *B* statements, what you do is encourage the group to work together. You reward the group for working together. You don't focus on individual initiative. So, what you believe is that long-term job security for everyone in the company is important. In addition, you feel that it is absolutely necessary to keep the organization as stable as possible. Therefore, you don't try to make rapid changes. Furthermore, you believe it is unnecessary to keep a clear division between management and labor. In fact, you encourage strong identification between management and labor.

Now just why are the Japanese and American business management styles so different? Over the last 20 years or so many researchers and management specialists have studied the contrasting styles of Japanese and American managers. What they have found is that the different styles of management reflect the different traditions and values of the two countries. While the Americans have treasured the values of individualism, self-reliance, and freedom from rules, the Japanese have preferred group identity, the interdependence of all workers, and the interdependence of workers and management along with a complex system of rules.

The researchers believe that the contrast between these two management styles has its roots in the geography, history, and the traditions of the two countries. Japan, as you know, is small, isolated, and poor in natural resources. As a result, it is necessary for Japan to bring together the available wealth and labor in a cooperative effort to succeed economically. The United States, in contrast, is large and has many areas that are still unpopulated. In the past, the United States had unlimited natural resources and populations that moved from place to place. In addition, the people in the United States seem to love breaking rules. They also love competition.

So researchers are now seeing that the American tradition may not work as well for modern industrial production as the Japanese system does. This is because modern industrial production demands supportive cooperation among workers and between workers and management, not competition within the company. Did you know that the word *corporation* comes from a word that means "a single body"? Now, both scholars and businesspeople believe that a shift in the direction of the Japanese cooperative system is just what American industry needs to improve its performance.

Laura, why don't you talk about Ouchi's work now? He's a great example of what I'm talking about.

Laura: Yes, great idea. I was just thinking the same thing

As Brian mentioned, one scholar who has taught the principles of Japanese business management to American managers is Professor William Ouchi. He asserts, in his widely read book, *Theory Z: How American Business Can Meet the Japanese Challenge*, that if U.S. managers take steps to strengthen close relationships between workers and their firms, U.S. productivity will increase dramatically and eventually be greater than Japanese productivity. Four important steps that he mentions are: (1) lifetime employment contracts, (2) promotions in small but regular steps, (3) nonspecialization of executives, and (4) consensus decision making with input from all employees— at all levels. Although these measures suggest a slowing down of three corporate processes— (1) innovation, (2) advancement, and (3) decision-making—Ouchi claims that in the long run these changes will lead to higher levels of agreement, morale, corporate strength, *and* profits.

Phil: Excuse me, Laura. I've heard that many American companies have already adopted the Japanese corporate model. Could you name some of the well-known ones, please?

Laura: Of course. There's IBM, Intel, Procter and Gamble, Hewlett-Packard, and the Cadillac and Saturn divisions of General Motors, to name a few. Oh, and lots of power companies such as Wisconsin Power and Light and Florida Power and Light.

These firms have divided employees into project teams that manage their own jobs, and they have protected jobs during bad economic times by cutting back everyone's working hours so they do not have to fire anyone. They have also allowed workers to manage quality control procedures. These changes have produced encouraging results. There has been a decrease in complaints among workers and also a decrease in disputes between labor and management along with gains in both quality and productivity. If this trend continues, it may turn out that Japan's most valuable export to the United States is a philosophy of business organization.

Phil: But didn't some of the Japanese management practices get started in America?

Laura: Yes, in a way. W. Edwards Deming, an American, brought many innovative management concepts to Japan after World War II. The

Japanese quickly put them to use, but American companies just weren't ready until recently.

Phil:	Laura, Brian, I think this would be a good place to take a short break. OK?
Laura and Brian:	Sure. That's fine.
Phil:	OK. We'll take a short break and when we come back we'll open up the discussion to everyone in the audience here and at the Downlink sites. And thanks so much to Laura Gordon and Brian Mani for doing the background presentation tonight.
Audience:	(applauds)

Persuading and Giving In

1 **Listening to People Persuading and Giving In. Page 101.**

Executive:	Our company is one of the most successful of its kind in Japan. We are sure to be successful here as well.
City official:	That will be good for your company, but exactly how will it help our town?
Executive:	Well, first of all, we will hire only local people to work in the factory.
City official:	Does that include all the employees? Even those in management positions?
Executive:	Yes, for the most part. We will, of course, have some of our personnel from Japan in management positions to get things started and to teach our management system.
City official:	That sounds good. Now what about your waste products? What will you do about them? We don't want any industrial waste problems here!
Executive:	There really isn't any waste to speak of. Not only that, the industry is very quiet as well. So you will have no noise pollution from us.
City official:	I'm sold. It sounds like an ideal situation. How about you, Mayor? What do you think?
Mayor:	Well, I'd like to know more about your management system. I'm not so sure the people in our town will be happy with that system, not to mention the fact that I have my doubts about how well your product will sell over here.
Executive:	You may have a point there. But our company is willing to take that chance. What's more, if the management system is not satisfactory, we're willing to change it if necessary to keep the employees satisfied and to keep our production rate up. And I might add that our company is willing to pay top dollar to the city for the use of that land by the railroad tracks where we want to build our factory.
Mayor:	I see. In that case, you've talked me into it!

Question 1: Where is the company executive from?
Question 2: What does he want to do?
Question 3: Who is he trying to persuade?
Question 4: Who will work for the company?
Question 5: Who will manage the company?
Question 6: What does the company executive say about pollution problems?
Question 7: What is the mayor concerned about?
Question 8: What enticing offer does the executive make?
Question 9: Is the mayor persuaded?

2 Listening for Expressions for Persuading and Giving In. Page 101.

See conversation in Activity 1.

PART 4

Focus on Testing. Page 104.

You will hear a short segment from a radio interview. After the interview, you will be asked some questions. Circle the letter of the best answer to each question.

Interview

Host: Good evening. I'm Frank Taylor, your host for *Business Day,* the program that knows America's business and keeps you informed. Our guest today is June Randolph from the University School of Business. June is an expert on the work of W. Edwards Deming, and she has agreed to explain Deming's seven-step quality improvement process. June, thank you so much for joining us today.

Guest: My pleasure, Frank.

Host: First, I'd like to ask a simple, but very important question. Is the seven-step quality improvement process useful for all businesses or only very large corporations?

Guest: Oh, it's definitely useful for all businesses, of all types and all sizes. In fact, it's useful for any organization or group that needs to get a job done well or to provide a service. I've even found it useful at home with my family.

Host: Really? In what way?

Guest: Well, the seven-step process helps us look at a problem or project in a very systematic way. We analyze the situation, take steps to deal with it, improve it, and then check our results. If we like the results, we then take steps to make sure we keep improving in the future.

Host: Can you give us an example of what you mean?

Guest: Sure. At our house, we had a problem with training our dog, Gracie, to stay out of the garbage. Now the first step in the improvement process is to understand the reasons for improvement. In this case, with our dog, they were pretty obvious: (1) She was making a big mess in the kitchen every day that none of us enjoyed cleaning up, and (2) she was eating things that were not good for her.

Host: And the second step is to collect data on the current situation, right?

Guest: Right. So we counted exactly how many times a month Gracie got into the garbage. We even tried to note the exact times of the day, but sometimes this was difficult because she usually did this only when no one was home.

Host: Of course!

Guest: The third step is to analyze the data. We found out that she only did it about three days a week. That was really a surprise to us. It had seemed as if she was doing it all the time, but it turned out that she was doing it only when we ate meat.

The fourth step is to plan and implement a solution to the problem. With our dog, that was easy. Every time we ate meat, we gave her a little of it in her bowl and also took out the garbage right away after dinner, so she wouldn't smell any meat in the garbage.

Host: And what were your results? The fifth step is to check your results, right?

Guest: Right. The results were great. And then the sixth step is standardization. This means that you take steps to make sure your results continue into the future. So all of us in the family agreed to take turns taking out the garbage on time! And to take turns giving Gracie some meat in her bowl if she left the garbage alone. The seventh step, of course, is to make plans for the future, for further improvement.

Host: Well, this is very interesting. It sounds like you got great results, but I wonder whose behavior actually improved as a result of using the seven-step process, the dog's or your family's?!

Question 1: What groups can profit from the seven-step quality improvement process?

Question 2: Who got into the garbage?

Question 3: What did steps two and three of the seven-step process reveal?

Question 4: What is the fourth step in the quality improvement process?

Question 5: What was part of the solution that the Randolph family found for their problem?

Question 6: What did the family members agree to take turns doing?

Chapter 8 ▌Breakthroughs

PART 2 ▌What to Do When You Don't Understand

Lecture: Discovering the Laws of Nature

Student 1: You know, I don't usually have trouble in science class, but I'm having a really hard time understanding this stuff. How about you?

Student 2: Yeah! Me, too. Let's get together later and compare notes, OK?

Student 3: Hey! Are you guys talking about comparing notes later? Great idea! This class is impossible. I just don't get this stuff.

Student 1: Yeah, I know. But I think that together we can probably figure it out.

Student 2:	Right. Come over about 6:00. I'll order a pizza.
Students 1 & 3:	Sounds great!
Student 2:	Shhhh. Here he comes.
Professor:	Good morning. I'm going to tell you a little about the history of physics today. You know, physics has not always been a separate science. In fact, long ago physics was part of the religious and metaphysical study about the nature of the cosmos. So is our current view of physics the one true and final view? Or is it like other views of the past, just a temporary belief about nature that may change in the future?

If we look at history, we find many examples of common beliefs about nature that turned out to be false or foolish. For instance, for many centuries millions of people believed that the earth was the center of the universe. Others believed that lead could be turned into gold . . . or that doctors could cure sick people by bleeding them.

Let's look at some ideas about physics and how they changed over time. The first great age of physics began with the ancient Greeks. They developed many theories about the beginnings of the universe. These theories were based on the four basic elements of nature: earth, air, fire, and water. The Greek philosopher Plato caused a revolution in physics by showing the connection between nature, the physical world, and philosophy, the ideas of humans. He also did not think the earth was the center of everything. In contrast, another Greek, named Aristotle, imagined the universe with the earth at the center and the sun and the planets traveling around it in never-ending circles. Ptolemy, an Egyptian astrologer, confirmed this view.

As ridiculous as it might seem now, this view was accepted by most people for the next 1,800 years, until the work of Sir Isaac Newton. Of course, before Newton's time there were some philosophers and scientists who had serious doubts about Aristotle's ideas. For example, Copernicus, Kepler, and Galileo all attempted to prove that the sun and not the earth was the center of the solar system.

However, it was Newton who finally demonstrated that the sun is the center of our solar system by using mathematics. He also showed that mathematics was the key to understanding the unity of nature. He showed that the stars in the distant skies as well as the earth under our feet obey the same mathematical laws. What's more, for Newton the mathematical principle of gravitation was the unifying idea, *the* paradigm that explained all events in the physical world. Gravitation was *the* unifying principle, or unified field theory of its time, the principle that provided the model for all other forms of knowledge.

Surprised? That's nothing. Listen to this . . . While Aristotle's paradigm lasted 1,800 years, Newton's lasted only about 200 years before it was seriously questioned. The problem with Newton's theories was not that they were wrong, but that they just didn't cover everything. When scientists began to look at atomic and subatomic particles, they found that Newton's mathematical equations simply did not explain what they were observing. So again there was a need for another unifying theory to explain how the objective world works.

The person who was able to come up with this theory was Albert Einstein. In the early twentieth century, Einstein gave us a new way of describing natural events. He gave us a new way of perceiving the world. His Special Theory of Relativity proposed that time and space were not constant and separate. He said that time and space were not independent principles of nature. Rather, they were relative to each other and even interchangeable. The unifying principle that Einstein proposed was light, because the speed of light remains constant, remains the same no matter where it travels.

Einstein went on to develop a General Theory of Relativity that joined elements of gravity, space/time, and matter into a cohesive or unified system. This theory was later used as a basis for theories of the origin of the universe. But Einstein was not completely happy with his work. He did not believe that his theories explained the events in the world of subatomic particles, such as electrons. You see, an observer cannot say that an electron is in a certain place at a certain time, traveling at a certain speed. An observer can say only that there is a *probability* of finding an electron in such and such a place at such and such a time when it is traveling at such and such a speed.

Einstein was puzzled by this problem most of his adult life. He tried and tried to find a unified field theory that could explain all electric, magnetic, optical, and gravitational events and locate them in space and time. He died, as we know, without succeeding. Nevertheless, he tried until the end of his life to prove his belief that "God does not play dice with the universe," that everything is not just left to chance.

So how long will Einstein's paradigm last? You think it will last a long time, don't you? It certainly does explain some aspects of our world very well. Ah, yes, but so does the mathematics of Newton.

So where do we stand now in terms of a unified field theory? Is it a myth, or perhaps a religious notion that we inherited from our ancestors? Or is all of nature truly unified in ways we can't see yet, but may discover one day. Is the unified field theory within reach, or is the search for it just a wild goose chase? Neils Bohr, one of the fathers of quantum theory, has suggested that we simply may not be looking in the right places. He believes that mathematical models are not able to describe all events in nature. Perhaps now we must use symbols and metaphors from other areas of human interest to explain the world. And this brings us back to where we started: combining physics, the study of nature, with religion and myth or metaphysics.

Well, I think this is a good spot to break. Next time we'll continue our look at the search for a unified field theory. So be sure to review the chapters on Einstein's Special and General Theories of Relativity and begin the next chapter on quantum mechanics.

Giving and Receiving Compliments

1 Listening for Appropriate and Inappropriate Compliments. Page 117.

Conversation 1
Ron and Mr. McGovern are in the hall after class.

Ron:	Mr. McGovern, you are such a very good teacher. I like your class so much. I'm learning so much. I like you so-o-o much.
Mr. McGovern:	Oh, uh . . . thank you, Ron. Well, I'm on my way to an appointment right now. I'll talk to you later.

Question 1: Ron's compliments to Mr. McGovern are inappropriate. What's wrong with Ron's timing?
Question 2: What's wrong with the number of compliments?
Question 3: What's wrong with the phrasing?

Conversation 2
Sandra and Mr. McGovern are in the professor's office during office hours.

Sandra:	Oh, Mr. McGovern, that was a great class. I never understood the second law of thermodynamics before, and now I feel like I could explain it to anyone else who doesn't understand it.
Mr. McGovern:	Thank you, Sandra. I appreciate your saying that.

Question 1: Are Sandra's compliments to Mr. McGovern appropriate?
Question 2: Why or why not? Consider location of the interaction, number of compliments, and phrasing in your answer.

Conversation 3
Helen, Larry, and Martin are chatting at a retirement home.

Martin:	Larry! Helen! Hello! Who's winning?
Helen:	Oh, hello, Martin.
Larry:	Hi, Martin. Not me! I can never seem to beat Helen at checkers. Just between you and me, she's definitely the checkers champion around here.
Helen:	Oh, I wouldn't say that. I just win a few games now and then.
Martin:	Oh, no, Helen, Larry's right. You're definitely the best player here.
Helen:	Well, thank you both very much.
Larry:	Hey, Martin, you were looking pretty good last night at the party. I couldn't believe how well you danced! I didn't know you knew how to do all that.
Martin:	I don't! It was my first time— my daughter pulled me out onto the dance floor and I had to do it. But I wasn't really any good. In fact, I was terrible. You know that law of nature that says, "You just can't teach an old dog new tricks"!

Helen:	Come on, Marty. That's not a law of nature! This is the generation dedicated to the principle of lifelong learning! And I don't mind telling you that you looked just fine out on the dance floor. And what's more, your daughter looked simply beautiful!
Martin:	Well, thanks. Coming from you, that means a lot. You're quite a dancer yourself.
Helen:	Oh, I can't take all the credit. My partner helped some.
Larry:	Oh, no, I hardly did anything. Helen really is a wonderful dancer. She's so graceful and light on her feet. She should give lessons. Better yet, she should go on stage in New York or be in the movies. She's as good as any of the dancers you see there.
Helen:	Now Larry, flattery will get you nowhere today. You're losing this game of checkers, and I'm not going to let you win no matter how many compliments you give me.
Martin:	That's telling him, Helen!

Question 1: How does Larry first compliment Helen?
Question 2: What is Helen's response?
Question 3: Why do you think she says this?
Question 4: How does Martin compliment Helen?
Question 5: How does Helen respond this time?
Question 6: What do Helen and Larry tell Martin about his dancing?
Question 7: Who looked beautiful on the dance floor?
Question 8: How does Martin feel about the compliments from Helen?

Conversation 4
Later in the day at the retirement home Helen, Larry, and Martin continue chatting.

Larry:	Martin, what's wrong? You look a bit worried.
Martin:	Well, I'm not worried exactly, but I am confused and feeling very old. I wish I had Helen's attitude about the principle of lifelong learning. You always seem so in touch with current ideas, Helen.
Helen:	I appreciate your saying that, but what brought all this on?
Martin:	Well, I was trying to help my grandson with his physics homework, and I'm afraid I wasn't much help at all. I don't really understand some of the new theories.
Larry:	Well, if you ask me, Martin, you were wonderful to even try to help him. A lot of grandfathers wouldn't take the time.
Martin:	Thanks, I needed that. But I still wish I knew more about what's happening in the field of physics these days.
Larry:	Why is that so important to you?
Martin:	It seems to me that young people today have a different view of the world than we did when we were young, and I'd like to understand it.
Helen:	Well, that's admirable, Martin. Sounds to me like you *are* interested in lifelong learning after all. In fact, I've been meaning to tell you that you're one of the brightest, most stimulating, most adventuresome and forward-thinking men I know.
Martin:	Why, thanks, Helen! That kind of flattery will get you everywhere!

Question 1: What's wrong with Martin?
Question 2: Is the compliment Martin gives Helen appropriate?
Question 3: How does Helen accept this compliment?
Question 4: How does Larry try to cheer Martin up?
Question 5: What does Helen say to encourage Martin?
Question 6: Does it work?
Question 7: How does Martin respond?
Question 8: What does he mean by this?

<table>
<tr><td>**PART 4**</td><td></td></tr>
</table>

PART 4   Focus on Testing. Page 122.

You will hear a short presentation. After the presentation, you will be asked some questions. Circle the letter of the best answer to each question.

Presentation

The German-American physicist Albert Einstein was born on March 14, 1879, and died on April 18, 1955. He contributed more than any other scientist to the break-throughs in our perception of physical reality. No other scientist has received so much public attention for his or her work.

Einstein was not always so successful, however. He lived in Munich until he was about 15 years old. At that time, the family business failed and he and his family moved to Milan, Italy. After a year, Einstein still had not completed secondary school, and he failed the examination to study electrical engineering at the Swiss Federal Institute of Technology. In 1896, at the age of 17, Einstein returned to Switzerland. He graduated in 1900 as a secondary school teacher of mathematics and physics.

After two difficult years on a teacher's salary, he obtained a position at the Swiss patent office in Bern. The patent-office work required Einstein's careful attention, but during the two years he was employed there, he also completed an astounding amount of work in theoretical physics. For the most part, these papers were written in his spare time and without the benefit of books to read or colleagues to talk to.

Einstein submitted one of his scientific papers to the University of Zurich to obtain a Ph.D. degree in 1905. In 1908 he sent a second paper to the University of Bern and was offered a position as a lecturer there. The next year Einstein received a regular appointment as associate professor of physics at the University of Zurich.

By 1909, Einstein was recognized throughout German-speaking Europe as a lead-ing scientific thinker. He worked for a brief time as a professor at the German University of Prague and at Zurich Polytechnic. In 1914, at the age of 35, he advanced to the most prestigious and best-paying post that a theoretical physicist could hold in central Europe: professor at the Kaiser-Wilhelm Gesellschaft in Berlin. Einstein remained on the staff in Berlin until 1933. At that time he came to the United States and held a research position at the Institute for Advanced Study in Princeton, New Jersey, until his death in 1955.

Question 1: When did Einstein die?
Question 2: Why did Einstein's family move to Milan?
Question 3: What was Einstein's first job?

Question 4: What did Einstein do in his spare time when he worked at the patent office?

Question 5: Which institution gave Einstein his Ph.D. degree?

Question 6: Where did Einstein die?

Chapter 9   Art and Entertainment

PART 2   Distinguishing between Fact and Opinion

Radio Program: The Rise of Rock 'n' Roll

Announcer: Welcome to *Music in America,* a production of Wisconsin Radio. This is program number six: "The Rise of Rock 'n' Roll."

Lecturer: So far in this series on music in America, we've talked about music and how it enhances the lives of all people. Musicologists agree that music is a universal phenomenon. Even though music may be a universal phenomenon and every society may have music, it is very different from culture to culture. Music reflects the social order. I think musicians and their audiences use music to reaffirm their feelings about themselves and their society. So it seems to me that the music of a particular culture reflects that culture's values. Therefore, I also think that music has the most meaning for the people from the culture in which it was created.

Now, from that perspective, let's look at the rise of rock 'n' roll in America. The term *rock 'n' roll* comes from Alan Freed, who was a popular disc jockey in the 1950s. He got the phrase from a line in an old blues song that goes, "My baby rocks me with a steady roll."

This story reflects an important element in rock 'n' roll, that is, its origins in the blues. As you know, the blues are part of the black musical tradition in America. But I think that the actual beginning of rock 'n' roll music occurred on April 12, 1954, in New York City when Bill Haley and the Comets recorded "Rock around the Clock." When you have a chance, listen to this famous song. It is a perfect example of how the blues harmonies of black music were mixed with the hillbilly country sounds of white music to become the earliest form of rock 'n' roll. This early form of rock 'n' roll was called rockabilly. This name still nostalgically refers to the type of music in which you can hear blues harmonies and country rhythms blending with the guitar sounds of rock 'n' roll. You can easily hear this rockabilly influence in Elvis Presley's music, especially in songs like his 1950s hit "Heartbreak Hotel."

Rock 'n' roll music of the '50s was, for the most part, youth music, the music of young people. And not all people enjoyed it, not even those people with youthful spirits. Pablo Casals, the famous classical cellist, said that rock 'n' roll was "poison put to sound." Mitch Miller, the famous bandleader, said, "The reason kids like rock 'n' roll is because their parents don't." Most likely teenagers in every society have rebelled against or resisted their parents in some way. In the '50s in the United States, rock 'n' roll was a focus for this adolescent rebellion.

Songs of the '50s, however, did not speak out strongly against the values of the adults in the society. But the songs of the 1960s certainly did. Teenagers who listened to rockabilly in the '50s became college students in the '60s. In the '60s there was a mood of confusion and instability. The Vietnam War was beginning; the civil rights movement in the early '60s pointed out many racial injustices in America. College students looked to folk values of the past for strength and peace of mind. The music that supported these values was called folk-rock.

In the early '60s, the star of the folk scene was Bob Dylan. His song "The Times They Are a' Changing" was a protest against tradition and indifference. In the song "Blowin' in the Wind," he asked that people stop being indifferent, that they become involved with important issues in the world.

Many people thought that Bob Dylan was more a poet than a songwriter. A lot of his poetry dealt with the dishonesty of people in authority, and frequently his songs became songs of protest.

In the middle '60s, with Dylan's music, protest-rock was born. Dylan generally provided his own accompaniment at folk-rock concerts using only acoustic guitar and mouth organ, a simplicity of style that was connected to a return to simple, basic folk values. At the Newport Folk Festival in 1965, he appeared on stage with an electric guitar and was booed off the stage. Although his concert audiences obviously didn't care for the electronic sound, record buyers apparently did, and protest rock became a major movement of the electronic age.

Some other participants in this movement were P. F. Sloan, who wrote "Eve of Destruction," about the fear of nuclear war, and Tom Paxton and Phil Ochs, whose songs protested segregation, the Vietnam War, and racism, as well as the evils of atomic warfare.

Right along with folk-rock and protest-rock came the British sound. In 1960, a group called The Silver Beatles was playing in the Indra Club in Hamburg, Germany. They had made a record that showed the influence of Elvis Presley and 1950s rockabilly on their music. After several name changes and a change of drummers, they became the Beatles.

By 1963, the Beatles had a gold record, "She Loves You," and in 1964 they had four singles on the best-seller charts. Then they came to America. When they appeared on the Ed Sullivan show, three out of every four TV sets in New York were tuned in to watch them. Because of the way they looked, wearing stiff white collars under collarless jackets— almost like choirboy outfits— and having well groomed if somewhat long hair, they appeared respectable to adults. Their appearance was a far cry from the black leather jackets and greasy hair of the '50s rock 'n' rollers, and it seemed to parents even further from the bare feet, stringy hair, and vacant eyes they associated with folk-rock and protest-rock.

The Beatles also had a good sense of humor. When they played for the Queen Mother and Princess Margaret in 1963 at a royal command performance, John said, "The people in the cheap seats can clap. The rest of you just rattle your jewelry." Unlike Dylan, the Beatles did not start out writing protest songs per se; they wrote humorous put-downs of values and conditions, not just of people in power. "A Hard Day's Night" is typical of this.

Most people like the Beatles now, but I remember that in 1966, their music got mixed reviews. The American composer Aaron Copland said that their music had an un-analyzable charm, while Richard Rodgers, who wrote Broadway musicals, said it was monotonous and boring. Some music critics said it wouldn't last.

By 1967, it was clear that it would. Richard Goldstein, the rock critic, said the Beatles were creating the most original, expressive, and musically interesting sounds in popular music. A good example of their original sound is "Sgt. Pepper's Lonely Hearts Club Band." Probably most of you have heard this one.

A major British invasion came with the Beatles. For example, there were the Rolling Stones, who were outrageous compared to the Beatles. Their statements were not gentle or humorous, and they challenged social rules with the suggestive words in their songs. "Satisfaction" and "Let's Spend the Night Together," now famous worldwide, are good examples. When they were on the Ed Sullivan show, the words "the night" were changed to "some time" because of censorship regulations.

Although the British did bring their own unique sounds, the blues, as I said before, is a major factor in all rock 'n' roll music. Eric Clapton, the famous British guitarist, said, "Rock is like a battery that must always go back to the blues to get recharged." An interesting combination of blues melody and soft-rock can be heard in Procol Harum's "A Whiter Shade of Pale."

Soul music also emerged in the '60s. Soul music emerged with the civil rights movement as an expression of black pride. African-Americans were now a people who no longer would accept second-class citizenship. They were proud of their identity and proud of their music. And the rest of the country loved it, too. The most important soul music came out of Motown—Motortown—the city of Detroit. The essence of soul music is apparent in "Natural Woman," a song made famous by Aretha Franklin, soul singer extraordinaire.

Today's popular music has come a long way from the rock 'n' roll of the '60s. On our next program, we'll finish talking about the '60s and continue with the rise of rock through the present day. Yes, rock 'n' roll is definitely here to stay.

Expressing Doubt or Disbelief

Listening for Expressions of Doubt.   Page 136.

1 **Conversation 1**

Carl discusses a project with Professor Johnson.

Carl:	Professor Johnson, I'd like to talk to you about my art project for my senior thesis.
Prof. Johnson:	No time like the present, Carl. Have a seat. What would you like to do?
Carl:	Are you sure it's okay? I know how busy you are.
Prof. Johnson:	It's fine.
Carl:	Well, I'd like to do something really imaginative and creative, something like my friend Howard did for his master's thesis.
Prof. Johnson:	What was that?
Carl:	He filled the administration building entrance hall with white paper cups and that was his project.
Prof. Johnson:	And he got his master's for that?
Carl:	Yes, he did.
Prof. Johnson:	I find that hard to believe. You'll have to think of something else, Carl, another type of project.

Question 1:   What expression does Carl use to express doubt?
Question 2:   Why do you think he uses that expression?
Question 3:   Professor Johnson expresses disbelief twice in this conversation. Is he polite to Carl?
Question 4:   The first time he expresses disbelief through intonation alone. What words does he use?
Question 5:   What expression does he use the second time?

Conversation 2

Mr. Jones chats with Mr. Smith about his son's band.

Mr. Jones:	My 12-year-old son is in a rock band, and the band is going to make $30 million in the next three months.
Mr. Smith:	Get outta here. The Rolling Stones only make $58 million in a whole year!
Mr. Jones:	Yes, they really will. And the most amazing thing is that they have a 12-year-old manager. She does all the negotiating for the concerts.
Mr. Smith:	Oh, sure!
Mr. Jones:	Yes, and she's really first-rate. These 12-year-olds are booked for concerts in New York, Chicago, Denver, Los Angeles, Atlanta, Detroit, and Philadelphia in the next four weeks alone.
Mr. Smith:	Yeah, right, and I'm Mick Jagger.

Question 1:   Is this conversation formal or informal?
Question 2:   When the second speaker says "Get outta here," does he sound amused or angry?
Question 3:   How does the second speaker sound when he says, "Oh, sure!"?
Question 4:   When the second speaker says "Yeah, right, and I'm Mick Jagger," does he sound rude?
Question 5:   Why do you think the second speaker expresses disbelief this way?

Conversation 3

Jenny and Al talk about dancing.

Jenny:	I'd really love to be a prima ballerina.
Al:	Well then, you'll have to do more than take lessons once a week. Nureyev danced until his feet bled, and he kept on dancing.
Jenny:	I find that hard to believe. How do you know that?
Al:	I saw it in a movie. He was so dedicated you wouldn't believe it! With bleeding feet he just danced and danced and danced some more. I saw it all in the movie.
Jenny:	Could he really do that?
Al:	Yes, it was the most incredible thing I've ever seen.

Question 1:   Are Jenny's expressions of disbelief formal or informal?
Question 2:   Is she polite or rude?
Question 3:   What are some expressions Jenny uses?

Conversation 4

Rachael attends Professor Starr's music appreciation class.

Prof. Starr:	Today I'm going to talk about Mozart, the musical genius who performed concerts on the pianoforte for the royalty of Europe at the age of eight.
Rachel:	Oh, come on!
Prof. Starr:	It's true. Not only that, he was already composing music at the age of five.
Rachel:	I doubt it.
Prof. Starr:	Well, why don't you see me after class for my list of references if you'd like to look into the matter further. But for now we'll concentrate on a discussion of Mozart's music.

Question 1:   Are Rachel's expressions of disbelief formal or informal?
Question 2:   Is she polite or rude?
Question 3:   Does the professor seem impatient with Rachel?
Question 4:   What are some expressions Rachel uses?

Focus on Testing. Page 140.

You will hear a short review of a music festival. After the review, you will be asked some questions. Circle the letter of the best answer to each question.

Music Review

Bethel, New York, August 29, 1969. The Woodstock Music and Art Fair in Bethel, New York, was advertised by its youthful New York promoters as "An Aquarian Exposition" of music and peace. It was that and more, much more. The festival, quickly nicknamed "Woodstock," may have turned out to be history's largest "happening." As the moment when the U.S. youth of the '60s openly displayed its strength, appeal, and power, Woodstock may rank as one of the most significant political and sociological events of the age.

By a conservative estimate, more than 400,000 people, the vast majority of them between the ages of 16 and 30, showed up for the Woodstock Festival. Thousands more would have come if police had not blocked off some of the access roads. Other roads turned into long, ribbonlike parking lots as spectators simply left their cars rather than wait for hours in a traffic jam. If the festival had lasted much longer, as many as one million youths might have made the pilgrimage to Bethel to participate in the Woodstock Festival.

What lured our country's youth to Woodstock? An all-star cast of top rock artists, including Janis Joplin, Jimi Hendrix, and the Jefferson Airplane. But the good vibrations of good groups turned out to be the least of it. What the youth of America and their worried elders saw at Bethel was the potential power of an entire generation, a generation that in countless disturbing ways had rejected the traditional values and goals of the United States. Over 400,000 young people, who had previously thought of themselves as part of an isolated minority, experienced the thrill of discovering that they were, as the saying goes, "what's happening." They were the current voice of America.

To many adults, the festival seemed like a monstrous Dionysian orgy, a wild party where a mob of crazy kids gathered to take drugs and groove and move to hours and hours of amplified noise that could hardly be called music. The significance of Woodstock, however, cannot be overestimated. Despite the piles of litter and garbage, the hopelessly inadequate sanitation, the lack of food, and the two nights of rain that turned Yasgur's farm in Bethel, New York, into a sea of mud, the young people found it all "beautiful." One long-haired teenager summed up the significance of Woodstock quite simply: "The people," he said, "are finally getting together."

Question 1:   Which item describes the festival?
Question 2:   What was the nickname for the festival?
Question 3:   How many people went to the festival?
Question 4:   How old were most of the people who came to the festival?
Question 5:   Why did the young people go to the festival?
Question 6:   According to the reviewer, which of the items was *not* a problem at the festival?

Resident Advisors Training Session: Dealing with Conflicts

Head Resident Advisor (RA): OK, guys! Today's the last session before your final test to qualify to become a resident advisor. Next week's test will be on today's topic—conflict resolution—and then the week after next, the students arrive. This year we have a record number of international students entering the university. I understand that many of you are international students, too. That will be a great help I think. Let's see, how many of you are international students? I see seven hands up. That's about 30 percent. Great!

Now, how many of you have had previous training in conflict resolution? Six out of twenty– that's pretty good. Well, today's session may be old hat for you. So please feel free to interrupt if you've got But before we go into conflict resolution, let's review the principles of making friends we talked about last week. These principles can be useful if you've got a student who's having trouble making friends or having conflicts with others as well as. Believe it or not, these principles are based on Dale Carnegie's 1937—yes 1937—bestseller *How to Win Friends and Influence People*. And I think they're still as true as they were then. Giving students this information can help prevent conflicts. Look at your handout on the seven principles of making friends as we review these principles.

Principle #1: Try to praise people. Speak honestly about how or why you appreciate them.

Principle #2: Be indirect when you talk about someone's mistakes.

Principle #3: Talk about your mistakes first, not others'.

Principle #4: If possible, try to ask questions; don't give orders.

Principle #5: If people make mistakes, let them save face by praising all improvements.

Principle #6: Give people a fine reputation to live up to, that is, set a good example.

And finally, principle #7: Always try to be encouraging.

So now that we've refreshed our memory about these seven principles, let's look at the steps to take if you're going to do conflict resolution with, for example, two roommates, or any two students in the dorms who have a conflict. You can be sure these steps will be on next week's test.

The first step is to get the two people who are having the conflict to cool off or chill out. Anger is the emotion that people have the most difficulty controlling, and when people are angry they don't make good decisions. Therefore it is not surprising that anger sometimes leads to rage or violence. How can you get people to cool down? Here are a few ways:

- You can distract them. For example, tell a joke. It's hard to stay angry when you're laughing.
- You can encourage them to exercise, such as playing a game of basketball or another sport. Anger is a high arousal state, and exercise changes a high arousal state to a low arousal state.
- You can get them to write their angry thoughts instead of saying them to the other person. Verbalizing anger may feel satisfying, but it increases the arousal state, which will certainly not help resolve the conflict.

After you've gotten the angry person to cool off, go to Step 2: Get the people to talk and listen to each other. How do you do that?

Well, first, have one student state the problem completely. Then the second student should restate what the first is saying to make sure he or she understands. Encourage the second student to begin these restatements with things like, "What I hear you saying is…", "One concern you have is …", "What bothers you is . . .", or "What you're afraid of is . . .". Then have the students change roles. The second one should state his or her view of the problem, and the first one should restate what is said to make sure he or she understands. During the process, you, as the advisor, should keep asking, "Is there anything else?" until there is nothing else either of the students wants to say.

The third step is to be clear about what each student needs. To be sure that each student's interests are being considered, make a list. Be sure you give the person time to think about what his or her most important needs or priorities are in the situation.

Remember the old Jack Benny joke. Do you guys know it?

Group of RAs:	No, never heard it. Which one? Huh?
Head RA:	Well, a robber comes up and pulls a gun on Jack Benny and says, "Your money or your life," and Jack Benny hesitates. The robber becomes impatient and says again and again, "Your money or your life." Finally Jack replies, "I'm thinking … I'm thinking."
Group of RAs:	(Laughter)
Head RA:	In other words, give each person time to figure out what his or her priorities or most important needs are.

There's one thing you have to be careful about during this part of the process. When students in conflict are talking about their feelings, tell them to make "I" statements. In other words, they should talk about themselves and their feelings and concerns, not the other student's faults. They should say for example, "It bothers me when people don't look at me when they talk to me" instead of "You never look at me when you talk to me." They should say "I feel confused when people say 'you know' and I don't know" instead of "You always assume I know things that I don't." And here's one more example: They should say, "I get nervous when people make plans for me without consulting me" instead of saying "You're always trying to tell me what to do."

OK, so now what do you do after the two students have heard and restated each other's views of the situation and made lists of what they each need? Step 4 is for you to help them brainstorm solutions. The rule to follow here is that these solutions must honor all their concerns.

Then consider each of the brainstorming ideas. Make these ideas into trial balloons and test them out. Discuss each solution in turn and see which one will fly by discussing the consequences of actually doing it. Remember: the real solution may be a combination of several ideas. So at this stage in the process you must keep asking both people, "Are you still feeling happy about the process?" Remember that there is no one right way. At this point you are just generating ideas, and you want to make sure that both students trust that you are not choosing sides.

The fifth step is to evaluate the solution. Each step is important, and this one is no exception. In fact, this one is so important that it's worth writing it out in black and white. Yes, put it on paper. Each student takes a sheet of paper and writes out the pros and cons for each of the brainstormed solutions. Just the action of putting on paper the possible solutions and the advantages and disadvantages of each of them can help both people clarify their views. At this time, let people express their reservations. Listen for statements like, "I hear what you're saying, but…" " I have a problem with…" " I guess so, but…" "one drawback I feel is…" or " I'm not sure that will work for me because…" Remember, Socrates said "Know thyself." It's very good advice and is really important in conflict resolution. Unless you are really clear about what you want, it's difficult to come to compromise.

Also, when you are doing conflict resolution, notice the body language. For example, is the speaker talking with folded arms or hands on the hips? Does the speaker shake a fist or wag a finger? Does the speaker move into or back away from the other person's space?

Next is Step 6: this is where you help the students choose one of the solutions or make a combination solution. In this step, both people must agree on a solution, one that is acceptable to both of them. This step will take some more negotiation. There must be some give-and-take. Be sure to have both parties buy into the agreement. If you hear one person say, "I trust you completely," that's good, but if you hear "Do whatever you think is best" or "Whatever you say" watch out. It's a sign that someone has acquiesced but hasn't really bought into the situation. The person does not really like the agreement, and that could mean trouble later. To make this step in the process work, start with the big picture, that is, the basic problem and all its consequences and the best solution and all its consequences. Each person should restate what he or she thinks the big picture is. Then help the two students create a shared vision and make commitments to action within a time frame. Work on the agreement until everyone is satisfied.

Finally, the last step: agree on contingencies, ways to monitor, and a time to reevaluate.

No matter how good your agreement is, how well intentioned each person is, and how clear both people are, circumstances change and there must be a way to deal with these changes. An unexpected event could happen after your agreement, but before you can start to implement the new plan. Part of the contingencies should be a way to get out of the agreement, specifically a way to get out without loss of face. And be sure to agree on some way to measure the outcome. It should be a yes/no measure. Either they did accomplish various parts of the agreement or they didn't. How will the agreement be monitored? Everyone has to agree on this. When will the agreement be reevaluated? Everyone should agree on this too. Any questions?

So there you have it guys – seven steps to conflict resolution. The test is next Wednesday. Good luck, and I'll see all you 'round the dorms.

| PART 3 | **Acquiescing and Expressing Reservations** |

1   Listening for Acquiescence and Reservations. Page 151.

RA:	I'm glad you guys have agreed to get together to resolve your conflict. Let's start with James. What's the problem, James?
Mohammed:	Why should he start? I'm the one who was insulted.
RA:	Whatever you say, then let's start with you, Mohammed.
James:	If you think that's best.
Mohammed:	I want a new roommate because James hates me.
James:	What do you mean I hate you? I don't hate you. Where did you get that idea?
Mohammed:	Well, you always sit facing me with your feet on the desk.
RA:	Oh! I see what the problem is. James, in Mohammed's culture, if you show someone the bottoms of your feet, it is a great insult.
James:	Oh, OK. I didn't mean anything insulting by that. I was just comfortable with my feet up. I can move my feet.
Mohammed:	OK then.
James:	Yes, but the question really is, is that enough? I don't know enough about Mohammed's culture and I'm afraid that I'll do something wrong again.
RA:	I think you guys should give being roommates another month. If there are still problems, we can see about changing roommates. What do you think?
James and Mohammed:	I'm willing to go along with that. OK, let's try it.

Question 1:   Why does the resident advisor allow Mohammed to speak first?

Question 2:   What expression does James use to acquiesce?

Question 3:   What is the problem?

Question 4:   What expression does James use to express reservations?

Question 5:   What do James and Mohammed agree to try?

Question 6:   What expressions do they use to show that they have acquiesced?

2   Listening for Suggestions about Conflict Resolution. Page 152.
See the Resident Advisors' Training Session.

3   Listening for Ways to Express Reservations. Page 153.
See the Resident Advisors' Training Session.

PART 4   Focus on Testing. Page 155.

Listen to Professor Taylor and some students discuss an upcoming exam. Then listen to the questions. Circle the letter of the best answer to each question.

Classroom Discussion

Professor Taylor: Let me review what will be on the exam next Monday and what will be on the final exam. For Monday's exam we'll cover the history of the conflicts in the Middle East and in Northern Ireland. We will not cover the conflicts in Africa. That will be on the final exam. You will be responsible for everything we've covered in lectures and discussion sections as well as the readings of course. In addition, you will be responsible for the class presentations your classmates made.

Mary: Will it be open book?

Classmates: (Laughter.)

Professor Taylor: No, it won't be open book.

Jim: What kinds of questions will there be?

Professor Taylor: The first part will be definitions, so that could be matching or short answer. I don't know because I haven't written it yet. The second part will be true/false and the third part will be an essay in which you have synthesize the concepts we've covered so far. You'll have to take a point of view and defend your position with specific examples. So there will be true/false and short answer questions for sure.

Penny: What about the exam after that?

Professor Taylor: Well, Penny, normally I'd say wait and see, but I do want to give you guys a head start because that will be a ten-page take home exam.

Students: Ugh. Whatever you say.

Professor Taylor: OK, guys. That's it for today. Study hard this weekend. See you Monday.

Question 1: What will be on Monday's exam?
Question 2: For which of the following will the students not be responsible?
Question 3: What kinds of questions will be on Monday's exam for sure?
Question 4: What kind of exam is the final exam?
Question 5: What advice does the professor give the students?

Chapter 11   Medicine and Science

PART 2   Cohesion and Reference

Discussion: Organ Transplants

Richard: Hey, listen to this. Remember that kid, David, the five-year-old who was dying of an incurable liver disease? You know—his condition was irreversible and his parents were frantically searching for some sort of a solution?

Susan: Oh, yeah. I remember. They had been told that David's only hope was a liver transplant from a compatible donor.

Richard: Right. David needed to get a healthy liver from another child who had just died, and he was put on the waiting list for a compatible donor.

Susan: So what happened?

Richard: Well, the waiting list for a liver transplant was so long that David's parents took matters into their own hands. They made nationwide appeals on TV and radio looking for a donor. It was in the papers, too.

Susan: Yeah, I remember that, but were they successful?

Richard: Yeah. Another five-year-old child, two thousand miles away, was hit by a car. The child was declared legally dead.

Susan: That means that the boy's brain is dead, but his body organs were still functioning, right?

Richard: Right. So anyway, this boy's parents hoped that their son's liver could help. Within a few hours, their boy's liver was removed and flown in a picnic cooler to David's doctors, who replaced David's diseased liver with the new one.

Susan: Gosh, that's fantastic.

Richard: Yup. And a week later David is playing with his toys in his hospital room, and his prognosis is very good. Pretty great, huh?

Susan: Yeah, pretty terrific for David. But, you know, there is a downside to this organ transplant thing.

Richard: Really? What's that?

Susan: For people who are dying of degenerative organ diseases, it's wonderful that there have been such great advances in immunosuppression and surgical techniques that people such as David can be given a second chance at life. But there are a few big ethical questions.

Richard: Like what?

Susan:	Like who should be allowed to live.
Richard:	Allowed?
Susan:	Yup, allowed. The patients needing organs vastly outnumber donors, those who can give organs. It's been estimated that only 10 percent of the people who can donate organs actually do donate them. Because of this, each year, thousands of people who could be saved by a routine transplant die.
Richard:	With such a small number of donated organs, I think that selecting recipients should be a question of national concern. What if there's only one organ available and many needy patients? Who should receive it? The nuclear scientist or the retarded child? And what about the alcoholic or smoker who voluntarily contributed to the degeneration of his or her own body? You're right. Transplants are a big ethical question!
Susan:	Yeah, and besides, who should make this decision and by what criteria? There is this one well-known example. It's the old lifeboat example. You know it?
Richard:	I heard it once, but I've forgotten it. How does it go again?
Susan:	OK. Well, imagine that you are one of 16 people in a lifeboat designed to hold only 13 people. As the sea becomes rougher, it is clear to all of you in the boat that the boat will sink unless at least three people jump into the sea. The people who go overboard will die. So how would you decide who stays in the boat and who must go? What criteria should be used to make these decisions and who should make them? Should the person with the highest rank—such as the ship's captain—make the decision? If so, do you trust his or her fairness? Should women, children, and married men always be saved first? Or perhaps the old and the sick should go overboard, because they have only a short time left to live? Maybe you think that each person is equal to every other person? In that case, the only fair method of decision would be some sort of a lottery.
Richard:	The lifeboat story is a good analogy, Susan. I don't know what the answer is, but I know that I wouldn't want organs just to go to the highest bidder—you know—the person with the most money.
Susan:	Me either! The ethical dilemma is obvious. What if people start to make a business of buying and selling organs? Can we let private interests in this country control organ transplants? In other situations like this where the public welfare is affected so dramatically, the government here has always intervened. You know, like with trucking strikes or with toxic waste disposal.
Richard:	Uh-huh, the idea of buying and selling organs is definitely ugly. I thought that, recently, laws have been proposed that would make this a crime. And that these laws would place the allocation of this precious commodity entirely in the hands of the federal government. Even in a capitalist country there is something unacceptable about the idea that life or death might depend only on the checkbook—only on the amount of money in your bank account. Not only that but . . .

Susan:	Hold on a minute. Even if we decide that organs ought to be distributed fairly, with no discrimination for any reason, we still have another major problem. We still have too many needy people and not enough donors.
Richard:	Oh yeah, right. I forgot about that for a minute. That was David's problem. I don't know how the government can help with that.
Susan:	Well, in my class we talked about this dilemma from a number of points of view. First, look at the donor side of the problem. The class came up with some interesting suggestions, I think. How about increasing the number of available organs by simplifying the donation process? Or how about writing laws that require everybody to donate organs if doctors say the brain is dead? And listen to this. We could establish a national organ bank and put all brain-dead people in the same hospital.
Richard:	What for?
Susan:	Well, that way doctors in that hospital would keep their organs alive artificially until they are needed. I suppose this would be something like harvesting the dead, though.
Richard:	Yeah, I agree. So much for increasing the number of donors. What about the recipients? Any good suggestions?
Susan:	Maybe. We discussed the usefulness of the recipient to society.
Richard:	Like the lifeboat example.
Susan:	Exactly. Why not give those who might benefit society the most the best chance to live? The response to that argument has often been that few people, if any, have the wisdom to see what the social good is now. Nor can they see what it will be in the future. What if the convicted criminal we choose to push overboard today changes, and ten years from now helps hundreds of young people with drug problems.
Richard:	Right. Who can know the future for sure?
Susan:	I don't know. But we came up with a couple of other solutions, which have to do with basic health and humaneness. For instance, there could be an agreed-upon standard of health that every person is entitled to. People who are furthest from this state of health— but not yet irreversibly damaged—would be treated first. This means that the people who are the worst off would get the organs first.
Richard:	Hey! Now you're talking. That sounds great.
Susan:	Maybe. The problem with this position is still the shortage of organs and the large number of needy people. What if three people are in immediate danger of dying from kidney failure, but there is only one kidney? Then this solution doesn't help.
Richard:	Of course. Boy! This is really a complex issue!
Susan:	Uh-huh. And what about those people who have destroyed their organs with alcohol or drugs? Should we discriminate against them and put them last on the list? And first help the people who suffer from genetic or infectious diseases?
Richard:	Good point. I don't know. Maybe the fairest thing would be a lottery. At least then the decision would not be made by any one person or

group, and the people who do not receive organs in time might die more peacefully, knowing that their chance to live had been as good as anyone else's. What do you think?

Susan: Well, I don't know. At least they would know that no one discriminated against them for any reason. But special exceptions would probably have to be made. Like for the president, for example. If the president needed a transplant, should he or she be allowed to have it before the person who won the lottery?

Richard: Well, it looks like we aren't going to come up with the perfect solution— agreeable to everyone— this morning. It's really overwhelming to realize that certain ethical choices can mean that one person will live and others will probably die.

Susan: Right. So what else is happening in the news? Or better yet, why don't we look at the comics for a while?

PART 3 # Taking and Keeping the Floor

1 **Listening for Expressions for Taking and Keeping the Floor.   Page 171.**

Conversation 1
Erik and Sylvia are talking in the cafeteria after class.

Erik: Sylvia, I hear they're doing great things now in the field of genetic engineering.

Sylvia: Well, Erik, our biology professor spoke to us today about how experimenting with genes can be dangerous. He said—

Erik: That's true, but—

Sylvia: Wait, Erik. Let me just tell you the main point he made. He said that newly created genes could accidentally enter the gene pool and cause unimaginable-

Erik: Yes, but Sylvia—

Sylvia: Let me just finish what I was saying. These new genes could cause unimaginable genetic changes in the world. And what if these changes were worse than the problems the new genes were developed to correct?

Erik: Yeah, I see what you mean. I hadn't thought of that.

Question 1: What nonverbal cue might Erik have used when he said, "That's true, but—"

Question 2: What nonverbal cue might Erik have used when he said, "Yes, but—"?

Question 3: What nonverbal cue might Sylvia have used when she said, "Let me just tell you the main point he made"?

Question 4: What nonverbal cue might Sylvia have used when she said, "Let me finish what I was saying"?

Conversation 2

A teaching assistant and some students are in class.

> *TA:* Well, to continue with some examples of issues that fall into the area of ethics, I'd like to talk about some of the problems with euthanasia.
>
> *Sally:* Oh, are the youth in Asia having problems these days?
>
> *TA:* That's very clever, Sally—now where was I? Oh, yes, the issue of choosing to die instead of living in pain and suffering because of serious disease or aging. The first problem seems to be whether we ever have the right to take another life or not. The law, in fact, says that we certainly do not.
>
> *Gina:* If I could interrupt, I believe some states allow for extenuating circumstances. It would be quite interesting to see how various governmental bodies deal with an ethical issue such as this.
>
> *Fred:* Excuse me for interrupting, but I already have that information because of the research I did for a term paper I wrote on a similar topic for another class. I could bring it in next time, if you like.
>
> *TA:* Sure Fred, that would save us quite a bit of time. Thank you.

Question 1: Was Sally's interruption about youth in Asia polite or impolite? Why?

Question 2: Was Gina's interruption about states allowing for extenuating circumstances polite or impolite? Why?

Question 3: Was Fred's interruption about research for a term paper polite or impolite? Why?

PART 4

Focus on Testing. Page 174.

You will hear a short human interest story. After the story, you will be asked some questions. Circle the letter of the best answer to each question.

Human Interest Story

This week a 14-month-old girl named Marissa Ayala donated a cupful of her bone marrow to her 19-year-old sister, Anissa. As Marissa lay anesthetized on an operating table, a surgeon inserted a 1-inch-long needle into the baby's hip and slowly withdrew the bone marrow. The medical team then rushed the marrow to a hospital room where her older sister, Anissa, lay waiting. If all goes well, if rejection does not occur and a major infection does not set in, the marrow will give life to the older sister, who otherwise could die of chronic myelogenous leukemia. Doctors rate the chance of success at 70%.

This dramatic story becomes even more poignant when we realize that Marissa's parents decided to make a baby—to conceive Marissa—in order to create a compatible bone marrow donor for their daughter Anissa. To many people, the fact that the Ayalas were able to accomplish this seemed like a miracle. To others, it seemed more like a profound horror. It called up brutal images—baby farming, harvesting living bodies for spare parts. Many saw in the story of the Ayala family the near edge of a dangerous slippery slope into a dark abyss.

A bone marrow transplant represents very little risk to the donor. And the Ayalas, of course, say they never considered aborting the fetus if its marrow did not match Anissa's. Still, what disturbed many people was that the baby was brought into the world to be used—and used without her consent. And the question remains: Would the baby have agreed to her own conception for such a purpose? And what if amniocentesis showed that the bone marrow of the fetus was not compatible for transplant? Should the Ayalas have been allowed to abort the fetus and then try again?

Just what sort of harvesting of living bodies is all right? Most organs come from cadavers, but the number of living donors is rising. There were 1,788 last year, up 15% from 1989. Of these, 1,773 provided kidneys, nine provided portions of livers. Six of the living donors gave their hearts away. How? They were patients who needed heart-lung transplant packages. To make way for the new heart, they gave up the old one; doctors call it the "domino practice."

There will never be enough cadaver organs to fill the growing needs of people dying from organ or tissue failure. Federal law now prohibits any compensation for organs in the United States. In China and India, however, there is a brisk trade in such organs as kidneys. Will the day come when Americans have a similar marketplace for organs? Turning the body into a commodity might, in fact, make families willing to donate organs. Would a family be willing to say, "We sold Joey's kidneys"? I don't think so.

Question 1:   Where did the bone marrow for the transplant come from?
Question 2:   What are the chances that this procedure will save Anissa?
Question 3:   What disturbed many people about this story?
Question 4:   Why do living patients sometimes donate their hearts for transplants?
Question 5:   Which country mentioned in the story prohibits people from selling organs?

Chapter 12 | The Future

PART 2 | Critical Thinking

Discussion: The World in the 21st Century

Dad:	Wow! Far out! Here's the first paper I wrote when I started college. I remember this paper well. Wanna hear it?
Ted and Jenny:	Sure, Dad. Let's hear it.
Dad:	OK. Here goes. "What will the world be like in the year 2000?" How's that for an opening line?
Ted:	Sounds kind of funny now.
Jenny:	Yeah, but I'm curious to hear what you thought our world would be like. Go on, Dad.
Dad:	OK. "The 21st century may bring many serious problems. According to a study commissioned by President Carter in 1975, the number of poor and hungry people will rapidly increase between now and the year 2000. At the same time, there will be a decrease in the available food to eat and land on which to plant food crops. The four billion

people living on earth today will grow to over six billion by the year 2000 and to over ten billion by the year 2030."

Jenny: You're right about that projection, Dad. There are over six billion people on earth, and there are 240,000 more each day. What else did you say in your paper?

Dad: "This means that the population of the world will more than double in less than 40 years. The report estimates that 100 million people will be born each year. Because of the population increase, it is likely that the gap between the industrialized countries and the developing countries will continue to widen."

Ted: Yeah? I think that's definitely happening. Did you say why in your paper?

Dad: No, I didn't write about it in my paper, but my guess is that the industrialized countries use up more and more of the world's resources, while the developing countries produce more and more people.

Ted: Yeah. Makes sense. I did a paper for my environmental engineering class, and I learned that there are 300 billionaires in the world (mostly in industrialized nations) and that they have as much money as the three billion people beneath them.

Jenny: Right. But it's doubtful that industrialization is the answer for everyone. You know, I just read that a lot of the people in China are moving from the country to the cities, and soon there won't be enough work for everyone in the cities. The article said that there will be at least 30 million workers in the cities without jobs.

Ted: That doesn't surprise me. Unemployment in urban areas seems to be a problem everywhere.

Dad: Yeah. And there are other problems that I included in my paper. Listen to this.

           "The Carter Commission said that oil reserves, water reserves, and forests will all be seriously depleted because of the increase in population. Furthermore, this will lead to more deserts. Also there will be greater amounts of carbon dioxide in the air. So more and more plants and animals will become extinct."

Ted: For sure, but here's some good news. I read somewhere that the African black rhino is doing OK. You know there are only about 500 of them left, but it looks like they'll survive the century.

Dad: That's because of the new poaching laws, right?

Ted: Right.

Dad: Listen to this. "The commission also predicted that the cost of everything will increase at alarming rates, primarily because of scarcity. Food costs alone will increase over 100%. The cost of energy, gas, and electricity will rise 150%. Our incomes, however, will not increase. Therefore, our actual buying power will be considerably less."

Ted: I think that's true already. I definitely feel like I have less money to spend than when I started college four years ago. My scholarship is still the same amount of money it was then, but my expenses have increased a lot.

Jenny: You know, Dad, I remember studying that Carter Commission report, too. Didn't it also say that renewable resources such as wood and land will not be replenished after they are used up, so there will be less and less land, wood, and water to feed and protect people as the population increases?

Ted: Yeah. I read that starting in the year 2000, we will need as much food in the next 40 years as we have in the last 8,000. And that for many countries, starvation will become the most serious problem in the twenty-first century.

Dad: You got it. I did make some suggestions in my paper to solve these problems. Listen and tell me what you think. "What can be done? First, the basic problem is that there is no minimum standard of living. People need a minimum amount of food, clothing, and shelter. The United States, which is economically and socially one of the most influential countries in the world, should make a commitment to solving this problem. The United States might lead a global program of distributing food and resources throughout the world. Ideally, this should be done without political 'strings' attached. An international consensus must be reached, possibly through the United Nations, to lessen human suffering and to take care of basic human needs."

Ted: Wait a minute, Dad. I hate to be a pessimist, but I'm beginning to doubt if the United States has that much influence anymore. I used to think so, but I'm not sure anymore. And I don't know how the United States could take care of the incredible problem that by 2050 the amount of fresh water available to everyone is very likely to be 25% of what we had in 1950.

Dad: Wait, wait. I didn't mean that the United States should do it all, only that the U.S. could be a leader in working toward solving this problem. We shouldn't have to do it alone. Listen. "Although this sort of cooperative global program may relieve the immediate needs for food and shelter for some people, more long-term economic planning is needed to reverse dangerous losses of natural and human resources. One long-range plan is for a cooperative solar energy project. Some say that a full commitment of international resources of scientists, technology, facilities, and money could help replace the world's dependency on oil. The sun could be used as a permanent source of energy and could be made available to all peoples of the world.

"Another proposal to change the bleak future predicted by the Carter Commission is that exports of food products and oil exports should be priced according to the incomes of the consumer nations. That is, prices should be based on ability to pay. Then lower-income nations could build themselves up without depleting all of their own natural resources. Also, technical and economic help should be given as payment to lower-income nations for nonrenewable resources. This would give developing countries the needed technology and monies to develop farmland, build irrigation systems, and complete other useful projects.

"Now, the big question is: Can any of this really be implemented? Can the bleak future forecast by the Carter Commission Report be averted? Most people would say 'probably not,' but it is this negative response that is at the heart of the problems we face. We feel intuitively that the economics and politics of international relations have become too big, too complex for anyone to comprehend or change them. We sense that somewhere, somehow, things have gotten out of control and that we have lost the power to determine our own future. It's as if we have become victims or prey to the systems we humans spent hundreds of years creating.

"There is also another reason why people may be pessimistic about the possibilities of averting a bleak future. It is because we are presented daily with almost certain proof by the media that the entire planet faces catastrophe, if not from political and economic strife, then from nuclear weapons in the hands of terrorists. And yet, it seems that nothing is being done about it.

"In the face of these things, a feeling of helplessness easily turns into apathy and when we feel powerless, we lose interest in even trying to change things."

Jenny: Well, I remember reading that Paul Schmid, one of the directors at the Institute for the Future in California believes that it is very hard to get people to change. And that the only thing that makes people change is disaster. He gave examples like Hitler, the civil rights movement, and the Vietnam War.

Dad: Yup. I said that in my paper too.

"If we can begin to think through some of our beliefs, we may realize that much of what we have come to believe about human nature may not be true. For example, some say that it is not natural for human beings to cooperate. I think it doesn't matter if human beings are basically cooperative or not. I think that the main problem is a basic ignorance of global economics. People need to understand that what is best economically for the whole world is also best for each individual. If people would take courses in economics and would try to understand other cultures, this would help reach the goal of a cooperative global economy, one that is based on mutual aid rather than mutual destruction."

Ted: Yay, Dad! You tell 'em. But what about the effects of technology? Did the Carter Commission make any predictions there?

Dad: Yes, son, but right now I'm hungry. Why don't we continue this over dinner?

Ted and Jenny: Great idea! Let's get something to eat.

Dad: Fine. How about that new Chinese restaurant down the street?

Jenny and Ted: Sounds good to me. Let's go.

Speculating about the Future;
Reminiscing about the Past

1   **Listening for Expressions of Speculation and Reminiscences.   Page 188.**

Speaker A: Good morning.

Speaker B: Good morning. And how are you today?

Speaker A: I didn't sleep too well and I feel a bit tired, but I'm really eager to get home. Well, let's get back to work. Where were we? As I recall, before I went to sleep, you were working on the calculations for our time of arrival.

Speaker B: That's right. You've been asleep exactly 3 years, 21 days, 5 hours, and 10 minutes.

Speaker A: Now, now, there's no need to be sarcastic. Just tell me when we'll arrive home on earth, will you?

Speaker B: Well, my guess is that we'll arrive at the spaceport in Dallas on February 23, 2047.

Speaker A: Your guess? You're supposed to know these things. And where did you learn that expression, anyway?

Speaker B: Same place you did, of course. Back on earth. And you know as well as I do that some of our instruments were not functioning for a while. I can only speculate how long they were off. So based on this speculation, I can only guess our time of arrival. But don't worry, there's a good chance we'll arrive in February, as I said.

Speaker A: Oh great! This reminds me of the time you broke down and miscalculated all the readings from the instruments. I'm surprised we got home at all that time.

Speaker B: Well, that's not the case this time! I assure you I'm perfectly fine.

Speaker A: OK, OK. Well, anyway, it will be good to get home.

Speaker B: But don't be surprised if things are a lot different now. There's a good chance that Dallas will seem almost foreign to you.

Speaker A: Yeah. I'll never forget the time we took our first trip. What a jolt that was, arriving home and everyone was ten years older. The clothing styles, the music— everything was different.

Speaker B: Mmm. That takes me back to when you first decided to become a space pilot.

Speaker A: What? How do you know about that?

Speaker B: I know everything you know. Remember the time you and Salina Gravitz went to that party in Chicago and then—

Speaker A: Enough reminiscing! If you don't quit doing that, I have a hunch that a computer I know quite well is going to have its circuits rearranged!

Speaker B: Oh, all right! But don't forget, it's bound to be lonely out here without me to talk to.

Question 1:   Who are the two speakers?
Question 2:   What are they doing?
Question 3:   What is their relationship?
Question 4:   What topics do the speakers speculate about, and what expressions do they use to introduce their speculations?
Question 5:   What topics do the speakers reminisce about, and what expressions do they use to introduce their reminiscences?
Question 6:   Why does Speaker A want Speaker B to stop reminiscing?

PART 4

Focus on Testing. Page 191.

You will hear a short presentation. After the presentation, you will be asked some questions. Circle the letter of the best answer.

Presentation

The future, which can seem so close— just days, hours, or even seconds away— is somehow always too distant to be seen clearly. But distance has not stopped generations of seers and forecasters from squinting in that direction. Even Henry Adams, the respected historian, made predictions about the future. In 1903, he declared: "My figures coincide in setting 1950 as the year that the world must go smash." Sorry, Henry. The end of the world may indeed be coming, but your prediction for 1950 is definitely off the mark.

In this century, an entire futurology industry has been developed to meet the planning needs of corporations, governments, and military establishments. At the same time, the average person has become more and more interested in social trends and future talk. Numerous books on future trends, such as *Global Trends 2005* and *Next: Trends for the Near Future*, are best-sellers. But being a best-seller does not mean that the information is right. We can't actually see the future. In the 1890s it was widely predicted that the United States would have no trees left by the 1920s. It was assumed that all the trees would have been chopped down for firewood. But something unforeseen happened. Oil and gas stoves were developed. Now the major threat to the trees is acid rain.

Futurologists in recent decades correctly predicted the rise of the number of "couch potatoes" addicted to television and videos, the increase in the number of home offices, and the prevalence of multiple marriages in one lifetime. They missed out, however, on many other important developments, such as the economic power of OPEC and the mass arrival of women in the workplace.

Many future forecasters become either excessively optimistic or excessively pessimistic about the future. Edward Bellamy, in his popular 1898 novel *Looking Backward*, described Boston in the year 2000 as a gentle, ideal city where everyone enjoys equal pay and where crime has all but disappeared. But the discovery in World War I that scientific advances could also produce weapons turned speculation about the future to the darker side. Bellamy's wonderful utopian city became the high-tech slave societies of Yevgeny Samyatin's novel *We*, and the dark and haunting visions depicted in both Aldous Huxley's *Brave New World* and George Orwell's classic novel *1984*.

Question 1:   Who tries to see into the future?
Question 2:   When did Henry Adams make his prediction about the end of the world?
Question 3:   Why is it difficult for futurologists to make accurate predictions?
Question 4:   What did futurologists *not* predict correctly?
Question 5:   How did Edward Bellamy feel about the future?
Question 6:   Why did some writers become pessimistic about the future?

Acknowledgments

First we wish to acknowledge the expertise, imagination, and inspiration of our editor, Annie Sullivan, whose incredible humor, dedication, and multiple talents contributed so much to this edition. She rocks! We also wish to express our deepest appreciation to Tina Carver at McGraw-Hill for pursuing this fourth edition and treating us with style.

The skills, ideas, and creativity of Marilyn Bernstein, Steven Carlson, Jill Wagner-Schimpff, Steven Hollander, Judy Tanka, and Steven Marx who worked on the first three editions laid the foundation for the fourth. We are indebted to Erik Børve for publishing the ground-breaking first edition and grateful to Mary McVey Gill for her efforts in gathering the original team, her excellent editorial work, and her friendship.

We are also grateful to others who have provided creative suggestions and other support. Steve Aron, Connie Bendal, Mary, Louise, and Elizabeth Dunn; Annie Gardiner, Sue Garfield; Osha Hanfling, Alan Kaiser, Dean Lerner, Eliot Levinson, David Marimont; Manouso Manos, Andreas Paecpke, DeeDee Quinn; John Schumacher, Ann Stromberg; Pat Sutton; Nancy Van Gundy, Patricia Walden and of course the folks down at the Plant: Alice, Joe Bankman, Gray Clossman, Peter Detkin, Barbara Fried, Frank Koenig, Michelle Oastes, Greg and Dorit Scharff, Barr and Susan Taylor, and David Yohai.

We thank the staff at the Palo Alto Public Library and San Francisco State University for their assistance and support.

Photo Credits

Page 1 © Michael Newman/Photo Edit; *Page 2* © Robert Isaacs/Photo Researchers, Inc.; *Page 5* (left) © Bettmann Archive; *Page 5* (right) © AP/Wide World Photos; *Page 7* © Hulton Archive; *Page 9* © Underwood & Underwood/Bettmann Archive; *Page 13* © BENELUX Press; *Page 15* © Reuters New Media, Inc./CORBIS; *Page 20* (left) © AP Wideworld; *Page 20* (right) © Corbis Stock Market/Straus/Curtis; *Page 24* © Guy Sauvage/Vandystadt/Photo Researchers; *Page 29* © Lindy Powers/Index Stock Imagery; *Page 30* Patrick Ward/CORBIS; *Page 37* (bottom) Joe Sohm/Chromosohm/The Image Works; *Page 38* © Michael Grecco/Stock Boston; *Page 40* © Jonathan Nourok/Photo Edit; *Page 43* © Mehau Kulyk/Science Photo Library/Photo Researchers; *Page 45* © Sanford Roth/Photo Researchers, Inc.; *Page 51* Photo courtesy of NASA; *Page 53* © Angelo Cavalli/Superstock; *Page 57* © Elizabeth Crews/Stock Boston; *Page 58* © David Young-Wolff/Photo Edit; *Page 61* © Steve Skloot/Photo Researchers, Inc.; *Page 63* © Pablo Bartholomew/Getty Images; *Page 65* © Elizabeth Crews/The Image Works; *Page 66* © Klaus Lahnstein/Getty Images; *Page 67* © Hella Hammid/Photo Researchers, Inc. *Page 71* © Mark Richards/Photo Edit; *Page 72* (left) *Page 52. Page 31*; *The Liberator*, 1947; René Magritte; Los Angeles County Museum of Art, Gift of William Copley; Photograph © Museum Associates/LACMA / 2001 C. Herscovici, Brussels / Artists Rights Society (ARS), New York; *Page 72* (middle) M.C. Escher's "Hand with Reflecting Sphere" © 2001 Cordon Art B.V. - Baarn-Holland, All rights